BALLS

BALLS

TALES FROM FOOTBALL'S NETHER REGIONS

PAUL BROWN

MAINSTREAM
PUBLISHING
EDINBURGH AND LONDON

First published in Great Britain in 2004 by
MAINSTREAM PUBLISHING COMPANY (EDINBURGH) LTD
7 Albany Street
Edinburgh EH1 3UG

ISBN 1 84018 930 4

A catalogue record for this book
is available from the British Library

Typeset in Frutiger, Kartoon and Van Dijck
Printed and bound in Great Britain by
Mackays of Chatham plc

CONTENTS

INTRODUCTION

Small boys, jumpers for goalposts: enduring image, isn't it? But the so-called beautiful game is rarely so innocent, so clean-cut, or so damned romantic. Behind the dreamy façade of the world's favourite sport lies a superfluity of madness, badness and plain stupidity. Not that there's anything wrong with that. Indeed, we football fans would simply have it no other way. Fans all over the world respect Pelé for his football skills but, boy, is the guy dull? If every footballer was like Pelé the game would be a technically superb, but ultimately anodyne, experience. (Granted, as we shall see later on, everyone would know a whole lot more about erectile dysfunction.)

Pelé's own favourite footballer was George Best. And now we're talking. Best was a footballing genius who played with a skilful swagger that was a joy to watch. Meanwhile, off the pitch, Best drank for Northern Ireland, assaulted coppers and got more lady action than cheap wine. There's nothing big or clever about the fact that Best drank his career away, but it's a great story, and he's a great character. Without these great stories and characters, football would be a pretty sorry affair. Think Gazza, Maradona, Garrincha and Robin Friday: their combined life stories feature excessive drink and drugs, womanising, car crashes, plastic breasts, a rubber penis and a kidnapped swan – oh, and football. Every one of these life stories is a ripping yarn.

And those are just the footballers. Throw fans, managers, chairmen and referees into the mix and you find that football is populated throughout its many echelons with a legion of bona fide insaniacs. There are colour-blind referees, colourful commentators, dodgy kits, dodgier haircuts, footballers called 'Primrose', players with prosthetic body parts, dangerous goal celebrations, suicidal own goals, pathetic penalty misses, God-fearing goalkeepers, gun-toting fans, musical travesties, cinematic turkeys, Nazi footballers, shocking scandals, horrendous tragedies, bung-taking managers, UFO-spotting chairmen and matches involving elephants, robots, prisoners and lesbians.

What follows is an anthology of amazing true stories from the world of football, revealing the bad, mad, hilarious and heartbreaking reality behind the beautiful game. Vital questions that will be answered include: who is the former First Division superstar allegedly now living as a fully post-op transsexual? What possessed a World Cup superstar to kidnap 120 Cameroonian pygmies? Why did a professional football team deliberately score 149 own goals in one match? Which ex-goalkeeper genuinely believes he is the Son of God? And does FBI 'most wanted' terrorist leader Osama bin Laden really support Arsenal?

We're through the looking glass here, people, and those responsible for sullying football's great reputation will be named and shamed. But, as Adam Ant once sang, ridicule is nothing to be scared of. While many of those featured on the following pages deserve a slap in the face, many of them merit a jolly good pat on the back. From the dark recesses of footballing history emerge many hidden tales of heroism and triumph.

To embrace football is to accept its flaws as well as its perfections. Far more than just 22 men attempting to kick a bit of dead cow between two sticks, football is a huge, living and breathing cultural behemoth. And sometimes you have to take a look under the bonnet to really appreciate something. Behold the glory of football – the greatest game in the world.

1. VIOLENCE

Thoughts of football violence usually conjure up images of Burberry-clad skinheads rampaging through far-flung cities in the name of England. But the actions of these vicious dunderheads has little to do with football. Real football violence occurs on the pitch in the form of punch-ups, horror tackles and goolie-grabbing antics. Hold onto your helmets.

One of the greatest ever mid-game dust-ups happened at the 1974 Charity Shield match between Liverpool and Leeds United at Wembley. Charity was in short supply. Leeds' Johnny Giles had already whacked Liverpool's Kevin Keegan once and, when Giles caught 'Mighty Mouse' for a second time, Keegan reacted. Unfortunately Keegan took out his revenge on the wrong man. He punched Leeds captain Billy Bremner and the tough Scot duly cuffed Keegan back. A top-notch boxing match ensued and both players were sent off. (Keegan had also been sent off four days earlier in a friendly match against Kaiserslautern.) Disgusted at the referee's decision, the pair ripped off their shirts, threw them to the ground and walked from the pitch bare-chested. Both were fined £500 and banned for 11 games – three for fighting and eight for taking off their shirts.

BALLS

The following year, in a match between Derby County and Leeds at the Baseball Ground, Francis 'Franny' Lee and Norman 'Bite Yer Legs' Hunter indulged in a memorable bout. Hunter held a substantial size advantage over Lee, but the smaller man was equally aggressive. Bite Yer Legs split Franny's lip with a cracking left hook and the pair continued to trade punches even after they'd both been shown the red card – while both sets of players swapped handbags around them.

World Cup history has also seen its fair share of on-field violence. In 1962, TV commentator David Coleman introduced highlights of Chile's 2–0 win over Italy with the words, 'Good evening. The game you are about to see is the most stupid, appalling, disgusting and disgraceful exhibition of football possibly in the history of the game.' The trouble began even before a ball was kicked, with Italian journalists accused of slighting the beauty and morals of Chilean women. FIFA saw the match as a potential problem and called in legendary English referee Ken Aston. But Aston, contacted at short notice, was not allowed to bring his own linesmen. Instead, he was stuck with an inexperienced Mexican and a diminutive American. 'They weren't very good,' Aston later said, 'so it became almost me against the 22 players.'

The so-called 'Battle of Santiago' kicked off with a booking within 12 seconds. After 12 minutes, and a succession of bad challenges, Italy's Giorgio Ferrini was sent off. Ferrini refused to leave the pitch and Aston was forced to drag the player off, with the assistance of armed police. Then Chile's Leonel Sanchez broke Italian captain Huberto Maschio's nose with a left hook. Aston had his back to the incident and the linesman refused to acknowledge he had seen it. Italy's Mario David responded by kung fu kicking Sanchez. David was also sent off. Armed police entered the field of play three times and Aston himself was forced to 'manhandle players left, right and centre'. 'I wasn't reffing a football match,' he said, 'I was acting as an umpire in military manoeuvres.'

But even the Battle of Santiago pales in comparison to the mass brawl that occurred in Mexico in 1997 during a 'friendly' match between the Jamaican national side and local team Toros Neza (The Bulls). Nine minutes into the game a Mexican player objected to a Jamaican tackle in the strongest possible terms and responded by punching and kicking the tackler to the ground. Within seconds a huge battle erupted involving all 22 players, and coaches and officials from both sides. Eventually a number of Mexican fans became involved and the Jamaicans fled to the safety of their changing room – only to return seconds later carrying assorted chair legs, bottles, bricks, wooden boards and rocks. A pitched battle ensued, involving boxing punches, karate kicks, wrestling moves and various implements being thrown and bashed over heads.

The entire incident was captured on camera by a local TV crew and the footage was feverishly aired across the world. The match was, obviously, abandoned, and Jamaica were fined £20,000. Jamaican coach Rene Simoes defended his players and blamed the poor ref, saying he did a terrible job of refereeing what amounted to nothing more than a physical game. Simoes even managed to take something positive out of the game, saying, 'This has moulded our players into a stronger unit.' Military unit, perhaps.

It wasn't the first time the Jamaican team had found themselves in trouble on Mexican soil. During a 1996 visit, the team were accused of causing £10,000 worth of damage to the Continental Plaza hotel. The Jamaican coach said the allegations were 'pure lies'.

So perhaps St Kitts and Nevis should have known better than to invite the Jamaicans to participate in their fourth Annual Island Football Festival in 2002. Midway through the match between the hosts and the visitors, Jamaican striker Walter Boyd claimed to have been deliberately struck on the head by assistant referee Anthony Bergan's flag. Boyd responded by punching Bergan in the face. A ruck ensued and the match was held up for 45 minutes while order was restored. Luckily for the Jamaicans this one was not caught on camera, although FIFA did get to hear of it and the side were again fined – this time to the tune of £9,000.

Perhaps the image that best sums up badly behaved footballers is that of Eric Cantona's incredible kung fu attack on fan Matthew Simmons at Crystal Palace's Selhurst Park. The photo was taken on 25 January 1995, and Cantona – wearing his black Manchester United away kit with a yellow number seven on the back – is pictured in midair, arms outstretched, legs horizontal. Simmons, in a black leather coat, grey trousers and white button-up shirt, has thrown up an arm to protect himself, but Cantona's right boot has found its target and connects forcefully with Simmons' chest. An elderly lady steps back out of the way. Other fans, including a child in a Manchester United hat, stand open-mouthed. The photo captures a quintessential moment of football lunacy, and it was splashed on newspaper front pages around the world.

The kung fu kick was by no means Eric Cantona's first brush with controversy. The Frenchman was born in Marseille on 24 May 1966 and began his football career with Auxerre. In 1987, he hit the headlines after punching out his own goalkeeper. Cantona moved to Olympique Marseille in the following year and was soon banned from playing for the French international team after insulting coach Henri Michel. He was suspended by Marseille for throwing his shirt to the ground after being substituted and was eventually sold to Montpellier. There he was again suspended for duffing up another teammate. He returned to Marseille, but was sold again, this time to Nimes. During one match he was sent off for throwing the ball at the referee. He was summoned before a French FA committee who told him he would be suspended for one month. Cantona called every member of the committee an idiot and his suspension was duly doubled. The aggrieved star signed a cancellation of his Nimes contract and announced his retirement in December 1991.

However, within weeks Cantona was looking for a new club in

England. He arrived at Sheffield Wednesday where the club wanted to sign him for an initial trial period, but Cantona refused to be subjected to a trial and walked out. In January 1992, he signed for Leeds United, before controversially crossing the Pennines to join Manchester United in November. On his return to Elland Road in Manchester's colours, Cantona spat at a Leeds fan and was fined £1,000. Then he was sent off in a Champions League match against Galatasaray for calling the referee a cheat. On his way from the pitch he fought with Turkish policemen and was eventually banned for four European matches. In 1994, Cantona was sent off twice within the space of five days, against Swindon Town and Arsenal. He was suspended for five matches. At the World Cup finals in the USA he was handcuffed and ejected from a press box after attempting to deck an official. He was then suspended again after being sent off in a pre-season friendly match against Rangers. And then came the Crystal Palace incident.

In a bad-tempered game that eventually ended 1–1, Cantona had received some rough treatment from Palace's Richard Shaw. Early in the second half, the Frenchman retaliated. He was immediately sent off, and was escorted from the pitch by Manchester United's kit man, Norman Davies. As he headed for the tunnel, Cantona was subjected to the customary catcalls from Palace fans. One particular fan ran 20 yards to a McDonald's advertising hoarding at the front of the stand to remonstrate with Cantona. Standing just feet away from the Frenchman, Matthew Simmons unleashed his volley of abuse. 'He said terrible things about my mother, wife and children,' Cantona later said. Enraged, Cantona leapt over the hoarding and launched an astonishing two-footed kung fu kick at Simmons. He followed this up with a couple of punches for good measure. Kit man Davies was swiftly joined by the United players, and they desperately tried to drag their teammate away. One fan threw a cup of tea over Cantona. Paul Ince stepped in and began to throw punches at angry Palace fans. Eventually Cantona was pulled towards the players' tunnel and into the dressing room.

BALLS

The repercussions of the extraordinary episode were huge. Newspapers and television bulletins across the world showed images of the incident, and Cantona and his kung fu attack became notorious. According to newspaper reports at the time, Sir Alex Ferguson and the club's board of directors and lawyers discussed sacking the player, but he was simply too important to Manchester United. Cantona was banned for eight months by the FA and also stripped of the French captaincy. Then, on 23 March, he was charged in Croydon Magistrates Court with assault and sentenced to 14 days in prison. The sentence was reduced to 120 hours of community service on appeal.

Following the appeal verdict, United held a press conference. Cantona entered to a barrage of questions and light bulb flashes. He sat down and slowly announced: 'When the seagulls follow the trawler it is because they think sardines will be thrown into the sea. Thank you.' Then he stood up and left.

Paul Ince's charge of assaulting a fan was dropped when it was discovered that the supporter he had clobbered was a former hooligan associated with West Ham. Cantona's victim, Matthew Simmons, was charged with provocation and was fined and banned from all football grounds. Cantona made his comeback for Manchester United on 1 October 1995 in a 2–2 draw with Liverpool. He scored, of course.

Surely the worst foul ever seen on a football pitch was committed in the 1982 World Cup finals in Spain. France and West Germany were drawing 1–1 in the second half of the semi-final in Seville. French substitute Patrick Battiston had only been on the pitch for five minutes when Michel Platini played him through on goal. Battiston had only the goalkeeper to beat – but this was no ordinary goalkeeper.

Harald 'Toni' Schumacher had risen from poverty to stardom, despite the fact that he declared himself to be bereft of natural talent. A tough character, Schumacher broke all ten of his fingers over his career. Before every match he would repeat to himself a well-worn mantra: 'You are a tiger, the ball is your prey.' Brutally honest, he once replied to a journalist's question about a poor performance with the comment, 'I played like an arsehole today.'

Schumacher had already clashed during the semi-final with Didier Six and Manuel Amoros. But his assault on Battiston was something else entirely. As the Frenchman bore down on goal, Schumacher came rushing out at high speed and flung himself legs first at his opponent, catching him across his midriff. Battiston was brutally scythed down and lay immobile on the pitch. He had lost three teeth, and was carried unconscious from the pitch with an oxygen mask over his face. Michel Platini later revealed he thought Battiston was dead because he was unable to find a pulse. With a worldwide audience anticipating a red card for Schumacher, the referee incredibly ignored the incident, watched the ball roll out of play and signalled a goalkick. Schumacher may not have been sent off, but his reputation as a football bad boy was nevertheless cemented.

The player later claimed his innocence by saying, 'It was too late. I couldn't stop and I couldn't avoid him.' German coach Jupp Derwall added, 'Schumacher says he went for the ball, but he had too much power in his movement to avoid the collision. He is very sorry for what happened, but it was an accident.' Others took a dimmer view of the incident. Schumacher revealed in his autobiography, *Blowing the Whistle*, that his own mother told him, 'It was dreadful, Harald.'

Schumacher became known as 'The Beast of Seville'. 'Am I some kind of wild animal?' he asked in his book. The French certainly thought so. Schumacher topped a newspaper poll to find the least popular man in France, knocking Adolf Hitler into second place.

With Battiston on his way to hospital, the semi-final unfolded into a classic. France, with the Spanish crowd uncharacteristically on their side, scored two goals in extra time to lead 3–1. But West Germany, with a half-fit Karl Heinz Rummenigge joining the game from the bench, staged a remarkable comeback and scored two goals within six minutes. Extra time finished 3–3 and the match went to penalties. Typically Schumacher was the hero, saving two penalties in the shoot-out, which West Germany won 5–4. The Germans progressed to the final, but lost 3–1 to Italy.

In 1990, at the World Cup finals in Italy, Holland's Frank Rijkaard committed a horrible deed against Germany's Rudi Voller that was worse than any traditional act of violence. Twenty minutes into the game, Rijkaard kicked Voller. The enraged German striker then clattered Dutch goalkeeper Hans van Breukelen. Rijkaard stepped in, and he and Voller began to throw hands. Both players were sent off and, as they turned to leave the pitch, Rijkaard hocked up a large ball of phlegm and spat twice at Voller. The second projectile landed in Voller's curly grey perm and dangled like a spittle earring in full close-up view of the world's television cameras.

And then there was perhaps the most pathetic piece of bad boy behaviour in World Cup history. It was 2–2 in a second-round match between England and Argentina in St Etienne. Two minutes into the second half England's David Beckham, lying on the ground after a challenge, aimed a petulant kick at Argentina's Diego Simeone. The midfielder was sent off and England struggled on through the 90 minutes and extra time, finally losing the match on penalties.

Twenty million English fans had watched the match on television and many blamed Beckham for their country's World Cup exit. The 23-year-old Brylcreemed star was vilified by the media and became public enemy number one. *The Sun* said, 'He should be ashamed.' *The Mirror* printed a cut-out David Beckham dartboard. An effigy of Beckham was burned outside a London pub, and the player was threatened by West Ham fans at his first away match following the incident.

'This is without doubt the worst moment of my career,' Beckham said at a press conference. 'I will always regret my actions. I have apologised to the England players and management and I want every England supporter to know how deeply sorry I am.'

Both Sir Alex Ferguson and the Archbishop of Canterbury declared their support for the player but, for a time, it seemed Beckham would have to move abroad, possibly to Real Madrid, to escape the pressure. However, Beckham managed to stick things out and, remarkably, became England's favourite footballer, give or take a finger or two flashed by the player at fans following the Euro 2000 defeat to Portugal. And what did Beckham do once he had ridden out the storm? He moved abroad, to Real Madrid.

Former Rangers player Duncan Ferguson's most famous foul was so bad he ended up in prison for it. The 6 ft 4 in. striker had already been in trouble for a variety of unsavoury incidents including head-butting a policeman, punching a fisherman and beating up a man on crutches. Then, during a match against Raith Rovers, Ferguson head-butted defender John McStay. The 'Glasgow kiss' earned the £4 million-rated Ferguson a three-month stay in the city's tough Barlinnie prison.

In 2002, 37-year-old heroin and cocaine addict Carl Bishop broke into a house in Formby, Merseyside. The burglar piled up boxes of booze and was preparing to carry them outside when he was confronted by the home-owner – one Duncan Ferguson. The footballing ex-con avoided Bishop's attempt to hit him with a vodka bottle and instead punched the intruder to the ground. Ferguson then grappled with Bishop until the police arrived, leaving the would-be thief 'battered and bruised' and requiring two days of hospital treatment. This time it was Bishop who was imprisoned, being sentenced to four years for trespassing with intent to steal. Incredibly, Bishop was the third burglar stupid enough to break into a home owned by Duncan Ferguson. In 2001, Michael Pratt and Barry Dawson made the same mistake. Pratt was lucky enough to escape (although he was later jailed after admitting to the burglary) but Dawson was restrained by Ferguson in the footballer's forcible fashion.

Another footballer whose house you wouldn't want to break into is Roy Keane. The Irishman's 2002 autobiography, *Keane*, caused uproar when it revealed he had deliberately set out to injure Manchester City midfielder Alfie-Inge Haaland. The feud between the two players began in April 1997 during a match between Keane's Manchester United and Haaland's Leeds United. Frustrated by niggling tackles and shirt-pulling, Keane kicked out at Haaland, but only succeeded in injuring himself. Keane heard his cruciate ligament snap and crumpled to the floor in agony. Haaland stood over him and said, 'Get up, stop faking it.'

Keane never forgot about Haaland during his rehabilitation. He says in his book that Bryan Robson told him, 'You'll get your chance, Roy. Wait.' That chance came four years later, in April 2001. Haaland, now with Manchester City, arrived at Old Trafford for a Manchester derby.

'He had the ball on the far touchline,' said Keane. 'Alfie was taking the piss. I'd waited long enough. I fucking hit him hard. The ball was there (I think). Take that, you cunt. And don't ever stand over me again sneering about fake injuries. And tell your pal [David] Wetherall there's some for him as well. I didn't wait for Mr Elleray to show the card. I turned and walked to the dressing room.'

Haaland was left with damaged knee ligaments and never started another game for Manchester City. He never fully recovered, and was released by City before retiring from the game in 2003.

Keane was given a five-match ban and fined £150,000 by the FA. He denied he had set out to injure Haaland, and said the autobiography's ghost writer Eamon Dunphy had used 'a degree of artistic licence'. This was despite the fact Keane had previously said he had read the book before publication and was 'happy with it'.

Keane's autobiography also stirred up further controversy surrounding his departure from the Irish World Cup squad in 2002. Keane was sent home by boss Mick McCarthy after a potty-mouthed altercation. Keane was unhappy with the squad's training facilities, and he confronted McCarthy at a team meeting. The meeting disintegrated into a war of words, and Keane admits telling McCarthy, 'You're a fucking wanker, and you can stick your World Cup up your arse.' According to Keane's teammates, although Keane denies this, the player also told his manager, 'You're not even Irish, you English cunt. You can stick it up your bollocks.'

'I cannot and will not tolerate that level of abuse being thrown at me, so I sent him home,' said McCarthy.

Again, Keane had no regrets. 'I saw him on *Football Focus* saying, "I don't appreciate being called an effing w and an effing c",' he said in the autobiography. 'The next thing you know, [Steve] Staunton is there in a press conference shaking his head saying he has never witnessed anything like it. He has never heard wanker or cunt before? He has played for Liverpool under Graeme Souness and he's never heard that? And Niall Quinn. Who is he? Mother Teresa?' Keane later told *The Observer Sport Monthly* that he hoped McCarthy, Staunton and Quinn 'rot in hell'.

Roy Keane was fined and banned for his violent behaviour, but few footballers receive any real comeuppance for their indiscretions. Vinnie Jones carefully cultivated a 'hard man' persona over the course of his career. On the pitch he captained Wales, won the FA Cup with Wimbledon and played for the likes of Leeds and Chelsea. He didn't last long at Leeds. That probably had something to do with the time he shoved a shotgun up manager Howard Wilkinson's nose after being dropped from the side. He also smacked Bobby Davison in the mouth during a training session. Jones once threatened to rip Kenny Dalglish's head off and 'crap down the hole', called Gary Lineker a 'jellyfish', closely marked Paul Gascoigne's testicles, very nearly bit journalist Ted Oliver's nose off, presented the FA-baiting

Soccer's Hard Men video and was sent off 13 times. He also claims that he and pal John Hartson once fought off an entire carload of thugs who had insulted his missus.

Following in the footsteps of stars like OJ Simpson, Jones swapped sport for cinema, starring in Brit gangster flicks *Lock, Stock and Two Smoking Barrels* and *Snatch*. He then moved to Hollywood to star in films with the likes of John Travolta and Nicolas Cage. Jones is now a multi-millionaire film star with luxury homes on both sides of the Atlantic. Proof indeed that footballing bad behaviour does occasionally pay dividends.

2. SEX

Footballers are drawn to pretty women like bees to honey. They have a dangerous obsession with 'birds' – and not the sort former Liverpool goalkeeper and keen ornithologist Mike Hooper was so fond of. Their pursuit of women sees them trawling through nightclubs, booze in hand. Sex can very often be a footballer's downfall.

George Best is football's most famous womaniser. In 1970, just hours before Manchester United's FA Cup semi-final against Leeds United, manager Wilf McGuinness caught Best in a very compromising position with a young lady on the stairs of the team's hotel. McGuinness intended to send his star player home but was persuaded otherwise by Sir Matt Busby. He would live to regret that decision. United disappointingly drew 0–0 after Best fell over the ball in front of an open goal.

Another footballer with a renowned eye for the ladies was Frank Worthington. Worthington made his name as a footballer when he led Huddersfield Town into the First Division in 1970. Liverpool spotted his talent and moved to sign him in 1972. But the deal broke down when Worthington failed a medical due to high blood pressure. The condition was attributed to the player's boozing, drug taking and womanising lifestyle. 'George Best had a reputation with the ladies but I had more than my fair share – they were great days,' Worthington later recalled. 'I admit I snorted cocaine and smoked dope. It was all part of the crazy scene at the time.' Liverpool manager Bill Shankly advised Worthington to take a break and return for a second medical. But Worthington's 'break' involved a boozy trip to Majorca, during which he was said to have shacked up with six blood pressure-raising Swedish beauties. He duly failed the second medical and signed for Leicester City instead.

And don't talk to Colin Street about footballers and sex. Late one night in 1980, Colin went looking for his wife Tina on country roads behind Nottingham racecourse. According to newspaper reports, he found her in a state of undress in the back of a Jaguar with England goalkeeper Peter Shilton. When the footballer understandably refused to open the car doors, Colin phoned the police. Shilton attempted a hasty escape, but wrapped the Jag around a lamp-post in the process. The goalkeeper was breathalysed and found to be well over the alcohol limit. He was banned from driving for 15 months and fined £350. He admitted taking Tina out for a meal, but denied any wrongdoing. That didn't stop fans up and down the country from regaling him with chants of 'Shilton, where's your wife?' and 'Peter Shilton, Peter Shilton, does your missus know you're here?'

In 1998, *The Sun* found a videotape in then-Aston Villa striker Dwight Yorke's dustbin. What the newspaper was doing trawling through Yorke's garbage was never revealed. The tape showed Yorke and teammate Mark Bosnich in bed with two women and another man. Stills published in the newspaper showed Yorke and Bosnich dressed in women's clothing, and pictured Bosnich being whipped. The Australian goalkeeper was later banned for nine months by the FA and sacked by Chelsea after losing an appeal against a drugs test that was positive for cocaine. He later admitted to a £1,400-a-week habit. But was his former girlfriend exaggerating when she told the *Sunday Mirror* that Bosnich would 'sit slumped watching porn all day, munching Chinese takeaways and staring vacantly at piles of cocaine'? As for Yorke, he jumped into bed with Page 3 legend Jordan, real name Katie Price, and fathered her child, Harvey, who was born in 2002.

England stars Kieron Dyer, Rio Ferdinand and Frank Lampard failed to learn from Yorke's and Bosnich's tale. On a holiday in Ayia Napa, the trio unwisely filmed themselves as they indulged in a 'sex orgy' with a string of drunken girls. The footballers recorded themselves chatting up the girls at a pool bar and then lured them back to a hotel room where a hidden camera had been set up. Predictably, the tape ended up in the hands of the *News of the World*. 'I haven't got a clue about the exact number of women I had,' said Dyer, 'four or five, maybe. But I regret it deeply.'

Football sex scandals sell newspapers, and barely a week goes by without another footballer or manager being sent scurrying into hiding by a fresh tabloid exposé. Even football's biggest names aren't safe. Seemingly unflappable England boss Sven-Goran Eriksson was severely rattled in 2002 by headlines relating to his affair with TV star Ulrika Jonsson. Jonsson had already been involved in a scandal in 1998 when she was beaten up by former boyfriend Stan Collymore in a Paris bar during the World Cup. She later obtained a court injunction to prevent Collymore from selling a video of the pair having sex. In 2004, Collymore was exposed as a fan of 'dogging', which entails hanging around in isolated car parks watching and participating in sex with strangers. In 2003, another sexual term entered the public consciousness as a result of footballing bad behaviour. According to newspaper reports, 'roasting' involves multiple Premiership footballers and one very drunk young lady. Even football's most famous marriage has been subject to intense media speculation. In April 2004, David Beckham was accused of having an affair with personal assistant, Rebecca Loos. Beckham described the stories as 'ludicrous'.

In 1998, a regular caller to a football phone-in radio show

hosted by Danny Baker and Danny Kelly caused widespread panic among Premiership footballers and managers. A football club barmaid, Joanne's first call revealed a sordid tale of 'having it off' with footballers. After more than 30 subsequent calls, Joanne became a legendary figure among football fans and found her exploits reported in the press. It was revealed that Joanne worked for a Premiership club with the letters 'e' and 'i' in its name and was intimately involved with three footballers from that squad, and the club's former manager.

Joanne, who described herself as looking like a cross between 'Martine McCutcheon, Cher, Dannii Minogue and Angelina Jolie', told tales of footballing threesomes, £500 lapdances, incriminating photographs and unsavoury bribes. All of Joanne's facts were said to check out, and she then set her sights on another Premiership club, scoring with two further footballers and another manager. She eventually moved to Australia with an Aussie Rules footballer, but kept in touch with two of her soccer conquests. Joanne also alleged that she had once been chatted up by Tottenham's Darren Anderton, who used the line, 'See this watch? Cost three grand.'

As if worrying about media exposés wasn't enough, in 1999, *New Scientist* magazine revealed research into a new condition called Sexually Acquired Reactive Arthritis (SARA). The condition is apparently prevalent among footballers because they have too much sex. SARA weakens joints, especially knee joints, and makes players more susceptible to footballing injuries. Researchers came up with these findings by counting up footballers' sexual partners, and by measuring the cloudiness of footballers' urine.

Brazilian football's greatest womaniser, and – according to many Brazilian football fans – greatest footballer, was Garrincha. Pelé is known as *O Rei* – The King. Garrincha is called *Alegria do Povo* – Joy of the People. The bow-legged winger, who played alongside Pelé at the 1958 and 1962 World Cups, was also something of a ladies' man. Garrincha – real name Manuel Francisco dos Santos – was born in a small Brazilian town called Pau Grande in 1933. The boy's left leg curved inward, and basic treatment to straighten it was not available in Pau Grande. He was also extremely small like a little bird – a wren or 'Garrincha', as his sister nicknamed him.

As he grew, Garrincha's remarkable footballing talent blossomed. Despite his small size and curved leg, Garrincha was exceptionally quick and boasted a mazy dribble. However, he was also extremely lazy and he had an 'infantile' level of intelligence. He was sacked from his job at a textile factory for idleness, but was later reinstated when the factory manager saw him play football and decided he wanted him in the company's Club Pau Grande team. Garrincha didn't even bother watching the 1950 World Cup. He couldn't see what all the fuss was about and went fishing instead.

Eventually, Garrincha was persuaded to head to Rio for trials with the city's top clubs. His application was typically half-hearted. He was sent home from Vasco after forgetting his boots, and blew his trial at Fluminese after leaving early to catch a train home. Then Garrincha was dragged along to Botafogo where his trial saw him pitted against Brazilian international defender Nilton Santos. Garrincha went past Santos several times, and once nutmegged him. Santos insisted his side sign Garrincha, saying, 'Better him with us than against us.' Garrincha scored three goals on his Botafogo debut and began to gain a reputation for his sublime skills – and for his clown antics.

After being called up to the Brazil side, he was chosen for a warm-up match for the 1958 World Cup finals against Italians, Fiorentina. During the match the 17-year-old Garrincha found himself facing an open goal. But, rather than slotting the ball home, he turned back and dribbled around three defenders and the goalkeeper. He waited for a defender to have another stab at getting the ball (the Italian fell against the goalpost) and then walked the ball into the goal, flicked it into the air, caught it, and walked back to the centre spot. The crowd was completely dumbstruck, and the only noise came from Garrincha's angry teammates, aggrieved that the player had been so irresponsible.

Garrincha didn't play in the first two games of the 1958 World Cup finals, but a player rebellion saw him – and also Pelé – included in the third match against the Soviet Union. Brazil completely outclassed the Soviets in a dazzling 2–0 win. That match set the precedent for the glorious brand of football now known as 'the beautiful game'. Brazil won the 1958 World Cup, and the side never lost a match in which Garrincha and Pelé played together. Pelé was injured, however, in the first match of the 1962 finals. Garrincha duly stepped up to become the tournament's star player, scoring four goals. He was also involved in controversy. He was repeatedly kicked and struck with missiles during games, and was sent off in the semi-final for retaliating after a bad tackle. He was nevertheless allowed to play in the final, and Brazil won football's top prize yet again.

That was the peak of Garrincha's career, and it was all downhill from there. His bent left leg was weakening rapidly, but Garrincha refused an operation after being advised against it by a faith healer. He also had financial problems. Botafogo had taken advantage of the player's naivety and had signed him up to a poor contract. What little money he had was stashed in fruit bowls in his Pau Grande slum house.

And then there were the women. Garrincha had married at 18, and he had eight daughters in Pau Grande. He also had two children with a girlfriend in Rio, and one child in Sweden with a local girl over there. He also dated the girlfriend of Botafogo's vice-president, and then left his wife for samba singer Elza Soares, who he later married. He also loved cars, although he was a notoriously bad driver. In various road accidents he ran over his father, knocked out Elza's front teeth and, tragically, killed Elza's mother.

By 1964, Garrincha's leg was so swollen that he could no longer refuse the orthopaedic operation. He went ahead with it, but never recaptured his form. He sunk into depression and began to drink heavily. After accepting he would never play football again he became a 'coffee ambassador', shaking hands with customers for the Brazilian Coffee Institute. After having another daughter with Elza, Garrincha's 15-year relationship ended and he married another woman, and had another child – his 13th. The drinking continued. In 1983, a bloated Garrincha was admitted to hospital in an alcoholic coma. He died on 19 January 1983 aged 49. His untimely death only cemented his reputation as a legend.

Certainly, Garrincha is still talked about in glowing terms today. In 2001, the great womaniser's penis became the subject of a heated courtroom debate. A biography, *The Solitary Star* by Ruy Castro, had contended that Garrincha's manhood was 25 centimetres (9.8 inches) long and that he was a great lover. The footballer's many daughters contested this claim in court, saying it was an insult to his memory. Judge Joao Wehbi Dib disagreed. He dismissed the case, saying the claim was a compliment. 'Having a big penis is a reason for pride in this country,' he said. 'Size of penis and sexual energy don't walk hand in hand, but Brazilians dream of both.'

In 2003, Neil 'Razor' Ruddock appeared in a ludicrous promotion for Wilkinson Sword's Quattro blade. In a pull-out newspaper supplement featured in *The Sun*, Ruddock was thrust into four bizarre 'scoring situations' with a quartet of 'busty beauties'. The advert revealed that the former Liverpool, Spurs and West Ham hardman often struggled with the ladies because of his unshaven appearance. So, a stubbly Ruddock was pictured alone and glum at home, in the gym, in a swimming pool and at the pub. However, after a quick shave, a smooth-chinned Ruddock was subsequently shown in those same locations in various states of undress with four 'beauties'. One caption read: 'Working out was a real chore for Razor until a close shave with Quattro led to the arrival of shapely Nikki to help him keep in trim and terrific form.' Interestingly, the left hand that Ruddock had draped over his half-naked conquest clearly bore his wedding ring.

Then the Impotence Association enlisted the 'most celebrated football player in history and the most popular athlete the world has ever known'. The one and only Pelé, wearing a bright yellow Mac, was shown on television standing in a football stadium lamenting the fact that erectile dysfunction is rarely discussed on terraces. The ad makes it clear that Pelé has no such problems in the bedroom department, but he can imagine how difficult it must be. 'Get more information,' he says. 'I would.'

Also in the world of sporting endorsements, Arsenal's Freddie Ljungberg became the new face of Calvin Klein underwear in 2003 – or, perhaps, the new lunchbox. The midfielder was pictured in ads wearing nothing but the skimpy Pro Stretch range of pants. 'I love fashion,' he explained. 'I like to mix different styles, a really nice shirt or jacket with some vintage jeans that are a bit beaten up. For me, that's fashion – when you can mix different stuff that you maybe don't think fit together.'

Some of the biggest selling items in the Real Madrid club shop are David Beckham knickers. The skimpy all-white pants bear the Madrid badge and Beckham's squad number, 23. 'They are a huge hit and a lot of people are buying pairs as Christmas gifts,' a salesgirl told *The Sun*. The newspaper accompanied the story with a photograph of 'Madrid beauty' Lorena, 22, wearing just the smalls and a smile. 'They are sexy and gorgeous, just like David,' Lorena commented. The pants are also available in men's sizes. 'People cannot get enough of David,' added a club source.

Of course, the England captain is unlikely to buy a pair for himself, as he is known to borrow his wife's underwear. Appearing on TV show *The Big Breakfast*, Victoria Beckham told presenter Johnny Vaughan, 'He likes to borrow my knickers.' She then tried to dismiss the comment as a joke, but Vaughan pursued the matter.

'I know you're not joking,' he said. 'You're trying to make out you are now, but he wears your pants. Is it thongs or big pants?'

'Thongs,' replied Victoria.

Beckham was subsequently subjected to a torrent of panty-related abuse from opposition fans. Chants were various, including, to the tune of 'Jesus Christ Superstar': 'David Beckham, Superstar, Wears Posh's knickers, And a push-up bra.'

In 2001, a pair of skimpy red and yellow AS Roma knickers got a very public airing. Respected Italian actress and Roma fanatic Sabrina Ferilli had promised in 1998 that, if her club ever won the Serie A title, she would perform a public striptease. When, three years later, Roma won their first championship for 18 years, the buxom screen siren duly obliged, stripping to her tiny club-branded pants at the Circus Maximus venue in front of an appreciative audience including the Roma squad, the city's mayor and many club fans. Ferilli called the act, 'My gift to the city.'

Some footballers should take more care over their choice of underwear – all too often it does not give the support required. Peter Beardsley and Paul Scholes are among the many top players who have been photographed midway through a sliding tackle with their tackle sliding midway out of their pants. Luckily, their misfortune is usually laughed off. In contrast, when Aussie Rules footballer Paul Hasleby was pictured in 2003 in the West Australian newspaper with his old chap hanging from his shorts he threatened to sue. The paper air-brushed Hasleby's appendage out of later editions and apologised in writing, but the player was still unhappy: probably something to do with the funny-shaped balls.

On rare occasions, footballers' penises come out of their shorts in less than accidental circumstances. In 2001, Francisco Gallardo of Seville proclaimed himself shocked to learn that the Spanish Football Federation were investigating his celebration of teammate Jose Antonio Reyes' second-half goal in his side's 4–0 win over Valladolid. Gallardo had jumped on top of Reyes, removed the striker's penis from his shorts and 'nibbled' on it.

BALLS

The entire incident was captured in close-up by television cameras. It was, unsurprisingly, in clear breach of the Federation's 'sporting dignity and decorum' rules.

Gallardo, however, was unapologetic. 'I don't think what I did was very noteworthy,' he told the Spanish press. 'I am sure I didn't offend anyone and, anyway, people at the ground were not even aware of the gesture. It was only when it was given coverage on the television and in the press that people realised what had happened. Anyway, I had completely forgotten about the celebration by the time the game had ended and it would be a shame if I was punished for such a minor matter.'

As for goal-scorer Reyes, who signed for Arsenal in January 2004, he wasn't too shaken up by the incident. 'I felt a bit of a pinch,' he said, 'but I didn't realise what Gallardo had done until I saw the video. The worst thing about it is the teasing I'm going to get.'

In 2002, a Dinamo Kiev player celebrated a goal in a Commonwealth Cup match against Kaunas in a similar manner. However, the Ukrainian football authorities were more understanding. They saw the incident as a hilarious prank and no punishment was issued.

It seems many top footballers have been photographed minus their shorts. One less-than-salubrious internet site offers pictures of 'O'Leary, Peter Taylor, Izzet, Vialli, Wise, Charlie Nicholas, Hansen, Keegan, Beardsley, Fashanu, Adams, Alan Ball, Clemence, Pires, Gazza, Petit, Dublin, Garrincha, Gullit, van Basten, Vinnie Jones, Phil Neal and many more caught starkers on camera!' Good grief.

And what of the fairer sex? Many detractors consider ladies' football to be a folly on a par with vegetarian sausages. As Sky Sports presenter Tim Lovejoy once noted, 'Whatever next? Monkey tennis?' Yet in the early 1900s, 'ladies' football' was all the rage.

In 1920, Dick Kerr Ladies, veterans of 67 matches, played

TALES FROM FOOTBALL'S NETHER REGIONS

St Helens Ladies at Goodison Park in front of 53,000 people. The team was formed in 1917 by Preston factory bosses WB Dick and John Kerr. With many workers away fighting in the First World War, women had taken over factory shifts. Working alongside the remaining men, the women challenged their male counterparts to a football match. The factory owners saw an opportunity to publicise their company and began to pay for the ladies to travel around the country and abroad. On a tour of the USA the ladies played nine games against men's teams, winning three and drawing three. In Holland and France they were treated like superstars. But their success had attracted the attention of football's paymasters.

The Football Association was so worried about the effects of the women's game upon the men's game that it immediately banned women from playing on men's pitches. 'The game of football is quite unsuitable for females and ought not to be encouraged,' a spokesman explained. The ban remained in place for over 50 years. The likes of the Doncaster Belles and Arsenal Ladies kept flying the flag for women's football. But it was in the USA, where an entire generation of schoolgirls grew up playing the game, that women's soccer really took off.

In 1999, Brandi Chastain became the most famous female footballer in the world when she helped the USA win the Women's World Cup. But was her image featured in newspapers by (mostly male) sports editors because she scored the USA's winning penalty in the final shoot-out against China, or because she then proceeded to whip off her shirt and run around the pitch in a sports bra? The unconventional celebration was seized upon as some sort of 'girl power' statement, but Chastain herself said that it was, 'Momentary insanity. Nothing more, nothing less.' Feminists called the celebration 'self-objectifying'. God knows what they made of her nude pictorial in *Gear* magazine, which did so much to bring women's soccer to the attention of the teenage boys of America. Chastain has also been criticised for her 'industrial' language in post-match interviews, including liberal use of words like 'Goddamn' and 'ass', which offended the conservative US TV networks. She particularly upset them when she defended her *Gear* photo shoot, saying she posed for the pictures because, 'I ran my ass off for this body.'

Also criticised for baring flesh were the Australian women's soccer team – the Matildas. In 2002, Aussie manager Chris Tanzey slapped a ban on his players stripping off after a topless Matildas calendar became a huge hit. He feared his stars could be exploited, saying dollar signs had popped up in some people's eyes upon seeing the calendar.

More clean-cut is Mia Hamm, who is considered to be the USA's best-ever soccer player, regardless of sex. A role model for soccer-playing kids, Hamm has appeared in TV ads alongside Michael Jordan, and is regularly mobbed by fans, Beckham-like, in her home country. When Hamm, Chastain and teammates won the 1999 World Cup in front of 60,000 spectators and a worldwide TV audience it seemed that women's football had a shot at becoming an established sport. 'Their approach to the game is very refreshing,' said FIFA's Keith Cooper on announcing an initiative to promote women's football. 'We have to acknowledge that women's football is becoming a major force. Numerically, women are half the world's population.' Good spot, Einstein. But, by 2003, the American Women's Soccer League had been suspended due to lack of sponsorship.

Perhaps women don't actually need their own exclusive football league. That's the opinion of Luciano Gaucci, the eccentric president of Italian club Perugia. 'Women have exactly the same rights as men,' he explained. To prove his point, in October 2003 Gaucci announced the signing of Hanna Ljungberg, a 25-year-old Swedish women's international player with 95 caps and 52 international goals to her name. (Gaucci's most famous previous signing was Al-Saadi Gaddafi, son of Libyan dictator Colonel Muammar Gaddafi.) Gaucci claimed Ljungberg would play in Serie A in 2004. 'Football isn't only about physical strength,' he said. 'I don't see why a woman shouldn't play. It's not against the rules.' Unfortunately, Gaucci's announcement was a little premature. Ljungberg snubbed Perugia, as did fellow Swede Victoria Svensson. Gaucci then set his sights on German striker Birgit Prinz. 'She's a good player,' he explained, of course adding, 'She's very pretty and has a good figure.'

In 2004, FIFA president Sepp Blatter – the most senior figure in world football – suggested that women's football might be more popular if the players wore skimpier outfits. 'Let the women play in more feminine clothes like they do in volleyball,' he said. 'They could, for example, have tighter shorts. Female players are pretty, if you excuse me for saying so, and they already have some different rules to men – such as playing with a lighter ball. That decision was taken to create a more female aesthetic, so why not do it in fashion?'

The response from female footballers was damning. 'That's typical of a bloke,' said England's Pauline Cope.

USA captain Julie Foudy suggested a compromise, saying, 'We'll start wearing tighter shorts when he starts doing press conferences in his bathing suit.' Don't tempt the man.

'As footballers we have to think practically,' said Norwegian player Lise Klaveness. 'If the crowd only wants to come and watch models then they should go and buy a copy of *Playboy*.'

Or perhaps they could buy a copy of the *World Society of Friends of Suspenders* magazine, from the 'international organisation pledged to the preservation of traditional ladies' hosiery' – a publication founded, and once edited, by one Joseph 'Sepp' Blatter. Could that be the same Sepp Blatter who, during a eulogy about David Beckham at the 2001 FIFA World Player of the Year awards, somehow shoehorned in a not very hilarious reference to the Victoria's Secrets lingerie company? (This joke did about as much good for his image as the time when he made the televised draw for the 2002 World Cup finals standing in front of a large backdrop featuring a stylised version of a traditional Asian symbol – the swastika.)

BALLS

Whenever a female footballer is said to have reached the ability level of a male counterpart, questions are inevitably asked of her sex and sexuality. Is she really a woman? And, if so, does she 'play for the other team'? A 2002 Norwegian women's football match between Askim Rodenes and Yven ended in controversy when a local reporter pointed out that one of the Askim players was actually a man. The referee checked his team-sheet and failed to find a man's name, although he did helpfully confirm, 'Men in the women's league is not allowed, as far as I know.' In fact, Askim's male coach Ragnar Johansen had played in goal under a false name. He told a newspaper reporter that he didn't think there would be any comeback because the referee was a 'nice bloke'.

In 2003, in a story straight out of a pulpy pot-boiler, a top UK women's football team was rocked by a lesbian scandal. Barney Davidson sensationally quit as manager of Gretna Ladies after lesbian affairs tore the team apart. Davidson, a former Leicester City player, had managed the 2002 Northern Women's League champions for five years. 'I'm gutted it has come to this, but I've had enough,' he told the *Daily Record*. 'If one girl is with a player then goes off with someone else, the two girls fall out and I've got a problem. Out of 17 players I would say about 8 are lesbians.' Some players, Davidson revealed, have boyfriends, but kick both ways. 'Some would deny it,' he said, 'but I know because I've been involved with the team for so long.'

In 2003, Chester-le-Street Ladies Football Club were ordered to drop their sponsorship logo – 'No BollX'. The logo referred to the title of a book by a local author. 'The girls love it,' said assistant coach Pauline Godward. 'One of the grandmothers did ask if it wasn't a little rude. But it isn't because it is spelt a bit differently. It is a normal phrase used every day by young people. We will continue to wear them no matter what.'

Durham County Football Association had other ideas. Secretary John Topping said it was obvious what was referred to in the logo, and the girls shouldn't wear it on their kit. The club dropped the logo, and instead found sponsorship with Newcastle hypnotist John Grierson. Mr Grierson also offered to give the ladies motivational talks before matches.

In Germany, Teutschenthal Ladies team are sponsored by a brothel. The X-Carree brothel in the city of Halle is owned by a local real estate firm. Teutschenthal's red and grey kits bear the logo, 'X-Carree: Always worth a visit.' 'The women have no problem with it,' said coach Andreas Dittman.

In 2004, a Spanish council withdrew funding from a Galician lower division side after spotting the club's 'sordid' sponsorship logo. Deportivo Carballio wore the name of a local brothel, Club Nymph, on their shirts until the council intervened. The brothel owner, Aquilino Gonzalez, defended his right to sponsor the club. 'We give a lot of trade to the region,' he said. 'Our ladies use the local butchers and hairdressers. I don't want to do any harm. I give to the community.'

Airdrie United are sponsored by Glasgow strip club Seventh Heaven. Jim Ballantyne, chairman of the Scottish Second Division side, arranged the deal after paying a personal visit to the club. Hoardings around the New Broomfield ground now bear photographs of scantily dressed exotic dancers, along with the phrase: 'Seventh Heaven – The Chairman's Choice.' 'Sexy football is coming to Airdrie United one way or another,' said Ballantyne. 'I will be the only chairman in Scottish football who'll still be in Seventh Heaven, even if we get gubbed 4–0 on a Saturday.'

In 2002, *The Times* asked the question: 'Just who is the former First Division superstar now living in the United States as a fully (post) operational woman?' Football fans across the country dropped their match pies and stood in open-mouthed wonderment. Who could it be?

David Beckham has been known to wear a skirt, Keith Weller wore tights when it was chilly, Gary Lineker donned a dress and make-up for a crisp advert, Paul 'Gazza' Gascoigne has been photographed wearing plastic comedy breasts, and John Hartson,

BALLS

Jan Molby and Thomas Brolin are just three players who have carried real man-tits around a football pitch. Hereford's Ronnie Radford is said to have worn a bikini top to keep his breasts at bay when he played and scored against Newcastle United in the famous 1972 FA Cup upset. But would any of them have the, erm, balls to go 'the whole hog'?

Times columnist Danny Baker was initially reticent to name names, worrying over the legal ramifications of 'outing' a former footballer as a bona fide transsexual. But, backed by reams of hard evidence, he eventually spilled the beans. 'It is Tony Powell, of Norwich City,' said Baker. 'Well, formerly of Norwich City and, I suppose, of "Tony" Powell too.'

Powell may not have been the biggest of household names, but a cursory glance at the record books confirms that he was indeed a First Division star, playing 275 times for Norwich City in the '70s. The 6 ft 1 in. Tony 'Knocker' Powell was a bantamweight champion boxer before becoming a footballer. He played for Bath and Bournemouth before joining the Canaries, where he made his name as a tough defender. He moved to the US in 1981 to play in the North American Soccer League, and was lost from British football's radar.

Powell, however, had been highly regarded at Norwich and, when the club's centenary celebrations were being planned, endeavours were made to track him down. Appeals were made in the *Norwich Evening News* and the *San Francisco Examiner*, and, eventually, the club discovered that Powell had abandoned more than his footballs.

'It was a right shock when we heard he was living as a woman,' said a Norwich City spokesman. 'No wonder it's been murder to track him down.'

The shinpads-to-stockings story made the national press, and the *Mail on Sunday* was able to track Powell down to a motel he now manages in Hollywood. The paper revealed that he had divorced his wife and was living with a 'male friend'. But Powell was quick to defend his manhood. 'It's ridiculous,' he told the paper. 'I don't know where all this started. I am all bloke. I have never worn a frock in my life!'

3. DRINK AND DRUGS

Excess. Footballers love it. Some buy fast cars and designer clothes. Others choose drugs and booze. An established drinking culture exists in British football, and the use of recreational drugs is not unusual. And then there are performance-enhancing drugs. When drink and drugs and football mix, all manner of unsavoury shenanigans can't be far away.

Football's drug of choice is alcohol, and footballers often find themselves in trouble when full of the demon drink. George Best is probably football's most notorious boozer. He battled alcoholism for many years, lost his glittering football career and ended up in numerous scrapes, before undergoing a liver transplant in 2002. Doctors told him at that time that one more drink could kill him. Less than a year later he was spotted boozing in his local pub.

Best was Pelé's favourite footballer, which is remarkable considering the Northern Irishman's international career never allowed him to grace a top-level tournament. Best joined Manchester United in 1963 aged just 16, and scored 115 goals in 290 appearances. He won two English League Championships and the European Cup with United. Blessed with speed, skill, an eye for goal and a penchant for flair, Best's was a unique talent. He was named European Footballer of the Year in 1968 for his genius on the pitch and was nicknamed 'The Fifth Beatle' by the European press for his mop-top haircut and celebrity image. Best was perhaps football's first real superstar, and he began to make the headlines with his activities off the field. 'I was born with a great gift,' he said, 'and sometimes that comes with a destructive streak. Just as I wanted to outdo everyone when I played, I had to outdo everyone when we were out on the town.'

When Sir Matt Busby left United in 1969, Best began to find it harder to resist his temptations. Tales of drunken binges and womanising filled the tabloids, and his playing career suffered. Best walked out on United on a number of occasions, and his first-team appearances dwindled. When he failed to turn up for a training session in 1974, his career at United was effectively over. 'George was a fantastic player,' said United manager Tommy Docherty, 'and he would have been even better if he'd been able to pass nightclubs the way he passed the ball.'

In an inglorious fade-out to a glorious career, Best turned out for Stockport County, Bournemouth, Fulham, Hibernian, Los Angeles Aztecs, Cork Celtic, Fort Lauderdale Strikers, San Jose Earthquakes, Dunstable Town, Brisbane Lions and then Ford Open Prison. He lined up for the prison side in 1984 after being jailed for 12 weeks for drink driving, assaulting a policeman and jumping bail. Best continued to drink and frittered away his career earnings. 'I spent a lot of money on booze, birds and fast cars,' he said. 'The rest I just squandered.'

In March 2000, Best was admitted to hospital with liver problems caused by heavy drinking. He underwent a liver transplant two years later and had pellets implanted in his stomach to prevent him drinking alcohol. He said he would never drink again, but was back on the booze within months. He was arrested for an alleged assault in 2003, and his wife Alex left him shortly afterwards, claiming he had beaten her and smashed up the

BALLS

house. In January 2004, Best was banned from driving for 20 months and fined £1,500 after again being caught drink-driving. The former footballing legend was again shamed on newspaper front pages. Despite all his talent, Best became most well known as a textbook case in drinking away your career. As his friend Michael Parkinson said, 'The only tragedy George Best has to confront is that he will never know how good he could have been.'

Tony Adams also admitted to being an alcoholic, but only after a booze-related prison sentence. The former Arsenal skipper served two months in Chelmsford Open Prison in 1990 for drink-driving. He also needed 29 stitches in his knee after falling down nightclub stairs in 1993. In 1996 he successfully quit drinking, and he later wrote openly about it in his autobiography *Addicted*.

Not all footballers have a problem with booze. The 1980s saw a promotional item appear called *Tom Caxton Homebrewing Made Easy with Emlyn Hughes* ('Team captain in TV series *A Question of Sport* and former captain of England and Liverpool'). The C60 'reusable' cassette featured Emlyn talking up the delights of homebrewing. 'If you're not playing a sport, then a good way of getting a different view of it is to watch it on TV,' explained 'Crazyhorse', 'and what could go down better watching the big match than a pint of your own homebrewed beer?' The cassette was presented free with the Tom Caxton homebrew kit. Emlyn advised users to carefully read the instructions and offered a variety of useful tips. 'You've got to be patient,' he said. 'You'll enjoy making your homebrew beer almost as much as drinking it. Almost.'

Rodney Marsh was known as 'The White Pelé', although he preferred to say that Pelé was 'The Black Rodney Marsh'. He made his name at Queens Park Rangers, where he averaged a goal every other game, before moving to Manchester City. There things began to turn sour, largely because Marsh was drinking a bottle of vodka a day. He won only nine England caps after falling out with Alf Ramsey and was eventually shipped off to Tampa

Bay Rowdies, before teaming up with George Best at Fulham. But, unlike his teammate, Marsh quit drinking when a doctor informed him his liver had swelled to twice its normal size. After his playing career petered out, Marsh became a TV pundit. In 1999, he declared that he would shave his head if Bradford City managed to avoid relegation from the Premiership. City survived, and Marsh kept his word. Marsh, whose name is Cockney rhyming slang for 'harsh', makes an appearance on a website called '1000 people more annoying than Mick Hucknall'. Visitors to the site have described him as 'singularly the most smug, self-centred pundit on TV' and 'a clueless knob'.

When Marsh left QPR, he handed his number ten shirt to Stan Bowles. It has been famously said of the talented Bowles that the only thing he couldn't pass was a betting shop. Bowles once turned up late for a big match and told his furious manager, 'You wouldn't believe it, that fucking horse just got beat in a photo-finish!' He was nevertheless allowed to play, and he scored within two minutes. Bowles became involved with betting syndicates and lost hundreds of thousands of pounds. He even bet during matches.

On a trip to Roker Park in 1973, Bowles spotted that opponents Sunderland were displaying their recently won FA Cup on a stand near the dugouts. 'Here you are,' Bowles told a teammate. 'I bet you a tenner that the first time I get the ball I knock that thing clean off the fucking stand!' Not only did Bowles dribble across the pitch and knock the trophy into the air, he later scored and then feigned injury to get a Sunderland player sent off. The Sunderland fans were furious and eventually invaded the pitch. The referee sent the players back to their dressing rooms, and it took 20 minutes for order to be restored.

Bowles once walked out on the England squad after an argument and went to the White City greyhound track instead. When a *Daily Mirror* photographer turned up to snap the missing England star, Bowles beat him up, saying, 'Street justice was called for and given.' But Bowles knew how to use the press to his advantage. After he was beaten up by police in Belgium when a prank backfired, he sold his story to the papers for several thousand pounds. He also made up stories and sold them for a profit. He once announced his retirement exclusively in the *Sunday People*, only to play again two days later.

As for booze, Bowles claims he wasn't a particularly big drinker but, in 1976, he did turn up hungover to compete in the TV sports show *Superstars*. Bowles sank his canoe and finished tenth and last. Athlete David Hemery won, and Malcolm MacDonald was eighth. Frank Worthington once said, 'Stan spent all of his money on gambling, booze and birds.' Bowles replied, 'Well, at least I didn't waste it.'

Many footballers have found themselves on newspaper front pages after boozy indiscretions. Former Liverpool midfielder 'Dirty' Don Hutchison was famously pictured in the tabloids with his pants around his ankles and a Budweiser beer label covering his manhood after a drunken binge in Ayia Napa. A year earlier Hutchison had showed his tackle to a group of students who were videotaping their graduation celebrations in a wine bar. 'Zoom in on this!' he proudly announced. When Liverpool manager Roy Evans heard of the Ayia Napa incident he allegedly raged, 'If Hutchison is flashing his knob again that's out of order!' The player was fined £5,000 and placed on the transfer list. Hutchison is still known to fans and teammates as 'Bud'.

In 1991, Everton's Peter Beagrie got notably sozzled during a pre-season tour of Spain. He drank late into the night following a friendly match with Real Sociedad and then hitched a ride back to his hotel with a friendly Spanish motorcyclist. Arriving at the hotel, Beagrie couldn't understand why the doors were locked. Frustrated, he hijacked the motorcycle and drove it up the hotel steps and through a plate glass window. Beagrie required 50 stitches. Imagine the egg on his face when he found out it was the wrong hotel.

TALES FROM FOOTBALL'S NETHER REGIONS

Paul Gascoigne, Steve McManaman and Teddy Sheringham were among the England squad members photographed drinking spirits in the infamous 'dentist's chair' during a 1996 tour of Hong Kong. The players were pictured sitting back in the chair wearing torn and soaked T-shirts, having booze poured down their throats. The England team re-enacted the incident after Gazza's classic goal against Scotland at Euro '96, when Gascoigne lay on his back and Sheringham and pals squirted water into his mouth.

In 2000, the Leicester City squad were kicked out of La Manga during a pre-Worthington Cup final trip to the Spanish resort. The players danced drunkenly on hotel tables, and Stan Collymore let off a fire extinguisher in the hotel bar before the squad were turfed out. When Leicester were surprisingly allowed to return to La Manga in March 2004, nine players were arrested after a boozy night out in connection with an alleged sexual assault.

Leicester's 2001 Christmas party also ended in disgrace, after Dennis Wise and Robbie Savage were involved in a fierce brawl. The fight started when Savage opened his present from Wise – a teddy bear sitting on a vibrator. West Ham's Christmas bash in the same year saw defender Hayden Foxe urinate on the bar at London's Sugar Reef club. Another player vomited on a table and the team were ejected, leaving a £2,000 bar bill unpaid.

Robin Friday took drunken, drugged-up mischief to strange new highs. Legend has it that Friday scored the greatest goal of all time, but no television cameras were present and only 11,000 people, packed into Reading's Elm Park, ever saw it. The *Reading Evening Post* called it, 'so stunning in its execution that it will be talked about for as long as football is played at Elm Park'. And it is still talked about, more than 25 years later.

It was 31 March 1976, and Reading were hosting Tranmere Rovers. Reading were chasing promotion from Division Four, and a large crowd turned up to see their club take a two-goal lead. Then, in the 69th minute, Friday took centre stage. The long-haired forward was standing with his back to Tranmere's goal, just outside the penalty area, when a long ball came to him at head height. In one move, Friday leapt to control the ball on his chest, turned and cracked a powerful 20-yard volley into the top corner of the net. Elm Park erupted, Tranmere players stood around open-mouthed, and even World Cup referee Clive Thomas held his head in disbelief. 'I can't believe a player like that isn't in the First Division,' Thomas later said. 'It was an amazing goal.' Reading won the match 5–0, with Friday grabbing a second goal with the last kick of the match.

Robin Friday was born in Hammersmith in 1952 and honed his incredible football skills at non-League Hayes. He also gained a reputation as something of a wide boy. He often turned up drunk, but was allowed to play as he had such a great talent. He once missed the start of a match because he was in the pub. Hayes started with ten men and waited for their star player. Friday eventually turned up virtually paralytic with drink and staggered around the pitch before, characteristically, scoring the only goal of the game. He was also involved in more serious indiscretions and was once jailed for stabbing a taxi driver in the face with a fork.

In 1972, Friday's career, and life, was almost ended in a terrible accident. He fell from scaffolding onto a metal spike, which went up his backside and just missed a lung. He spent six hours in an operating theatre and three months in hospital, but recovered in time to play for Hayes in the FA Cup against Bristol Rovers. Hayes won and went on to play Reading, where Friday was spotted by Reading manager Charlie Hurley. 'I was desperate for a striker,' he said. 'I knew Robin's reputation. I found out he had been in borstal, maybe the nick, I don't know. When you're in the Fourth Division you look at players on the pitch, not off it.'

Hurley signed Friday for £750 and the player described as a 'new striker sensation' by the *Evening Post* made an immediate goal-scoring impact. He scored twice on his home debut, netting over 50 goals for Reading overall, and helped the club win promotion in 1976 despite spending the pre-season in a hippie commune. He continued to drink heavily, dropped acid before matches and was involved in numerous punch-ups. He only turned up for training once or twice a week, but he regularly played full matches for the reserves as well as the first team. Friday made up for his wayward lifestyle with a succession of incredible and flamboyant performances. He was renowned for his great goals, which he often celebrated by kissing a policeman or flicking a V-sign at opposition fans. He distracted defenders at set pieces by pulling their shorts down and kicked balls out of play in an attempt to knock policemen's helmets off. He was regularly sent off and sometimes took revenge by defecating in the opposition's bath.

In December 1976, Friday moved to Second Division Cardiff City for £30,000. Arriving to sign for Cardiff, Friday stepped off the train without a ticket and was immediately arrested by British Transport Police. On the night before his Cardiff debut he spent all evening in the pub and ordered 12 bottles of lager to take home with him. He still scored two goals and ran rings around his marker – the mighty Bobby Moore.

'I can picture him now,' recalled Cardiff's club doctor, Leslie Hamilton, 'long hair flowing, cutting in from the wing, beating two or three players. He really was outstanding. His ball control was absolutely fabulous – I've never seen anything like it. There is no question he could have played for England if he'd sorted his head out.'

Friday only played 25 games for Cardiff, but he still became a legend. He performed outrageously, both on and off the pitch. He scored goals, was sent off for kicking Mark Lawrenson in the face and got arrested for stealing a live swan from a pond outside the team's hotel. Then, with First Division clubs and England beginning to notice the player, Friday quit.

His lifestyle had finally begun to affect his play, and he claimed he had simply had enough of people telling him what to do. He returned to non-League football and continued to drink heavily.

BALLS

He fell into poverty and died of an alcohol-related illness in 1990 aged just 38. Friday became a cult figure when Welsh pop group Super Furry Animals dedicated an anarchic 1996 single to him called *The Man Don't Give A Fuck*. The sleeve pictured Friday in typical pose – flicking a V-sign. A book chronicling his life and career, *The Greatest Footballer You Never Saw* by Paul McGuigan and Paulo Hewitt, followed in 1998, and Friday was named Reading's player of the Millennium in 2000. Few football fans ever saw Robin Friday play, but those who did will never forget him.

In 1994, former Arsenal forward Paul Merson admitted at a tearful press conference that he was addicted to cocaine, alcohol and gambling. He successfully underwent rehabilitation and returned to football ten months later. Another Arsenal player, David Hillier, was suspended for six matches in 1995 after testing positive for cannabis. In 1997, Charlton Athletic terminated the contract of Jamie Stuart after he tested positive for cocaine and cannabis. Mark Bosnich's career was derailed in 2002 when he tested positive for cocaine. The goalkeeper was sacked by Chelsea. And the likes of Frank de Boer, Fernando Couto, Edgar Davids, Josep Guardiola and Jaap Stam have all tested positive for the banned steroid Nandrolone. All claimed their innocence.

British football's highest profile drugs case occurred in 2003, when Manchester United's Rio Ferdinand missed a drugs test after training. The defender went shopping and claimed United couldn't contact him as his mobile phone was switched off. Ferdinand was excluded from the England international squad, which prompted a player revolt led by Gary Neville. A threatened strike never materialised, and Ferdinand was left to take his punishment. He was charged with misconduct under rule E26 (the failure or refusal by a player to submit to drug testing as required by a competent official), banned for eight months and fined £50,000.

A 2003 survey carried out by the BBC and the Professional Footballers' Association found that 46 per cent of footballers thought football had a drugs problem. The study revealed that 6 per cent of footballers – around 160 players worldwide – use performance-enhancing drugs. It also found that 4 per cent of footballers had been injected with an unknown substance.

In 1909, Manchester United happily advertised the fact that they had won the FA Cup final thanks to the effects of a popular brain and nerve tonic, which, like the original tonic version of Coca Cola, probably contained cocaine. Then, in 1925, Arsenal manager Leslie Knighton gave his players 'courage pills' before a Cup tie. He later recounted the incident in a startlingly honest chapter of his autobiography called 'I Dope Arsenal for a Cup Tie'.

'I was sitting in my office with my head in my hands, wondering how on Earth we could put West Ham out of the cup, when a card was handed to me,' he said. 'It bore the name of a distinguished West End doctor.' Knighton met the good doctor and received a bottle of silver pills that, the doctor explained, would tone up the players' nerve reflexes. One hour before the Cup tie on 10 January, Knighton and his players took the pills. 'I felt I needed to run, jump, shout,' said Knighton. 'There was something in those pills. I felt I could push down a wall with my fist.'

The manager and his players were high on amphetamines, but the experiment hit a snag when the match was postponed due to fog. With his hyperactive players having no football match to expend their energy upon, Knighton was left with the difficult task of getting his souped-up charges home. 'It was like trying to drive a flock of lively young lions,' said Knighton.

The match was due to be replayed two days later, and again the players took the silver pills, but again the match was postponed because of fog. On 14 January the players again necked the pills and the match was finally played. 'Just before half-time I noticed a change,' said Knighton. 'The Arsenal boys seemed like giants, suddenly supercharged. They tore away with the ball and put in shots that looked like leather thunderbolts. They monopolised the play. There was no defence against the pluck pills.'

Supercharged or not, Arsenal could only manage a 0–0 draw, and the tie went to another replay on 21 January. This time, however, the players refused to take Knighton's pills because of the side effects. They complained about the bitter taste, a burning thirst and a lack of sleep. Knighton, who had also experienced the side effects, agreed, and the pills were shelved. Without their pluck pills, Arsenal drew 2–2. The tie went to a fourth replay a few days later on 26 January. Again the players refused to take the pills. Arsenal were beaten by a last-minute West Ham goal and knocked out of the Cup.

In 1946, Stoke City boss Bob McGrory gave amphetamines to his star player, the very great Stanley Matthews. Matthews was suffering from flu, so McGrory contacted the local infirmary and asked for a prescription to be sent over so that the striker could play against Sheffield United. A bottle of pills duly arrived, and Matthews was told to take one. Within 30 minutes he had perked up considerably and played in the 2–0 win. 'I have to say the pills did the trick because I felt strong and active, good in myself and played a decent game,' said Matthews in his autobiography *The Way It Was*. Unfortunately, Matthews also suffered from side effects. After arriving home from the game he was overcome by a sudden urge to do copious amounts of housework. He dusted, cleaned, swept, and changed the bed sheets, and then went for a four-mile run. On his return, he got stuck back into the housework. Only when he found himself sweeping leaves in the garden in the middle of the night did he think to himself, 'Stan, it's three in the morning and you're out here sweeping leaves. What on Earth is wrong with you?' Matthews went on to have a highly understandable falling out with McGrory, the manager, who doped him and then dropped him.

Even during the reign of legendary Manchester United manager Sir Matt Busby players were given performance-enhancing drugs. Both Albert Scanlon and Harry Gregg revealed that they were offered Dexedrine, an amphetamine, at United in the '50s.

Harry Catterick led Everton to the League championship in 1963, but an investigation by *The People* newspaper found that the victory had been set against a backdrop of widespread drug taking. Albert Dunlop and four other Everton players revealed that they had been given Benzedrine and purple hearts (Drinamyl amphetamines) before matches. Everton strenuously denied this, but the newspaper managed to track down the chemist who had supplied the drugs and the nurse who had forged the prescriptions.

Football's most notorious drug cheat may well have been the very best footballer of all time. That accolade has been contested between Diego Maradona and Pelé for years. Maradona himself has no doubts over who is the best. 'Pelé is a great politician and seems to have a cosy relationship with the soccer establishment,' he said. 'They don't want to let me into their club. That's all right. I don't begrudge Pelé anything. I think he's cool and wonderful, but I'm sorry for him if people think I'm the best.'

The 5 ft 4 in. Argentinean midfielder was born in a Buenos Aires shanty town in 1960 as one of eight children. He played for Argentinos Juniors and Boca Juniors in his home country before moving to Europe to ply his skilful trade at Barcelona, Napoli and Seville. As an international footballer, he led Argentina to four World Cup finals tournaments.

It was at the 1986 World Cup, in a quarter-final match against England, that Maradona became a legend, on two contrasting counts. In the 52nd minute Maradona became labelled as the greatest cheat in football history when he punched Jorge Valdano's cross over Peter Shilton's head and into the England net. Tunisian referee Ali Bennaceur saw nothing wrong with the strike and allowed the goal. Maradona later said of the goal, 'It was partly the hand of Maradona, and partly the hand of God.'

BALLS

Just minutes later, Maradona cemented his reputation as the greatest footballer in the world when he scored a wonderful individual goal, running from the halfway line, beating half of the English team and slotting the ball home. Maradona and Argentina won the game 2–1 and went on to win the World Cup, beating Germany in the final.

At club level Maradona won the Italian Serie A league championship with Napoli in 1987 and 1990 and the UEFA Cup in 1989. But the player was suffering from weight problems and had been using cocaine since he was first introduced to the drug at Barcelona in 1993. Napoli chiefs accepted his habit, and the Italian club even devised a fiendish way to con drug testers.

'Diego could do whatever he wanted,' said former Napoli president Corrado Ferlaino, 'but he had to be clean by Thursday. However, if he was still at risk, he was given a small pump containing someone else's urine, which he slipped into his tracksuit. Then, in the testing room, he would fill the specimen jar from the pump in his tracksuit. He was saved that way many times.'

In 1991, however, Maradona's rubber penis ruse finally failed. Cocaine was found in his post-match sample and he was banned for 15 months. 'Maradona was asked whether he was clear after the game and he said he was,' said Ferlaino. 'But cocaine users often lie to themselves and, when he took the test, it was too late for him to cheat.'

Maradona's career never properly recovered, and the scandals continued to accumulate. First, his friend and manager Guillermo Coppola was jailed on drugs charges. Then Maradona was exposed in the Italian press as a close friend of the bosses of Napoli Mafia clan the Camorras. He was also photographed sharing a bath with notorious drug trafficking crime lords the Guiliani brothers.

At the 1994 World Cup Maradona appeared bloated and, in one notable goal-scoring celebration, completely possessed. In fact, he was high on ephedrine. Maradona failed the post-match drug test and was sent home in disgrace. He failed another drug test in

Argentina in 1997 and was subsequently not selected for the 1998 Argentinean World Cup squad. Instead Maradona was given a suspended jail sentence of two years and ten months for shooting journalists with an air rifle. The incident, in which four people were injured, was captured on tape by a television camera crew. The footage showed the footballer crouching behind a Mercedes, popping up every now and then to take pot shots at the press.

In 2000, while on holiday at the Uruguayan beach resort of Punta del Este, Maradona was admitted to hospital suffering from hypertension and an irregular heartbeat. Tests showed only 38 per cent of his heart tissue was functioning. Doctors blamed his brush with death on cocaine. Finally, Maradona decided to seek help. At the invitation of communist leader Fidel Castro, Maradona travelled to Cuba to undergo lengthy drug addiction treatment. 'I chose Cuba because of the dignity of the people,' he said. 'I trust Cuban medicine, and I know they will cure me.'

Maradona's legion of fans certainly hoped so. A hundred of them have even set up a religion in his honour. The followers of the Hand of God Church, known as the Diegoran Brothers, use Maradona's autobiography as their bible and celebrate Christmas on his birthday. 'We believe he is football's God,' said one follower. No doubt they would all have rushed out to buy Maradona's 2002 charity pop single 'Hand of God'. 'It doesn't matter if I sing well or badly,' he said. 'Go and buy the record because the money is for the kids.'

And then there was the Maradona musical, which premiered in 2004 to a full house at a downtown Buenos Aires theatre. *Number Ten: Between Heaven and Hell* was approved by Maradona (in return for a cut of the profits) yet it doesn't shy away from depicting the star's dark side. One scene sees the young Maradona being plied with cocaine at a cocktail party. The part fact/part fiction story also involves a fight with a corrupt Argentinean president, a bizarre clash with Prince Charles, the ghost of Che Guevara and several 'tear-jerking' ballads.

BALLS

Reaction to the production was mixed. 'It was beautiful,' sobbed one theatre-goer. Another said, 'They turned it into a fairy tale. They invented everything so he would look like an angel.'

The final insult to Maradona's playing career was the 2003 theft of his infamous rubber penis. The drug test-cheating fake willy, or 'gland of God', was stolen while being toured around Argentina. Police confirmed they were searching for the penis. 'We're confident we can sniff it out,' said a spokesman. 'It's quite an unusual theft but I suppose it is quite valuable because of its former owner.'

In April 2004, Maradona's health declined dramatically. The star, aged 43, was admitted to hospital with heart and lung problems and was kept on a respirator for a week. He discharged himself after 12 days, proclaiming he had seen death. But, within weeks, Maradona was back in hospital, this time in a psychiatric ward. Apparently admitted against his will, the footballing hero was sedated and placed in a straitjacket. His personal doctor denied that Maradona's condition had anything to do with drug addiction. Others were not so sure. His family, friends and fans feared that Maradona's amazing life story could be coming to a premature end. A serious question mark hung over Maradona's health and future well-being.

4. MADNESS

Footballers don't live in the real world. They're protected in bubble-wrap by their clubs from an early age, deified by supporters, plied with more money than they know what to do with and drip-fed a constant stream of ego-massaging lies. It's no wonder so many of them are completely bonkers.

Marco Boogers isn't mad. At least that's what he claimed when a newspaper found him in Amsterdam living in a caravan when he should have been in London playing for West Ham. Boogers cost former Hammers boss Harry Redknapp £1 million when he arrived from RKC in 1995. Redknapp had signed Boogers on the strength of a videotape, one of piles he regularly receives. He was quoted in the *Evening Standard* as saying, 'I tape over most of them with *Corrie* or *Neighbours*. Most of them are crap. They can fucking make anyone look good. I signed Marco Boogers off a video. He was a good player but a nutter. They didn't show that on the video.'

If Redknapp was looking forward to seeing Boogers play in the flesh rather than on tape he was to be sorely disappointed. In his first match Boogers was ineffective, in his second match he was sent off after what *The Sun* called 'a sickening horror tackle' on Man United's Gary Neville, and in his third match he never got off the bench. Then he disappeared.

BALLS

Rumours of a nervous breakdown abounded, but nothing was heard of the player, who became known as 'Mad' Marco Boogers, for several weeks. When he was eventually tracked down to his Dutch trailerpark hideout, Boogers loudly protested against his 'Mad' tag. West Ham weren't convinced. They passed their million-pound player to Groningen on a free transfer. Boogers went on to become player–coach at his home town club FC Dordrecht, managing to get sent off and become embroiled in a live TV bust-up with the club's president within weeks of arriving.

Speaking in the *Hammers News* magazine, former West Ham player Ian Bishop revealed more about his temporary teammate. 'I liked Marco,' said Bishop, 'but he used to whistle at you when he wanted the ball: once, and he wanted the ball to his feet; twice, he wanted it over the top. It was like *One Man and His* bloody *Dog*! Then we had all the stories about him living in a caravan. Mental hospital, more like.'

In December 2002, London's *Evening Standard* ran a piece on a former West Ham employee who was seeking to rubbish the tale of Boogers running off to live in a caravan. Bill Prosser used to organise West Ham's travel arrangements and also, for some reason, sponsored Marco Boogers' socks. He claimed the caravan story originated when he told a journalist, over a crackly phone line, that Boogers had 'gone by car again'. This was apparently and inexplicably interpreted as 'gone to live in a caravan'. 'When I read that Boogers is now playing in the lower leagues of Dutch football, I felt sorry for him and, well, the caravan story is on my conscience,' said Prosser. 'Oh, and I never got the socks I sponsored. You were supposed to get them at the end of the season.'

Then there is the case of Lars Elstrup, the former Luton Town striker and club record signing at £850,000. The Danish international won the 1992 European Championships with his national side, but, just a year after scoring the winner in the Euro semi-final against France, he quit football to join a religious cult.

Elstrup joined a group called Sangha, part of the Wild Goose religious sect, and changed his name to 'Darando', meaning 'the river that streams into the sea'. The Danish tabloids followed the group to the island of Funen, near Odense in Denmark, and printed tales of 'rampant free sex' involving 'Darando', also claiming that the sect's leaders were attempting to steal the star's career earnings. Elstrup certainly didn't find the happiness he was searching for in the loving arms of the cult. 'I tried to cut my wrists,' he said. 'I tried to hang myself. I was lying in bed for two years. I just wanted to die.'

After a brief footballing comeback with Odense, aborted when he walked out after the club refused to pay him during a trial, Elstrup found the tabloid headlines again. First, he was spotted waving his penis at shoppers in Copenhagen's busiest pedestrian street. 'In some respects I do this to provoke people,' he said. 'I am very aware of people's reactions and I love the fact that people recognise me as Lars Elstrup.' Whether people recognised him or not, they did throw small change at him. He made 27 krona, or £2.25, in an afternoon.

When Elstrup took his act to the streets of Odense, the locals were less generous. His willy-waving shenanigans were heckled and laughed at. He eventually lost his temper and slapped a giggling schoolboy about the face (with his hand, thankfully). When the authorities arrived, Elstrup got into a fight with a police officer, before being arrested. He told police he wished he'd hit the schoolboy harder. 'The kid deserved a fist,' he said.

He was subsequently expelled from the Wild Goose sect, who he unsuccessfully tried to sue. 'They're inhuman,' he said. 'They stole Devi, my dachshund!'

Despite ditching the cult, changing his name back to 'Lars Elstrup' and making a footballing comeback of sorts in the Danish Amateur League, Elstrup's behaviour remains more than odd. His official website, now sadly offline, detailed a multitude of bizarre beliefs, alongside a gallery of highly peculiar photographs. 'He works with healing the self, personal development, obtaining higher levels of consciousness, and sees man as being an energy,' read the bumf on his site. 'In his interaction with others, he supports the individual in finding his own inner truths and to get more contact with his self and God. He uses meditation, yoga, breathing exercises, therapy, that will help untie the inner knots, so life can be lived in a richer way.' And, yes, in the photographs on the website, Elstrup did have his knob out.

Several footballing drop-outs have turned to religion, swapping goals for God. The original 'God's Footballer' was Wolverhampton Wanderers' Peter Knowles. Regarded as one of the greatest footballing talents of the '60s, he quit the game in 1969, aged just 24, to become a Jehovah's Witness.

Knowles, the brother of former Tottenham star Cyril, felt that he couldn't allow himself to be worshipped by Wolves fans as a 'false idol'. Instead, he resigned at short notice and devoted all of his time to knocking on people's doors, offering copies of *Watchtower* and theories of creationism. Fans turned 'Oh My Darling Clementine' into a Peter Knowles terrace anthem, singing, 'Where's your Bible, Where's your Bible, Where's your Bible, Peter Knowles? In your handbag, In your handbag, In your handbag, Peter Knowles.' And singer/songwriter Billy Bragg immortalised Knowles in a track called 'God's Footballer' on his *Don't Try This at Home* LP.

Knowles scored 64 goals in 91 games, and the under-23 international was tipped to be on the verge of a full England call-up before his resignation. Wolves, ever hopeful, left the door open for a possible return for several years. But, despite many comeback rumours, Knowles never returned to football. Wolves finally ended Peter Knowles' contract in 1982, some 13 years after he last kicked a ball in anger.

Brazilian goalkeeper Claudio Taffarel became a legend after saving a penalty in the 1994 World Cup final and then saving two in the 1998 semi-final. 'That was God helping me,' Taffarel said after the semi. The goalkeeper, who won 101 international caps, was named a national hero by the Brazilian president and had a prayer published in his honour in newspaper *Jornal do Brasil*. By 2003, however, the 37 year old had lost his first-team place at Parma. He was offered a deal by Empoli, so he got into his BMW and headed along the A1 autostrada. Then his car conked out. Most people, on their way to signing a lucrative contract, would have telephoned the Italian AA, but not Taffarel. 'This was no mechanical coincidence,' he explained. 'This was God telling me to call it a day.'

And so, Taffarel hung up his gloves. He never did get to Empoli. 'He called us up and told us what had happened to his car,' said the club's sporting director, Giuseppe Vitale. 'He thinks it was destined to be this way, so he won't be joining us.'

And what of the World Cup winner who quit football because of the impending Armageddon? Argentinean goalkeeper Carlos Roa was the man whose penalty saves from Paul Ince and David Batty put England out of the 1998 World Cup finals. It was something of a last hurrah for the player because, as he announced to the gathered press, the world was going to end on 31 December 1999. Roa distanced himself from that claim somewhere around 1 January 2000.

But the teetotal vegetarian, nicknamed 'The Lettuce' by his teammates, still quit football. As a Seventh Day Adventist, he felt he couldn't continue to play on Saturdays. He claimed God had given him the opportunity to play in the World Cup and the strength to save the penalties against England. Now he wanted to pay God back and no longer play on the Sabbath by retiring from football.

His timing wasn't great. Manchester United had just offered Roa's club Real Mallorca £4 million for the goalkeeper. But even Mallorca's offer to Roa of a £2 million slice of the transfer fee, plus Man United's £1 million-a-year salary, couldn't convince him to reconsider. Perhaps not surprisingly, Roa's wife admitted she cried for a month when he broke the news.

Roa duly returned to Argentina and set up home at a remote ranch, spending his time farming and preaching to the locals. 'I am living a simple but hard life,' he said. 'Money isn't everything, God is more important. I think I'm very lucky. I have learned things that you don't learn on a football pitch, that people are kind, that they have big hearts and that we're all the same.'

Sadly, money became more of an issue than Roa might have anticipated. He returned to Mallorca to pick up an outstanding payment and inevitably ended up back between the sticks, before being subsequently transferred to another Spanish club, Albacete. He continues to keep goal remarkably successfully, what with the tail between his legs and all.

Roa's religious beliefs are nothing, however, compared to those of David Icke. The former Coventry City goalkeeper retired at the age of 21 due to arthritis in his joints. He went on to present the BBC's *Grandstand*, moved to the Isle of Wight to research a book on trainspotting and became a spokesman for the political Green Party. Then, after visiting Brighton medium Betty Shine, he decided he was, in fact, the Son of God.

Icke announced his belief to the world at a press conference at Gatwick Airport in 1991. He also declared that his spiritual advisor Mari Shawsun was the daughter of God and that his wife Linda (renamed Michaela after the archangel Michael) was the angel of God. Icke then proceeded to do the chat show rounds wearing a turquoise shell suit, turquoise being an apparent conduit of positive energy.

First up was *Wogan*, going out at primetime on BBC1. Jim Davidson was the night's top-billed guest, but most viewers tuned in to watch the tabloid-hyped man in the shell suit. They weren't to be disappointed. Within seconds of the start of the interview, Icke announced to host Terry Wogan, and several million television viewers, his belief that he was the Son of God.

'Why you? Why have you been chosen?' asked Wogan.

'People would have said the same thing to Jesus,' replied Icke. '"Who the heck are you? You're a carpenter's son."'

Icke proceeded to make a series of soothsaying predictions, involving huge earthquakes and other natural disasters interpreted as warnings to mankind, much to the amusement of the guffawing studio audience.

'The best way of removing negativity is to laugh and be joyous, Terry,' said Icke, 'so I'm glad that there's been so much laughter in the audience tonight.'

'But they're laughing at you, they're not laughing with you,' replied Wogan, in a damning put-down.

The studio audience burst into applause and, immediately, Icke was transformed from former footballer and likeable snooker anchorman, into a certifiable fruitloop with a carnival organ playing a perpetual circus tune inside his head. Icke was appalled by the reaction of the public. As a television presenter he had been respected, but now he admitted he couldn't walk down the street without being laughed at.

So Icke backtracked from his 'Son of God' claims and doomsday prophesies. They had, he claimed, been grossly exaggerated by the media. Icke-supporting group 'The Campaign For Philosophical Freedom' protested incredulously: 'With careful editing the *Wogan* show made David Icke out to be completely bonkers!' Of course, the *Wogan* show was actually transmitted as live, but that's by the by.

Icke left England and travelled the world to refine his beliefs. He stopped wearing turquoise shell suits, saying, 'Turquoise is an important colour, but you don't have to wear it all the time.'

On his return to the UK, he announced his new belief that global leaders and major celebrities, including the Queen, George W Bush, Tony Blair, Hillary Clinton and Kris Kristofferson, were in fact extraterrestrial twelve-foot lizards. His tales of multi-dimensional shape-shifting reptilian entities, known as the

BALLS

'Illuminati', secretly ruling the world apparently struck a chord with disenchanted humans. Icke became a celebrity once again, travelling the world to spread his conspiracy theories.

He also wrote ten books with exciting titles like *And the Truth Will Set You Free*, *Alice in Wonderland and The World Trade Center Disaster* and *Tales From the Time Loop: the Most Explosive Exposé of Global Conspiracy Ever Written and All You Need to Know to be Truly Free*. But detractors and claims of anti-Semitism dogged his new career, and he retired from public speaking in September 2003, declaring himself 'physically and emotionally exhausted.'

'If I'm mad like they say I am, why don't they leave me alone?' Icke said. 'Ever since I started exposing the reptilian elite, the opposite has happened. Why is that?'

It's because, David, you're as mad as tits on a vicar.

Of course, neither David Icke nor Carlos Roa is the most famous footballer, or even goalkeeper, to swap sport for religion. When Karol Jozef Wojtyla's football career was prematurely ended by the Nazi invasion of Poland in 1939, the 'powerfully built' goalkeeper of Wotsyla turned to a little-known religious group called 'the Catholic Church'. Karol Jozef Wojtyla, or Lolek to his pals, became Pope John Paul II.

Perhaps Isadore Irandir should have followed the likes of Icke, Roa and the Pope in quitting football when he found religion – because he clearly couldn't combine the two. The God-fearing goalie began every match kneeling in his goalmouth praying. Unfortunately, this ritual occasionally went on too long. In a 1970s Brazilian league game between Irandir's Rio Preto and Corinthians at the Bahia stadium, the mighty Roberto Rivelino used Irandir's ritual to his advantage. The Corinthians striker received the ball from the kick-off, looked up to see Irandir kneeling in prayer and blasted a 60-yard shot over the goalkeeper's head and into the net. Corinthians celebrated, and Irandir continued to pray. Then Irandir's brother ran onto the pitch, pulled out a revolver, fired six bullets into the ball and calmly walked off.

Of all footballing characters, surely none were as big and as colourful – or as mad – as CB Fry. Not only did Fry play football for Southampton, the ultimate sportsman also captained England at cricket and held the world long jump record. He was also a close friend of Adolf Hitler, a part-time nude model, almost a Liberal MP and very nearly the King of Albania.

Charles Burgess Fry was born in 1872, and he began his sporting career as a track and field athlete. In 1892 he set the world long jump record of 23 ft 5 in. The record stood for 21 years. Fry was also a world-class sprinter, and he would surely have won a gold medal or two at the first modern Olympic Games in 1896. Unfortunately his invitation to attend the competition was lost in the post. Something of a genius, Fry gained top class results in Latin and Greek at Oxford University and began to work as a journalist. He played cricket for Sussex in his spare time and later went on to captain England, where he once scored six first class centuries in successive innings. He also signed for Southampton Football Club, where his eccentric loftiness began to be noticed. Fry, a left-back, insisted on having his own changing room and bath, which caused conflict with his teammates. He played for Southampton in the 1902 FA Cup final against Sheffield United at Crystal Palace. Despite Fry's efforts, the Saints lost 2–1 in a replay. Fry was also courted by various rugby teams, but declined their offers because of his other sporting commitments.

But beneath Fry's sophisticated Olympian exterior lay a troubled man. He had suffered a breakdown while at Oxford and then became involved in a cruel and controversial relationship. Beatrice Sumner was ten years older than Fry and her past was littered with scandals. The pair married in 1898 but it soon became clear that Sumner was still involved with her previous lover and father of her illegitimate children, banker Charles Hoare. Fry was virtually penniless – he resorted to full-frontal nude modelling to pay the bills – and it was suggested that he suffered in a loveless marriage for 48 years because the affluent Mr Hoare continued to finance the couple's lifestyle.

During the First World War, the multi-talented Fry ran the Hamble Naval College. It was at this time he was inexplicably offered the Albanian throne. Albania's ruling family, the Weids, had fled back to their native Germany during the war. After hostilities ceased, the Albanians refused to allow the Germans to return. At the same time, Fry was asked by his great pal and cricketing partner Kumar Shri Ranjitsinhji to travel with him to Geneva. 'Ranji', an Indian Prince, had been chosen as a representative in the newly created League of Nations, and he asked Fry to accompany him as his scriptwriter.

The pair arrived in Geneva to find the Albanians searching for a new monarch. They were looking for an 'English gentleman' with an income of at least £10,000 per year. Ranji asked Fry if he would like to be crowned King Charles III of Albania. 'I accepted on the nail,' Fry later wrote. 'I was willing to be king of any nation.' Ranji set up a boozy interview with Albanian officials, and all went well. The only stumbling block was that the cash-strapped Fry did not have an income of anything like £10,000. Ranji did have the funds to help his friend, but he became reluctant to lose the services of his trusted companion to a foreign state. Fry couldn't come up with the cash, and the offer was withdrawn. 'If I had really pressed Ranji to promote me,' he wrote, 'it is quite on the cards that I should have been King of Albania yesterday, if not today.'

After narrowly failing to become a Liberal MP three times, Fry's mental health began to deteriorate. His marriage was said to be a major factor, with his daughter-in-law commenting, 'I should think anyone should have a breakdown married to her.' His son later said, 'My mother ruined my father's life.'

As the problems mounted, Ranji stepped in and took his friend to India, but Fry suffered another massive breakdown. He began to wear outlandish clothes and suffered from severe paranoia.

Then Fry developed an irrational fear of Indians, including his best friend. Ranji had nursed Fry through his illness, but the friendship was lost when a befuddled Fry left India. Ranji died in 1933 and was not around when his wayward former friend made his most flawed of judgement calls.

Fry first met Hitler in 1934 at the opening of an *autobahn*. The former footballer declared himself to be very impressed with the calibre of the Fuhrer's growing band of Aryan young men and tried to persuade the Nazis to create a Test cricket side. Hitler wasn't impressed with that idea, but he did manage to convince Fry of his anti-Semitic war-mongering beliefs in an hour-long meeting. Fry left Germany full of praise for the Nazis and even invited some of the Hitler Youth to his Naval College.

Despite his health problems, CB Fry lived to be 84. He died in 1956, and it is quite safe to say football will never see anything such as his like ever again.

If football played by humans is mad, imagine the lunacy of football played by animals. Elephant football is exactly what it says on the tin. Popular in Thailand, the game sees elephants attempt to kick or 'trunk' an oversized ball into a goal. Elephants are sacred animals in Thailand and are said to have a 'special love for sports'. They also enjoy racing, polo, tug-of-war and, of course, water spraying. Thai elephants play football against each other in 11-a-side matches on huge pitches, competing for the Jumbo Cup. They also compete on smaller pitches against, rather dangerously, teams of children. Team trainers refute the claims of People for the Ethical Treatment of Animals (PETA) that elephant football represents 'the ritualistic torture of baby elephants in the country's tourism industry'. Instead they see the game as a serious sport, albeit one played by big dumb animals who wouldn't know the offside rule if it smacked them in the trunk.

Elephant football actually dates back to the very beginnings of the professional game in England. In the 1890s the star attraction at the travelling Sanger's Circus was a penalty-taking elephant. The six-and-a-half-ton beast was said to be deadly from the spot and equally invincible when it came to saving penalties. When the circus arrived in Leicester, the management set up a publicity stunt involving Leicester Fosse football club. It was decided that some of the club's professional footballers would take on Jumbo the elephant in a gala penalty shoot-out. Four Leicester players took up the challenge and, in a packed big top, they were each asked to attempt to score two penalties and save two penalties against the elephant. The mighty Jumbo defeated the first three players in confident manner.

Then up stepped William Keech. Taking the matter extremely seriously, Keech looked the elephant in the eye, shaped to kick the ball into the left corner and knocked it to the right. Jumbo was fooled, moving to the left, and the goal was scored. Keech repeated his tactic for his second kick and again sent the elephant the wrong way. Then Keech took his place between the sticks and Jumbo stepped up to take its kicks. The elephant had obviously been watching Keech closely. It copied the footballer's technique, sending him the wrong way twice and scoring both kicks. The shoot-out ended 2–2, and sudden-death was required. Keech went first, again sending the elephant the wrong way. Jumbo had to score to remain in the competition, but the elephant's nerve seemed to fail. Keech saved the final kick and won the tournament, being presented with a specially engraved cup. But Jumbo never forgot the humiliation of his defeat – legend has it the elephant never lost a penalty shoot-out ever again.

Sanger's Circus later became known as Sanger's Royal British Menagerie and was incorporated into PT Barnum's legendary 'Greatest Show on Earth'. But Barnum, an American, didn't see fit to include soccer-playing animals in his show, and the spectacle of the penalty-taking elephant was lost forever.

It's not uncommon for animals to get involved in football

matches. There have been numerous instances of dogs running onto football pitches and chasing the ball during games.

In 2002, a cup tie between Lincoln Moorlands and Appleby Frodingham Athletic was abandoned when a police dog ran onto the pitch, stole a linesman's flag and bit three players. In the same year, a Scottish Cup match between Nairn County and Brora Rangers was called off because the pitch was covered with 'excessive dog excrement'. A 2003 cup quarter-final between Austrian sides Watten Wacker and SV Salzburg was held up for twenty minutes after a piglet invaded the pitch. Eleven thousand fans cheered as six security guards ran comically around the Innsbruck Tivoli stadium trying to catch the animal, which had escaped from a local farm.

A 2002 top flight Brazilian match between Botafogo and Gremio saw a lapwing save what would have been the winning goal. The bird swooped from the sky and deflected Botafogo striker Fabio's goal-bound shot away from the line. When aggrieved Botafogo player Ademilson was asked if the bird had been injured, he said, 'Unfortunately not. It flew away again.' The game ended 1–1, and Gremio fans chanted, 'Lapwing, lapwing!' as they left the ground.

Most impressively of all, in a Staffordshire Sunday Cup match between Knave of Clubs and Newcastle Town, a dog actually scored a goal. Knave were losing 2–0 when one of their players escaped from the Town defence. From 15 yards out, and with just the goalkeeper to beat, the Knave player managed to miscue his shot and the ball looked to be going woefully wide. Enter man's best friend. The dog ran onto the pitch, leapt into the air and headed the ball, which flew into the net. The goal was awarded, although celebrations were short-lived as the goal-scorer ran off to piss on a lamp-post, and Town resisted a canine-powered comeback to win 3–2.

Although we can possibly dismiss elephant football as a contrived tourist attraction, it is impossible to say the same of robot football. Not only do robot football organisers and participants believe they have a genuine alternative to real football, they actually intend to take over our beautiful game. Like a plotline from a *Matrix* or *Terminator* sci-fi film script, the stated aim of the RoboCup project is to, 'by 2050, develop a team of fully autonomous humanoid robots that can win against the human world champion team in soccer'. First stop the World Cup, next the enslavement of the human race.

The rules of robot football are pretty much the same as those of the real game, with goals, fouls and penalties all present and correct. The robots compete in different categories, including classes for humanoid robots, four-legged robots and robots with wheels. Robot players must move completely autonomously, without any mid-game interference from their designers. They use artificial intelligence 'independently and collectively' to decide playing and team strategies.

In principle, a good robot footballer has to be able to read the game via some sort of digital scanner, make quick decisions using an electronic brain and 'kick' the ball using some form of moveable appendage. The RoboCup organisers offer a more technical breakdown, saying, 'In order for a robot team to perform a soccer game, various technologies must be incorporated including: design principles of autonomous agents, multi-agent collaboration, strategy acquisition, real-time reasoning, robotics and sensor-fusion. RoboCup is a task for a team of multiple fast-moving robots under a dynamic environment.'

In 2003, 224 teams and 1,250 participants took part in the RoboCup in Italy. One of the stars of the tournament was Priscilla, a Swedish robot with human-like feet, 'complete with toe bones'. Priscilla played alongside teammates Elvis and Elvina in the Chalmers University of Technology team. Elvis was named because he has shaky hips. 'We are trying to make his leg lighter to give him more freedom,' said University scientist Professor Peter Nordin. 'But we don't want to give too much freedom to the robots as they will go crazy.' Good grief.

TALES FROM FOOTBALL'S NETHER REGIONS

The UK was represented by Bold Hearts from the University of Hertfordshire and Essex Rovers from the University of Essex. Alas, it seems that English robot footballers suffer from many of the same shortcomings as their human counterparts. In 1998, the England Robot Football squad reached the quarter-finals of the Robot World Cup. Unfortunately, according to one report, 'A thrilling match saw England eliminated, but only after seven goals had been scored against a talented Brazil side.'

5. STUPIDITY

Footballers have more money than sense. That's the reasoning wheeled out whenever a player gets into a spot of bother. But not all footballers are as dumb as a bag of rocks. Portsmouth goalkeeper Shaka Hislop used to work for NASA, Iain Dowie is a qualified rocket scientist and Graeme Le Saux has two A-levels and reads *The Guardian*. But they are the exceptions.

Perhaps football's aversion to intelligence can best be summed up by the tale of Pat Nevin and the *NME*. As a Chelsea player, Nevin favoured alternative music paper *New Musical Express* over traditional footballer reads like the *Sunday Sport* and *Razzle*. Unfortunately several members of the Chelsea squad took exception to their egg-headed teammate's reading matter. They regularly snatched Nevin's *NME* away from him and destroyed it – tearing it to pieces and throwing it into the shower. This happened every week for several months. Eventually Nevin put his superior intelligence to work. He sliced open the bottom lining of his kitbag and created a secret hidden compartment. Nevin then began to buy two copies of the newspaper. One was hidden under the lining, and another was placed in plain view. After his lowbrow colleagues had gleefully ruined the top copy,

Nevin could safely remove the second paper from its hiding place and read about the latest exploits of Echo and the Bunnymen and The Teardrop Explodes in relative bliss.

Many incidents of footballers behaving badly are fuelled by nothing more than gross stupidity. When Brazilian superstar Ronaldo arrived in South Korea for the 2002 World Cup he greeted his welcoming party with a slightly racist and entirely inappropriate Oriental impression that involved him grinning profusely while pulling back the skin around his eyes in order to achieve a cheeky Far Eastern look.

Cameroon striker Roger Milla was a household name in 1990 when, aged 42, he became the oldest player ever to play and score in the World Cup finals. Two years later he 'kidnapped' 120 pygmies. The footballer's intentions seemed good-natured when he arranged a football tournament for Cameroonian pygmies to raise money for their health and education, but the tournament was a failure. Less than 50 spectators turned up at the 50,000-seater Omnisports stadium to see teams like Bee-Sting of Lomie and Ants of Salapoumbe compete. Sadly, most of them had only come along to shout abuse at the diminutive players.

Then the 120 pygmies revealed they had been imprisoned in a single locked room at the stadium and watched over by guards – one of whom wore a Saddam Hussein T-shirt. 'You don't know the pygmies,' said a tournament spokesman, 'they are extremely difficult to keep in control.' The pygmies also complained of starvation, saying they had been fed just once over the course of the tournament's three days. 'They play better if they don't eat too much,' the spokesman explained. Milla didn't comment, but he did organise a further fundraising event in 1995. The pygmies, who live on the fringes of Cameroonian society in rainforests and are regarded by many fellow-countrymen as 'subhuman', beat Milla's side in a charity football match.

Paul 'Gazza' Gascoigne is remembered as the clown prince of British football. What is sometimes forgotten is that he was also arguably the greatest natural football talent Britain has ever produced. Gazza, who once stated his nationality as 'Church of England', was born in Gateshead in 1967. The midfielder began his career as an apprentice at Newcastle United, where he cleaned Kevin Keegan's boots. One day he took them home to show his mates and characteristically left the Golas on the Metro underground train.

Gazza made his first-team debut at the age of 17 and played 92 games for Newcastle, showing superb skill and scoring some wondrous goals. But Gazza also made something of a name for himself as a joker. He once booked a series of sunbed sessions for teammate Tony Cunningham, the black centre-forward. Then, after a demoralising 4–0 away defeat to Luton Town, after which Luton's players boasted in the press, Gazza orchestrated a stunning response in the return fixture. Showing immaculate skill, he led Newcastle to a 4–0 lead, before proceeding to run rings around the Luton team. He indulged in lengthy bouts of keepy-uppy and coerced teammate Kenny Wharton into literally sitting on the ball.

Tottenham Hotspur signed Gascoigne for £2 million in 1988. Arriving in London to finalise the deal, Gazza and his entourage took over a posh hotel and wreaked drunken havoc for 72 hours, all at Spurs chairman Irving Scholar's expense. The contract talks began with Gazza telling Scholar, 'We'd like to thank you for the best three days of our lives.'

Gazza's defining moment came at the World Cup finals in Italy in 1990. TV coverage of the tournament used revolutionary team line-up captions, featuring video footage of each player mouthing their own name. So Gary Lineker mouthed, 'Gary Lineker.' Chris Waddle mouthed, 'Chris Waddle.' And Paul Gascoigne mouthed, 'Fucking Wanker.' The coverage was supplied by Italian TV, and British stations had to grin and bear the clip and run it for the duration of the tournament. To compound matters, when the live TV cameras panned past him as the teams lined up during the national anthem, Gazza would stick out his tongue and make goggle eyes.

When England manager Bobby Robson called Gazza 'daft as a brush' before the tournament, he didn't know the half of what was to come. Gazza promptly turned up for training with hairbrushes down his socks instead of shinpads, feigned injury, drank beer and played marathon games of tennis in the midday sun. He also won a fortune during a squad race night. The players were betting large sums on videotaped horse races. What they didn't know was that Gazza had already watched the videotape, having bribed England physio Fred Street.

On another occasion, Gazza asked if he could skip dinner and have cheese and biscuits in his room instead, as he was feeling bloated. Bobby Robson agreed. Later that evening, on his way to dinner, Robson spotted Gazza, in full England tracksuit, heading out of the hotel door.

'Gascoigne!' shouted Robson. 'Where do you think you're going?'

'I'm going down the pub with my dad,' said Gazza.

'You what?' said Robson. 'I thought you were going to have cheese and biscuits in your bedroom.'

'I am,' said Gazza. 'I'll have them when I get back from the pub.'

The World Cup semi-final was the biggest game of Gazza's life. An insomniac at the best of times, he was unable to sleep on the night before the match and sneaked out of the hotel. Finding two Americans playing tennis, Gazza offered to take them on. Meanwhile, Bobby Robson realised his star player was missing. He scoured the hotel grounds and eventually found a sweating Gazza playing tennis single-handedly against both of the Americans. The footballer was despatched back to his room, but Robson saved his wrath for the Americans. 'Do you know who he is?' he bellowed. 'He has the biggest game of his life tomorrow and you've got him playing tennis!'

BALLS

And then came the semi-final against West Germany. Gazza famously cried after receiving a booking that would have kept him out of the final. In the event, England lost on penalties. But Gazza had been the tournament's brightest player, and his tears only endeared him more to the British public. He returned home a hero, arriving in London wearing a pair of plastic comedy breasts with 'Gazza' written across his stomach.

Returning to domestic action, he scored a stunning 35-yard free kick for Spurs against Arsenal in the 1991 FA Cup semi-final. But just minutes into the final against Nottingham Forest he made a dangerous and rash challenge that wrecked his knee ligaments. Gazza needed major surgery, and fought depression as he battled to regain his fitness.

After a year of rehabilitation Gazza was fit enough to sign for Lazio. On his first night in Rome, Gazza placed his shoes on the balcony of his hotel room and hid in a wardrobe to trick his minder into thinking he'd committed suicide. He then greeted the Italian press by standing up, asking for silence and farting at high volume. Lazio fans greeted Gazza with a friendly, if slightly misinterpreted banner reading, 'Gazza's boys, we are here, shake your women and drink your beer!' On the other hand, rival supporters offered a banner that read, 'Paul Gazza, you are fat poofta [sic].' Gazza responded by having Mick Hucknall-inspired curly ginger hair extensions fitted, presumably just so that they had something else to take the piss out of. But Gazza failed to find his feet in Italian football and was never more than a cult figure at Lazio.

Returning to Britain, Gazza joined Rangers in 1995. Still an England international, Euro '96 proved to be a great tournament for Gazza as he recaptured some of the old magic, scoring a memorable goal against Scotland. Off the pitch, however, Gazza was increasingly displaying obsessive behaviour: twitches, grimaces and outbursts, said to be linked to attention deficit disorder and obsessive compulsive disorder. He would also binge drink, and it was the booze that led him to the lowest point in his personal life, when he beat up his wife Sheryl. She divorced him, and Gazza admitted he contemplated suicide.

After disappointing spells at Middlesbrough and Everton, Gazza checked himself into an Arizona clinic to be treated for alcoholism. Gazza was still drinking, though, when he returned to England for a brief stint at Burnley. He was then variously linked with DC United, Dundee, Auckland Kingz, Carshalton Athletic and Exeter City, before signing for Chinese side Gansu Tianma in 2003.

A BBC television crew followed the footballer to one of China's poorest regions on the edge of the Gobi desert, and the resulting documentary, *Gazza – One Day At a Time*, made depressing viewing. Gazza appeared broken and battered by his addictions and obsessive disorders and seemed unable to accept that his best playing days could be behind him. He struggled to fit in with his new teammates and completely forgot he had signed on as a player–coach. Cutting a sad and lonely figure, Gazza spent his time away from the training pitch drinking and playing snooker. On a visit to an empty karaoke bar, Gazza crooned, 'England, I miss you!' As it happened, he was back in England within months following a contract dispute.

A trial with Wolverhampton Wanderers failed to bring Gazza a new playing contract, so instead he played in a charity match, turning up at the event with a broken nose sustained when he deliberately ran into a pub door. 'I ran into the door as a dare,' he said. 'I just thought it would be a bit of a laugh to head-butt the glass. And it was.'

Footballing stupidity on the pitch is best illustrated by missed penalties and own goals. Missing a penalty is pretty difficult to do. Football goalposts are 24 feet wide and 8 feet high. The goalmouth represents an area of 192 square feet. The average goalkeeper is just over 6 feet tall and less than 2 feet wide. In the goalmouth he takes up about 12 square feet. That leaves 180 square feet of empty goalmouth into which to slot a relatively tiny football. So how come the likes of Stuart Pearce, Chris Waddle, Gareth Southgate, Paul Ince and David Batty have all found it so difficult to do?

Probably the worst penalty miss of all time was Lancaster City player Peter Devine's fluffed effort in the 1990 Northern Premier League First Division Cup final against Whitley Bay. Devine tripped during his penalty run up and delivered only a desperate flap at the ball. His embarrassment was increased when video footage of the miss was broadcast on television and then became a staple clip on footballing gaffe videos.

Perhaps the only penalty miss that has been shown on television more often than Devine's is that of former Supremes singer Diana Ross. At the USA '94 opening ceremony in Chicago, the pop star was charged with the none-too-difficult task of kicking a penalty into an unguarded plastic goal. The goalposts would then collapse in an orgy of confetti and fireworks. Unfortunately, Ms Ross toe-punted her penalty well wide of the target, causing many an embarrassed smile. The goals still collapsed, the confetti still fell, the fireworks still went off and the tournament eventually got underway. Then, just days later, Diana Ross's penalty miss was surpassed by that of a pony-tailed Italian.

Roberto Baggio's fluffed effort in the 1994 World Cup final was one of the most famous and important penalty misses of all time. Baggio had done more than most to get Italy to the final in Pasadena against Brazil. For the first time ever, the World Cup final was decided on penalties.

Baggio needed to score to keep Italy in the game as he stepped up to face Brazil goalkeeper Taffarel. 'I knew Taffarel always dived,' said Baggio in his autobiography, *A Goal in the Sky*, 'so I decided to shoot for the middle. It was an intelligent decision, because Taffarel did go to his left, and he would never have got the shot I planned. Unfortunately, and I don't know how, the ball went up three metres and flew over the crossbar.' Baggio missed and Italy lost. The devastated striker was vilified by the Italian press and subsequently lost his place in the national team.

Can opposition fans distract stupid penalty takers? It is common for fans to leap up and down waving behind the goal in an attempt to put the kicker off. But, in 2003, one non-League supporter went a little bit further. Somerset's Morland Challenge Cup final between Norton Hill Rangers and Wookey FC finished 0–0 after extra time and had to be decided on penalties. As a Norton Hill player stepped up to take a sudden-death penalty, a female Wookey supporter behind the goal lifted up her shirt and flashed her breasts. Her devious tactic worked. The distracted penalty taker ballooned his kick over the crossbar, with the ball apparently ending up in the club car park. Wookey won the penalty shoot-out 3–2 and lifted the Cup. Norton Hill's fans were furious, with some penning a strongly-worded letter to the local paper, but the players took it on the chest. 'We've not complained,' Norton Hill captain Lee Baverstock told the *Gloucester Citizen*. 'At the time we were not happy, but we lost on the night and just decided to get on with it.'

In February 2004, Carmine Gautieri of Italian Serie B side Atalanta came up with a novel way of preventing rivals Avellino from taking a penalty. Angry that a last-minute penalty had been awarded against his side, Gautieri attempted to dig up the penalty spot. It took 20 minutes for the spot to be re-measured, re-filled and re-painted. By that time the pressure had clearly got to Avellino striker Marco Capparella. He struck his penalty kick against the crossbar, meaning Gautieri's gamesmanship had earned Atalanta a 0–0 draw and preserved the side's 20-game unbeaten run.

If penalty misses are stupid, own goals are idiotic. One of the earliest recorded own goals was scored in the 1877 FA Cup final between Wanderers and Oxford University. Wanderers goalkeeper Arthur Kinnaird caught a seemingly innocuous shot and fell backwards, carrying the ball over the goal line. Many spectators and reporters failed to realise that Oxford had taken the lead, as they were so unused to seeing own goals. Kinnaird's blushes were later saved, as Wanderers went on to win the match 2–1.

Arthur Kinnaird wasn't just a goalkeeper. He was the only man to play in Cup finals both in goal and outfield. He played in nine finals and scored in three of them. In the 1878 final, he started up front, scored and then went in goal after Wanderers' keeper broke his arm. Kinnaird was perhaps football's first celebrity, a kind of nineteenth-century David Beckham, albeit a Scottish one with a big red beard who played in long white trousers, a jumper and a cricket cap. Lord Kinnaird, as he was endowed, eventually became president of the Football Association. In 1911, he was presented with the FA Cup to commemorate 21 years in the post. It wasn't the original FA Cup, however. That was stolen from a shop window in 1895, after being loaned to boot manufacturer William Shillock by holders Aston Villa. A reward of £10 was offered, but the Cup was never returned. Villa were fined £25 – the cost of a new trophy.

For more own goal stupidity we must leave these shores. In 1994, Barbados won a Caribbean Cup qualifier against Grenada by deliberately scoring an own goal. Barbados needed to win the match by two clear goals to qualify for the final stage, otherwise Grenada would progress. Everything was going to plan, with Barbados holding a 2–0 lead. Then, with seven minutes left to play, Grenada scored to make it 2–1.

Now Barbados turned their attention to a bizarre Caribbean Cup rule. The tournament organisers had decreed that, should a game go into extra time, a winning golden goal would count as two strikes towards goal difference. With a proper goal eluding them, Barbados decided to put the game into extra time and look for a golden goal. They deliberately scored an own goal to level the tie at 2–2.

Then Grenada realised if they could score a goal at either end they would still go through. Now Barbados were forced to defend both goals. Amazingly, they managed to hold out, and the game went into extra time. Barbados' shady tactics paid off. They scored the winning golden goal four minutes into extra time, meaning, according to the tournament rules, that they effectively won the game 4–2 and progressed to the finals. There they failed to win a match and were eliminated at the group stage.

In a 1998 Asian Tiger Cup game between Indonesia and Thailand in Ho Chi Minh City, *both* sides attempted to score own goals in order to lose the game. Both teams had already qualified for the semi-finals, but this group stage match would decide their opponents. The winning team would top the group and go on to play hosts, Vietnam. Neither Indonesia nor Thailand fancied meeting the tournament favourites in the red-hot atmosphere of Hanoi, so both teams attempted to throw the match. Both proved equally ineffectual, and the score was tied at 2–2 with only seconds remaining. Then Indonesia decided to score an own goal. With Thailand bizarrely defending their opposition's goal, Indonesia's goalkeeper Mursyid Effendi grabbed the ball, turned and booted it into his own net. Indonesia lost the match and avoided playing Vietnam. They played Singapore instead and, fittingly, they lost.

The ultimate tale of own goal stupidity took place on the Indian Ocean island of Madagascar. On 31 October 2002, a professional football team deliberately scored 149 goals in one match. AS Adema were playing Stade Olympique L'Emyrne (SOE) in the final game of the island's league championship. SOE and Adema had stood neck-and-neck in the tournament, until SOE were held to a controversial 2–2 draw in the penultimate game of the season, in which the referee awarded a very late and dubious penalty against them. Adema were crowned champions, and SOE were highly aggrieved.

The final match offered an opportunity for SOE to protest their mistreatment. SOE kicked off – and immediately kicked the ball into their own net. One–nil. The ball was re-spotted, SOE centred and again scored an own goal. Two–nil. With their coach orchestrating proceedings from the dugout, SOE continued to fire shots into their own net from every kick-off. Adema's bemused players stood around open-mouthed, the referee struggled to keep a tally of the score and irate supporters besieged stadium ticket booths demanding refunds. At the final whistle, SOE had scored a massive 149 own goals to hand Adema a 149–0 victory.

This record-breaking farce was certainly an impressive protest. In netting 149 times in 90 minutes, SOE had scored one own goal every 36.2 seconds. It was a mighty achievement although, upon hearing the final whistle, you can't help but think they must have been disappointed not to have reached 150. The Malagasy Football Federation, however, were not impressed. They handed out bans to the team coach and four SOE players.

When SOE self-imploded they, of course, shattered the own goal record. But they also easily smashed another record that had stood for 177 years – that for the highest score in top class football. The previous record was held by Arbroath, who beat Aberdeen's Bon Accord 36–0 in an 1885 Scottish Cup tie. This was perhaps no surprise, as 'Bon Accord' were actually Orion Cricket Club, who had received an invitation to enter the Scottish Cup by mistake. They made up a name, turned up without boots and were 15–0 down at half-time. There was so little for Arbroath's goalkeeper Jim Milne to do that he borrowed an umbrella from a friend in the crowd and stood sheltering from the rain as the action continued at the opposite end of the pitch. John Petrie scored 13 goals in the match, and the score could have been much higher had referee Dave Stormont not taken pity on Bon Accord and disallowed seven Arbroath goals with dubious offside decisions. Arbroath fans claim their team could have further added to their tally had goal nets been invented, with precious seconds lost every time a goal-bound shot was retrieved from the crowd.

Remarkably, at the same time on the same day, just 20 miles

away, Dundee Harp were busy hammering Aberdeen Rovers by a similarly preposterous margin. At the end of the match the referee admitted he had lost count of the score, but believed it to be 37–0. Harp's honest officials said they had only counted 35 goals, and the score was duly recorded as 35–0. Harp happily looked forward to claiming the world record, until Arbroath's score, and their own honesty, scuppered their plans.

6. MUSIC AND FILMS

There are three types of football records. There are records about football by non-footballers, there are records about football by footballers and, worst of all, there are records not about football by footballers. Generally, records about football by non-footballers are celebrations of the beautiful game. With examples including 'World in Motion' and 'Three Lions', they are, although their merit is relative, usually the best. Records by footballers about football, like 'Back Home' and 'Anfield Rap', are generally made to coincide with an international competition or cup final. They are cash-ins, and are always rubbish. And records not about football by footballers, such as 'Diamond Lights' and 'Head Over Heels in Love' are flatulent ego-massaging exercises that scrape the very foot of the tub every single time.

Back in the 1930s, FA Cup final singles were somewhat different than they are today. In 1932, the FA Cup squads of Newcastle United and Arsenal released a joint spoken-word record called 'Meet the Teams'. The disc offers a 'few words' from Newcastle centre-forward Jack Allen and even fewer words from inside-right Jimmy Richardson:

Allen: 'You speak truly when you say "a few words". All
   I want is to hit that ball so hard into the net that no
   goalkeeper can get near it. Let Richardson, our inside-
   right, tell you what he feels about it.'

Richardson: 'Deeds, not words, that's me.'

Allen: 'That's the stuff, Richardson.'

Then, Arsenal striker Jack Lambert offers some insight into the making of a football record: 'Here I can say Jack's the boy for work. My motto as a centre is "forward". And I hope I can smash records at Wembley easier than I find making a record in front of the mike . . . I will do my best anyway.'

But it was Jack Allen who hit that ball so hard into the net that the goalkeeper couldn't get near it, twice, to give Newcastle a 2–1 win. Allen's first strike was the controversial 'over the line goal', from a Richardson cross which appeared to have gone out of play. Presumably, Richardson had few words to say on the matter. Deeds, not words.

The 1930s also saw the release of the first great football record. Gracie Fields, the Rochdale-born music hall and film star, was the most famous person in the UK next to royalty in the 1930s. Her 1931 record, 'Pass, Shoot, Goal' is a catchy and fitting paean to the beautiful game. The chorus, belted out in an incredibly high voice with a plinky-plonk piano backing, runs, 'Football, football, sends them up the pole, You hear their gentle voices calling, Pass! Shoot! Goal! Potty, dotty, right up the sausage roll, You hear their gentle voices calling, Pass! Shoot! Goal!'

At first glance, Gracie's ditty appears to be a charming, rose-tinted appraisal of the gentlemen's game. The meaning of the phrase 'right up the sausage roll' may have been lost to history, but there is much in the lyrics that the modern day football fan can relate to. However, as the song develops, Gracie sings of football violence and beating up the ref ('The poor referee is kicked by three or four, Right between his whistle and the half-time score'). Then, as the record fades out, Gracie can be heard having an argument with a fellow fan who has been pouring scorn on the team. 'You're going to get yourself a new team?' she cries, 'Go and get yourself a new face!' Charming.

In the modern era, football and music have become regular bedfellows, although their relationship is not always a comfortable one. Football and music became inextricably linked in the 1990s, the era of Euro '96, *Fever Pitch*, fanzines and Fantasy Football. Rock group Oasis played Manchester City's Maine Road. Five-a-side competitions became fixtures at pop festivals. Baddiel and Skinner released 'Three Lions'. Former Verve singer Richard Ashcroft revealed he used to be 'a bit useful'. Beckham married Posh Spice. Redknapp married Louise. It stands to reason that football and music – both passionate, exciting, important things – should go together like toast and melted butter.

A 2003 survey conducted by Manchester University revealed the musical tastes of Premiership footballers by polling their pre-match listening. Eminem was the most popular choice, with seven Premiership sides choosing the rapper's music in the dressing room. 'Eminem's music may play a role rather like the Haka in helping players reach an aroused competitive state,' explained music psychologist Dr Neil Todd. Manchester United psyched up by listening to Iggy Pop's 'Lust For Life', and Newcastle United prepared with Mark Knopfler's 'Local Hero'. Other dressing room favourites included U2, Oasis, Robbie Williams and Kylie Minogue.

Former footballers, now TV pundits, Terry Venables and Ron Atkinson have both tried to pass themselves off as Sinatra-style crooners. Current footballers Andy Cole and Lomana Lua Lua have both recorded rap records. Cole's misnamed 'Outstanding' failed to chart, and Lua Lua's has yet to be released, despite the fact that it is apparently a hit in the dressing room. Lua Lua occasionally 'jams' with former teammate Nolberto Solano, who is an ace trumpet player. Chelsea's Carlton Cole is a tip-top hip-hop

'MC'. West Ham's Christian Dailly is in a rock band called South Playground. And beardy former US international Alexi Lalas has released several albums, including one called *Ginger*. Even David Beckham has turned up on record, singing backing vocals on wife Victoria's really quite rubbish 'Out of Your Mind' pop single, although his contribution to the final recording can best be described as negligible.

The football–music interface also swings the other way. Most impressively, crooner Julio Iglesias played in goal for Real Madrid between 1961 and 1962. His career was cut short at the age of 20 when he was involved in a serious car crash. Legend has it that a hospital nurse gave him a guitar with which to pass the time, and the rest, as they say, is history. Rod Stewart was once on the books at Brentford before fame came to call. As a pop singer, Stewart later recorded a single with the Scotland World Cup squad. Spandau Ballet stars Martin Kemp and Steve Norman both played for Melchester Rovers in the 1980s. Kemp, who would go on to act in *EastEnders*, scored on his debut for the fictional comic book side in *Roy of the Rovers* comic. And both Shakin' Stevens and Mick Hucknall out of Simply Red lined up for Fulchester United, alongside half-man, half-fish goalkeeper Billy 'The Fish' Thomson in *Viz*.

Cue an Alan 'Fluff' Freeman-style hit parade of the top ten most memorable football records. It should be noted that 'memorable' does not always equal 'any good'. The ten records are ranked in order of chart performance. Blame the record-buying public for the following, mostly atrocious, offerings:

1. England New Order – 'World in Motion' (1990) – reached No. 1

Generally acknowledged as the best ever football song, New Order manage to retain their indie credibility by, for the most part, keeping footballers out of the equation. Beginning with the most famous piece of football commentary of all time, Kenneth

BALLS

Wolstenholme's 'Some of the crowd are on the pitch . . .', 'World in Motion' utilises New Order's trademark electro-pop, low-slung bass and nonsensical lyrics to great effect. The chorus is suitably singable, although strangely football-free, and suddenly it becomes clear why 'World in Motion' was a success – it's not really about football at all, it's a love song. Unfortunately, things go ever so slightly pear-shaped when the footballers eventually turn up. It's still unclear what Peter Beardsley, Paul Gascoigne, Steve McMahon, Chris Waddle and Des Walker contributed to the record. They were all at the recording, and appeared in the video, but can't be heard on the record. Instead, it is John Barnes who provides the song with its possibly unintentional comic interlude, with surely the very worst rap ever committed to vinyl. Granted, this was probably not Barnes' worst performance in an England shirt. There follows the obligatory chanty bit, and you have pretty much the perfect football single. The song gave New Order their first UK number one hit. A proposed 2002 remix, featuring a rap from David Beckham, was never released.

2. Baddiel & Skinner – 'Three Lions' (1996, 1998, 2002) – No. 1, No. 1, No. 16

Comic duo David Baddiel and Frank Skinner were the hosts of funny 1990s TV footy show, *Fantasy Football League*, when they wrote the lyrics of 'Three Lions', set to music by Ian Broudie of The Lightning Seeds. Clearly a homage to 'World in Motion' (even the 'Three Lions' bit is nicked from John Barnes' rap), the song is another sing-a-long terrace anthem, with lyrics that actually make some sense, and are about football, which is always nice in a football song. Citing England's numerous disappointments, the lyrics also recall 1966 and look optimistically towards a Euro '96 win that never happened. The song did better than the team. It spent two weeks at number one, and its catchy 'Football's coming home' refrain was sung heartily by Wembley crowds before England's Euro matches. In 1998 (32 years of hurt) it was re-

released to coincide with the World Cup. And although the attempt to update it should have failed (the new lyrics rattled on about Gazza and Stuart Pearce, neither of whom made it to France 98) it did top the charts. It comprehensively outsold the official England theme by England United – actually Echo and the Bunnymen featuring The Spice Girls, someone from Space and that guy out of Ocean Colour Scene. (Apparently the FA chose England United's '(How Does it Feel to Be) on Top of the World' after hearing an early demo, although you can't really imagine the then FA chief executive Graham Kelly being handed a grubby cassette at the back of a Bunnymen gig and remarking, 'Hmm, I really loved "The Killing Moon".') In 2002 (36 years of hurt) there was another 'Three Lions' re-release, but the song only reached number 16 in the run-up to the Japan and Korea World Cup finals. No doubt it will resurface again, as a real phenomenon among football songs, unlike, say, Ant and Dec's 2002 attempt to replicate the feel of the song with the awful 'On the Ball'.

3. England World Cup Squad – 'Back Home' (1970) – No. 1

The quintessential football squad song, 'Back Home' features the dubious harmonies of the 22 England players who travelled as champions to Brazil for the 1970 World Cup finals. Featuring the vocal talents of the likes of Jeff Astle, Alan Ball, Gordon Banks, Bobby Charlton, Geoff Hurst and Bobby Moore, the song is a strangely enduring one. It was chosen as the theme tune for Baddiel and Skinner's *Fantasy Football League*, which also regularly showcased the unique singing ability of Astle. Fittingly, England were knocked out by West Germany in the quarter-finals and were themselves 'back home' in time to watch the final on the telly.

BALLS

4. Gazza & Lindisfarne – 'Fog on the Tyne (Revisited)' (1990) – No. 2

Geordie folk-rockers Lindisfarne had three top ten hits in the 1970s, but their biggest single was a remake of 'Fog on the Tyne', with uncouth footballer-stroke-kebab connoisseur Paul Gascoigne on board. Gazza was hot property after his tears at Italia '90, and the public lapped up his first foray into the world of pop. The song was slightly rewritten for Gazza, the words are shouted rather than sung and an '80s tinpot beat replaces the original version's folksy instrumentation. The video features a shell-suit-and-chunky-necklace-wearing Gazza superimposed over images of Newcastle's Tyne Bridge. Such was the success of 'Fog on the Tyne' that the presumably ironically named Best Records released a follow-up just six weeks later. Unfortunately, 'Geordie Boys (Gazza Rap)' failed to match the success of its predecessor, only reaching number 31.

5. Fat Les – 'Vindaloo' (1998) – No. 2

This really quite rubbish effort was lapped up by lager-swilling Burberry boys in the run up to France '98. The brainchild of London drinking buddies Keith Allen (comedian and 'World in Motion' co-writer), Damien Hirst (dead sheep in formaldehyde artist) and Alex James (scruffy bassist of pop group Blur), 'Vindaloo' is a simple, shout-along tune designed to appeal to the lowest common denominator. The song failed to find a home on the terraces, despite the distribution of thousands of song sheets outside the England team's World Cup venues. Nevertheless, it was bought in spades and reached number two in the charts. Fat Les returned in time for Euro 2000, with a surprisingly straight version of 'Jerusalem'. It was a bigger hit than the group's failed festive single, 'Naughty Christmas (Goblin in the Office)'.

6. Liverpool FC – 'Anfield Rap (Red Machine in Full Effect)' (1988) – No. 3

Craig Johnston invented the Adidas Predator football boot. That was a good idea. Johnston also came up with the concept for 'Anfield Rap'. That wasn't. The accompanying video is a rare sight to behold. Johnston, Bruce Grobbelaar, John Barnes, John Aldridge and company wear Beastie Boys-style VW necklaces and backwards baseball caps and stand in front of a graffiti-covered wall. 'They don't just play, they can rap as well,' the song contends. The evidence that follows suggests otherwise. Bizarre highlights include 'World in Motion' rapper John Barnes offering the very nearly inappropriate, 'I come from Jamaica, My name is John Barnes, When I do my thing, The crowd go bananas.' The rhyming leaves something to be desired. Liverpool were deservedly beaten in the 1990 FA Cup final, courtesy of a Lawrie Sanchez goal and a penalty save by Dave Beasant, by rank outsiders Wimbledon.

7. Tottenham Hotspur FC – 'Ossie's Dream' (1981) – No. 5

Stand up Chas and Dave, two beardy cockney stereotypes who have made a career out of penning annoying 'Knees Up Mother Brown'-style, up the apples and pears, round the old Joanna, sing-alongs. 'Rabbit, Rabbit' and 'Snooker Loopy' have almost certainly never been brought to the attention of the Ivor Novello songwriting award judging panel. Between 1981 and 1991, Chas and Dave's favourite football team, Tottenham Hotspur, reached the FA Cup final four times. To celebrate these occasions, Chas and Dave released four FA Cup final singles. 'Ossie's Dream (Spurs are on their Way to Wembley)' was the most memorable, some say most annoying, of the four. Featuring the vocal stylings of Argentinean midfielder Ossie Ardiles, the song includes the memorable line, 'Ossie's going to Wembley, His knees have gone all trembly.' Ardiles himself then details how he plans to win the Cup for 'Tottingham'. Spurs did win the Cup in 1981, and Chas and Dave's 'Tottenham Tottenham' and 'When the Year Ends in One' proved equally inspiring in 1982 and 1991. However, 'Hot Shot Tottenham' failed to help Spurs overcome Coventry in 1987. Spurs have failed to reach the FA Cup final since 1991, and Chas and Dave remain in mothballs.

8. Scotland World Cup Squad – 'We Have a Dream' (1982) – No. 5

Following the less than prophetic 'Easy Easy' in 1974 and 1978's 'Ole Ola' featuring Rod Stewart, Scotland recruited *Gregory's Girl* star John Gordon Sinclair to sing 'We Have a Dream'. *Gregory's Girl* has a bit of footy in it, but Sinclair was nevertheless an odd choice. Perhaps understandably, Gordon Strachan was kicked out of the recording studio for laughing. The single, written by BA Robertson, hit number five in the charts. But Scotland's dream turned sour. They were inevitably knocked out in the first round. By 1998, Scotland's hopes seemed to have faded even further, as few football songs have been less optimistic than Del Amitri's dour 'Don't Come Home Too Soon' – essentially 'Yeah, We're Crap, but We Might Just Scrape a Draw Against Morocco'.

9. Glenn & Chris – Diamond Lights (1987) – No. 12

Tottenham's favourite fancy Dans, Glenn Hoddle and Chris Waddle, made a bizarre bid for pop stardom with this nightmarish tune. Like a mullet-wearing version of Robson and Jerome, the twosome looked excruciatingly uncomfortable in the pop world. The song itself has thankfully long been forgotten, but Hoddle and Waddle's awful *Top of the Pops* performance cannot be so easily erased from the memory. Wearing horrific '80s tops, the pair stood under disco lights and awkwardly swayed their way through a miming performance in front of a gaggle of unimpressed schoolgirls. Nevertheless, Waddle later explained that Hoddle's unique mind powers allowed him to avoid embarrassment. In 2000, that performance was voted number 28 in a Channel 4 viewer's poll to find the '100 TV Moments From Hell'. In terms of sheer inanity, 'Diamond Lights' eclipsed even Kevin Keegan's 1979 minor hit 'Head Over Heels in Love'. Coincidentally, Keegan also sported a dodgy barnet when he recorded that travesty.

10. Germany World Cup Squad – 'Far Away In America' (1994) – failed to chart

You're a tough-tackling football side keen to herald your arrival at the USA '94 World Cup finals. You decide to release a pop single to declare your intentions of winning the competition. Who better to team up with than celebrated gay icons The Village People, best known for camp disco tunes 'YMCA', 'Macho Man' and 'In the Navy'? This almost unbelievable team-up saw Germany's Stefan Effenberg, Oliver Kahn, Jürgen Klinsmann, Lothar Matthaus, Karlheinz Riedle and Rudi Voller team up with the Village People's Indian, Soldier, Construction Worker, Cop, Cowboy and Biker. The English lyrics, as presented on several internet lyric databases, are simply unintelligible. The catchy chorus runs, 'Far away in America, We're gonna making, Find a place is shaking, Play in America, We're gonna making, Get it up and shaking, You've gonna find to a light, baby, Come on and know it's all right, Far away in America, Let's go!' Despite no one having the slightest idea what any of that means, the record was a number one hit in Germany, proving that Germans must indeed have a keen sense of humour. Then again, fact fans, in German the word 'rock' does mean 'skirt'. Unfortunately, Germany crashed out of the 1994 World Cup, losing 2–1 to Bulgaria in the quarter-finals. More importantly, the Germans gave us 'Far Away in America', unquestionably the very worst football record of all time.

In the grand scheme of things, there are not a great number of football films. There are two main reasons for this. Firstly, most films are made in Hollywood or Bollywood and neither the US nor

BALLS

India are the most receptive of lands to football. Secondly, it is extremely difficult to film a fictitious football match without it resembling a scene from *Keystone Kops*. Football fans going to see football films demand, at the very least, realistic football scenes. And no matter how many stand-ins, cut-aways and special effects you implement, you simply cannot put Sean Bean into a football film and convince the audience he is any good (see *When Saturday Comes* for more information).

Gregory's Girl is an above average film, telling of a romance between John Gordon Sinclair's goalkeeper and Dee Hepburn's striker, but the football scenes are rubbish. *Bend It Like Beckham* was a huge hit in the US because of the girl power/girl's soccer angle, and in the rest of the world because of the David Beckham association. It was not, by any stretch of the imagination, a hit, because of its horrifically poor football scenes. Fellow British films *There's Only One Jimmy Grimble* and *Mike Bassett, England Manager* were minor hits because they were relatively funny and not because they represented any giant leap in depicting football on-screen. *Fever Pitch*, the screen adaptation of the Nick Hornby book, sensibly took its football scenes from actual TV footage.

A good football film needs to authentically re-create the game and the drama that naturally surrounds it. In practice, this means leaving the football to real footballers and the writing and direction to genuine football fans.

Take *The Arsenal Stadium Mystery*, a solid 1939 crime drama starring Leslie Banks and the entire 1937–38 Arsenal League championship-winning side. Banks is Inspector Slade of Scotland Yard, brought in to investigate the murder of a star player during a friendly match. The football scenes are left to the real Arsenal side, and the end result is suitably dramatic. The film only falls down when it allows the players and staff, including manager George Allison and captain Eddie Hapgood, to speak.

Few people have the talent to be both a footballer and an actor – just look at Vinnie Jones. Jones' unlikely turns in films like *Lock*,

TALES FROM FOOTBALL'S NETHER REGIONS

Stock and Two Smoking Barrels and *Snatch* make him the most successful footballer-turned-actor. But none of the former Wimbledon hardman's film roles can match the most bizarre entry into the footballers-in-films category.

1978 Footballer of the Year and former Charlton Athletic star Allan Simonsen played himself in *Skytten* (*Marksman*), a 1977 thriller about a deranged sniper (Jens Okking). One scene sees Okking shoot Simonsen dead during an international match. Bizarrely, the sequence was shot during a real match. The director asked the footballer to lie completely still for a few moments after attempting a header. Blood was added later, via the magic of special effects. Thankfully for Simonsen, bookings for simulation had yet to be introduced. *Internet Movie Database* (*IMDb*) reviewer, McBuff from Denmark, says the film 'misses the mark (so to speak)'. According to the *IMDb*, Simonsen actually 'starred' in another film, but *Hero: The Official Film of the 1986 FIFA World Cup* doesn't really count.

Another odd footballer-in-a-film occurrence is Julian Joachim in Hollywood blockbuster *Hannibal*. The Thomas Harris-penned Hannibal Lector flesh-fest features the player in a scene set in an Italian police station. On a TV set in the background of one shot, Joachim can clearly be seen playing for Aston Villa.

Pelé has starred in numerous films, including 1975's *This Is Pelé* – a retelling of the player's life story featuring a soundtrack composed and sung by the great man himself. But the very worst Pelé film is surely *Hotshot*, a 1987 picture saddled with the awful tagline, 'They've got nothing in common but the determination to be the best.' Featuring a less than star-studded cast including Mario van Peebles and Jimmy Smits, the film follows an American soccer player as he heads for stardom under the tutorage of Pelé himself. *IMDb* reviewer Skhemka calls it, 'Awful. Nothing to do with soccer. The actors are typical Americans who do not know what football ("soccer") is all about.'

Julio Iglesias certainly knows what football is all about. He played for Real Madrid before a car crash ended his career, and he's made a film about it called *La Vida Sigue Igual* (which roughly translates as *Life Rolls On*). The 1969 film stars Julio as himself and sees him overcome the disappointment of losing his football career by becoming a middle-of-the-road pop singer. Just like Pelé, Julio penned the soundtrack to his film. The title track features the lyrics, 'Some are born, Others will die, Some will laugh, Others will cry, In the end, How it works is, People go away, Others replace them, Life rolls on!'

Ian 'Lovejoy' McShane isn't a footballer. Any doubts over that fact can soon be removed by viewing *Yesterday's Hero*, a 1979 flick penned by the one and only Jackie Collins. McShane plays Rod Turner, a washed-up alcoholic of a former footballer who attempts a comeback with the help of his rock star ex-girlfriend Cloudy Martin (Suzanne Sommers). McShane joins 'Leicester Forest' under the management of Adam Faith, and all the seeds are sown for two hours of spectacularly bad Collins-scripted twittery.

Perhaps the best-loved football film is *Escape To Victory*. Unfortunately, other than representing an opportunity to see the likes of Bobby Moore and Pelé play in the same team, as a film it fails to inspire. Using football as a rather heavy-handed metaphor for war, the plot sees a bunch of Allied prisoners of war take on a team of Nazis in a propaganda match. A half-time escape is planned, but the players swap their chance of freedom for the chance of pulling back a four-goal first-half deficit. Sylvester Stallone is the obligatory heroic American, and Pelé is shoehorned into the side on the premise that he is a Trinidadian Allied soldier. Unfortunately, despite the cast of footballing legends, the football scenes are curiously unrealistic. Lest we forget, the Allies' squad line-up was:

1. Robert Hatch (Sylvester Stallone – USA)
2. Michael Fileu (Paul Van Himst – Belgium)
3. John Colby (Michael Caine – England)
4. Pieter Van Beck (Co Prins – Holland)

5. Doug Clure (Russell Osman – England)

6. Terry Brady (Bobby Moore – England)

7. Arthur Hayes (John Wark – Scotland)

8. Carlos Rey (Osvaldo Ardiles – Argentina)

9. Sid Harmor (Mike Summerbee – England)

10. Luis Fernandez (Pelé – Brazil)

11. Erik Borge (Soren Linsted – Denmark)

Substitutes:

Paul Wolchek (Kazimierz Deyna – Poland)

Gunnar Hilsson (Hallvar Thoresen – Norway)

Tony Lewis (Kevin O'Callaghan – Ireland)

Aside from Stallone and Caine, that is an undeniably impressive side. But, by the time the film was made in 1981, Bobby Moore was 40 years old. Pelé was 41 and had been retired for four years. Perhaps that in part explains why the Allies make such hard work of overcoming a Nazi team containing just three real footballers. According to the unofficial *Escape To Victory* website, the Nazi team contained two Schmidts and no less than four Kuntzs. The website owner, Spodrum, also defends the film's dodgy acting, saying, 'What do you expect? They were professional and ex-professional players, not actors!'

Director John Huston was on the right wavelength with *Escape To Victory*. He cast the likes of Caine and Max von Sydow to act, Stallone to appeal to the US market and the footballers to, well, play football. Unfortunately, the football scenes are too carefully choreographed to retain any sense of reality and the script isn't up to much either. Nevertheless, it's hard not to feel some empathy with Spodrum when he says, 'True the script isn't the best, but how many chances do you get to see Bobby Moore, Ossie Ardiles, Pelé and Michael Caine play in a game of footy together? And tell me that the Pelé goal isn't a brilliant moment.' For the record, despite a stirring second-half performance, the Allies fail to beat the Nazis. The match ends 4–4.

BALLS

Pelé's overhead kick notwithstanding, the best realisation of football on-screen is in Ken Loach's 1969 film *Kes*. Adapted from Barry Hines' novel *A Kestrel For A Knave*, the film is the gritty grim-up-north tale of young Billy Casper – a schoolboy who finds solace from his tough life in his love for a kestrel. The highlight of the picture is undoubtedly the much celebrated football scene. Loach used many non-actors to achieve a cinéma vérité documentary feel. One such non-actor was local teacher Brian Glover, who was recommended to Loach by Barry Hines for the role of bullying PE teacher Mr Sugden. As Sugden, Glover leads his ragtag bunch of pupils out onto a muddy field and removes his tracksuit to reveal a Manchester United shirt. 'I'll be Bobby Charlton today, boys,' he proudly announces. Glover goes on to fulfil the roles of team captain ('I'll have first pick, Tibbut'), star striker, referee and commentator in this hilarious but brutally realistic depiction of PE lesson football. Mr Sugden barges kids to the ground, leaving them writhing in agony. He awards, takes and retakes a penalty, and celebrates wildly when he scores.

The scene succeeds because it is real. It celebrates the muddy nether regions of football: the scrawny figure of Billy Casper standing lonely in the goalmouth; terrified boys hugging the touchline lest they be clattered by Mr Sugden; bigger boys attempting to kick their teacher only to be pushed aside. Even Casper's attempt to avoid the post-match shower (Glover: 'Put your hands up if anyone saw Casper under the shower') is painfully authentic. *Kes* deservedly made a star of Brian Glover, who died in 1997. Over thirty years after it was filmed, the football scene in *Kes* remains the very best ever committed to celluloid.

7. FASHION

If football offers fans an identity within our society, then football strips provide an identity within the football community. Wearing football colours with pride is as close as you can get to removing your heart and stapling it to your sleeve without causing severe health difficulties. Some strips are great but others do nothing but make the wearer look daft. When combined with an inappropriate sponsorship deal and a traditionally bad footballer's haircut things get downright silly. So which football kit is the worst of all time? Who had the dodgiest barnet? And which top Premiership star allowed the lure of the greenbacks to find him dressed up as a leprechaun in a national television advert?

In football's formative years there were only five commonly available shirt colours to choose from – black, green, red, white and blue. The referee took black, and green was considered unlucky, so most early club teams played in red, white or blue. Nineteenth-century football shirts were long-sleeved and made of heavy-duty material. Shorts were long 'knickerbockers' that hung below the knees. Players wore standard work boots with studs nailed into them. Long socks and, often, a cap completed the uniform. Stripes and quadrants were introduced to jazz up shirt designs, but the limited number of colours meant kit clashes were inevitable.

In 1890, Sunderland and Wolverhampton Wanderers both turned up for a League match wearing identical red and white striped shirts. In response, the Football League ordered all clubs to register their colours and keep a set of white shirts as a change strip. Goalkeepers wore the same colour kit as their teammates until 1909, when they were ordered to wear scarlet, blue or white shirts. In 1912, the same year that a rule change stopped them from legally handling the ball anywhere in their own half, goalkeepers were made to wear green shirts.

Kits continued to evolve in colour and design, with lace-ups, hoop necks, V-necks and pointy collars all finding favour. In the modern era, with fans lapping up replica shirts, kit redesign has become a regular and essential venture for clubs. Typically, professional clubs now change their home kit every two seasons and their away kit every season. Many clubs have also added a 'third kit'. Although many redesigned kits retain essential elements of club colours and tradition, many do not. The replica kit has become an item of fashion-wear among fans. But many football kits are unfashionable to the extreme.

Although Coventry City's famous chocolate-brown away strip of the 1970s (with white piping, V-neck and wing-sized collars) is popularly regarded as the worst football kit of all time, it certainly has a number of rivals. In the 1992–93 season, someone at Hull City thought it would be a great idea for the Tigers to take their big cat nickname somewhat literally. Hence the bizarre orange and black 'tigerskin' away shirt, manufactured by Matchwinner, that raised eyebrows at football grounds across the country.

In 1990, designers working on the new Newcastle United home strip saw fit to abandon the club's famous broad black and white stripes. Instead, Newcastle played home games in a peculiar 'barcode'-style black and white striped Umbro shirt, with thin stripes on one side and thick stripes on the other. This had the peculiar effect of making players appear nearer or further away in perspective, depending on the thickness of the stripes in view. In the late '90s, noticing that fans wore replica strips with jeans, Adidas produced a supposedly complementary blue denim Newcastle away shirt – marketing genius and fashion disaster.

In 1996 Manchester United boss Sir Alex Ferguson ordered his side to change strips at half-time during a match against Southampton at the Dell. Manchester were losing 3–0, a fact that Ferguson blamed on their grey Umbro away shirts. Apparently the players couldn't see each other. Manchester 'won' the second half but still lost the match 3–1. The shirt was never worn again, having appeared in six matches, four of which were defeats.

In the early '90s Brighton & Hove Albion's blue and white striped home strip with red lettering became known as the 'Tesco carrier bag'. In the mid-'80s Morton played in Scotland's only all-Tartan away kit. Surely no strip, though, can match non-League Corinthian Casuals of Tolworth's awful combination of blancmange-pink and chocolate-brown quadrants shirt and bright sky-blue shorts?

Italian giants Juventus originally played in pink shirts until, in 1903, English Juve player John Savage brought over a set of Notts County shirts. The black and white stripes were a hit, and Juve never played in pink again – until their centenary year, that is, when a special pink 'Juvecentus' commemorative away kit was launched.

Cameroon went into the World Cup finals of 2002 wearing a green Puma shirt that was unique, in that it had no sleeves. Although the *Stade d'Afrique* newspaper said the shirts represented a lack of respect for supporters and opponents, many fans loved the distinctive design. Unfortunately FIFA objected to the sleeveless number on the grounds that the World Cup logo had to be stitched onto the shoulder of participating teams' kits.

BALLS

'They're not shirts,' said FIFA spokesman Keith Cooper, 'they're vests.' The Indomitable Lions were banned from playing in the strips as they were, and were forced to sew on black mesh T-shirt sleeves, resulting in a kit that looked like it had been knocked up by a well-meaning granny. Cameroon's next kit was revealed at the African Nations Cup in 2004 – a figure-hugging skin-tight affair with lion's claw-marks torn down the sides.

In 1973 Leeds United became the first football club to customise their socks. The Mileta sports company supplied the club with 'sock tags' – essentially a tasselled pennant bearing the team name and shirt numbers. Leeds won the League that season but the sock tags had apparently not found favour with Norman Hunter and his 'hard man' colleagues. They were never worn again.

Of course, alongside the numerous footballing fashion travesties, there are many great football kits. Brazil's yellow 1970 World Cup shirt and Holland's orange 1974 kit are classics – striking and synonymous with success – and retro replicas are still popular among football fans today. France's international kit has always stayed proudly faithful to the country's national colours, and Real Madrid's all-white home kit has attained a level of reverence that befits the biggest club in the world.

Retro shirts retain a presence in British football grounds and classic and rare shirts are much sought after on internet auction sites like eBay. A signed 1966 England replica shirt sold for £2,500 in 2004, and unsigned vintage Brazil, Manchester United, Barcelona and AC Milan replica shirts all sold for over £400. Geoff Hurst's actual 1966 World Cup final shirt sold for £91,750, and Pelé's 1970 shirt went for £157,750. Pop group Half Man Half Biscuit eulogised the allure of exotic football strips, and Subbuteo, in the song 'All I Want for Christmas is a Dukla Prague Away Kit'.

The first football club to wear a sponsor's logo on their shirts were Kettering Town. On 26 January 1976, in a game against Bath

City, the Southern League club proudly took to the pitch with the name of local firm Kettering Tyres emblazoned on their chests. The groundbreaking 'four-figure' sponsorship deal was brokered by Town's chief executive and former Wolves striker Derek Dougan. The deal, however, lasted just four days. The FA had banned sponsorship in 1972, and the governing body ordered the club to remove the sponsorship logo. Dougan responded by abbreviating the tyre company logo to read 'Kettering T' and claiming the 'T' stood for 'Town'. He got away with the cunning ruse for a couple of months but, in April, the FA got wise and threatened the club with a £1,000 fine. Dougan backed down, but Town joined a consortium of British clubs, including Derby County and Bolton Wanderers, pressing the FA on the sponsorship issue. The FA finally agreed to allow shirt sponsorship from June 1977. Unfortunately, Kettering couldn't find a sponsor and played out that season with blank shirts. Derby, meanwhile, found sponsorship with Saab, Bolton wore shirts bearing the initials 'BEN' for Bolton Evening News and Liverpool signed a high-profile deal with Hitachi. Shirt sponsors have been around ever since – everywhere except for Barcelona.

Barça's famous deep red and Atlantic blue striped shirt has never featured a sponsor's logo, with the Catalan club insisting that such a deal would tarnish the heady tradition of the classic shirt. Barça are the only top class club in the world without a shirt sponsor, although financial problems in recent seasons may mean that will soon have to change. In 2003 the club considered shirt sponsorship deals from several top companies, although they have so far managed to hold out.

Wolverhampton Sunday League side Billas AFC are sponsored by an Indian restaurant. Not only do the side wear the curry house name on their shirts, but they have also ditched half-time oranges in favour of onion bhajis. The players claim the Indian snack-food helped Billas make an unbeaten start to the 2003–04 season. 'The lads come in for a drink and always guzzle down a plate of barbecued chicken tikka,' restaurant owner Mac Matta explained. 'One of them decided football and curries were the greatest things in life, so we decided to combine the two.'

Also in the West Midlands, under-nines team Sedgley Scorpions were ordered by the local FA to change their 'violent and offensive' logo. The club's badge bears the motto, 'Stuffem, Tankem, Ammerem', a familiar expression in the area. A political activist who became offended by the logo during a match against her son's team brought it to the attention of the football authorities. Sedgley were ordered to replace their shirts and club kit at a cost of around £2,500. 'This is political correctness gone mad,' said club chairman Gary Davis. 'The printer even thought the words were a bit of Latin.'

Shirt numbers were first added to kits in the 1933 FA Cup final between Everton and Manchester City. Everton wore numbers 1 to 11, and Man City wore 12 to 22. Everton won the Cup 3–0. It has since become traditional, whether in 1 to 11 numbering or in squad numbering (where each player retains his shirt number for the whole season or tournament), for goalkeepers to wear the number one shirt.

However, that tradition is not always adhered to. At the 1978 and 1982 World Cups, the Argentinean squads were alphabetically numbered, with Ossie Ardiles wearing the number one shirt in '78. At the 1974 World Cup the classic Dutch squad were also numbered alphabetically. Striker Ruud Geels wore the number one shirt and goalkeeper Jan Jongbloed wore number eight. But surely Johan Cruyff should have worn the number one shirt, as Cruyff is before Geels alphabetically? No. Always the exception to the rule, Cruyff was allowed to wear his trademark number 14 shirt.

The 1974 Dutch squad wore the famous orange Adidas 'three-stripe' shirts – except, again, for Johan Cruyff. The midfield maestro had a sponsorship deal with Puma and wore Puma King boots. He refused to wear rival company Adidas's trademark three stripes on his shirt sleeves and demanded a 'two-stripe' version.

Adidas bowed to the awkward Dutchman, and Cruyff played in the 1974 World Cup with a stripe torn off his strip. Cruyff had retired from international football by 1978, but twins Rene and Willy van de Kerkhof proved equally difficult with their demands for a Cruyff-style 'two-stripe' shirt. Again, Adidas obliged.

Individual sponsorship deals usually mean wearing a particular brand of football boot, driving a certain make of car, or filming an ad for a mobile phone company. So, David Beckham promoted Vodafone, Alan Shearer made ads for McDonald's and David Ginola appeared on TV washing his lovely locks with L'Oreal shampoo ('Because I'm worth it!'). Jack Charlton packed a suitcase full of Shredded Wheat on his way to USA '94, Ian Rush drank milk in a shed with two young boys, and Kevin Keegan shared a shower – and a bottle of Brut '33 – with Henry Cooper.

Other footballing endorsements have been more unusual. In 1996, Gareth Southgate was 'rewarded' for his European Championship penalty miss with a Pizza Hut ad, also starring fellow penalty-botchers Stuart Pearce and Chris Waddle. Hilariously, the ad found the trio trying to attract the attention of the waitress by shouting, 'Miss! Miss!' Then Gary Lineker became the face of Walkers Crisps and roped in the likes of Gazza and Michael Owen to help him. The ads saw Lineker variously dress up as a nun, a housewife, a punk rocker and the devil. But it was the special St Patrick's Day Walkers ad that caused the biggest stir. The company paid a very famous footballer £125,000 to dress up as a leprechaun. The footballer? Only Manchester United hardman Roy Keane.

In the 1960s, Terry Venables endorsed his very own patented invention called the Thingummywig – a hat with a wig attached. El Tel heavily promoted the item, but it never found success. 'It might sound bizarre now,' he later said, 'but it seemed a good idea at the time.' The former footballer, former manager, sometime TV pundit and wannabe crooner also ran a greengrocer's in Dagenham. Venables also co-wrote '70s TV cop show *Hazell*, which ran for 22 episodes on ITV in 1979. El Tel wrote a revival script in 2002 and earmarked Ray Winstone for the leading role. 'There aren't many people who can do good dialogue, but Terry can,' said Winstone.

Former Liverpool star Craig Johnston's invention was a lot more football-orientated, but no less revolutionary. In 1990, the Australian invented the Adidas Predator football boot, with unique 'fins and jets' – rubber attachments fitted to the upper part of the boot – and plastic blades instead of studs. The attachments are said to give more control and enhance the boot's 'sweet spots'. Several new models down the line, the boot is now worn by many top players, including David Beckham and Zinedine Zidane.

Manchester United players can enjoy the luxury of hanging their Predators on heated boot pegs. The expensive pegs were fitted in the home team's dressing room at Old Trafford in 2004, after complaints from some of the overseas players that their boots were uncomfortable to wear because they were too cold.

In the '60s and '70s it became popular for footballers to open their own clothes stores. This trend was pre-empted by Welsh hero Ivor Allchurch back in the '50s, when he set up a shop in Swansea selling sheepskin coats. In 1966, George Best and Mike Summerbee opened two fashion boutiques in Manchester. The clothes on offer – all big collars and bright colours – reflected Best's 'fifth Beatle' image. 'I cut a dash in the bars of Manchester,' recalled Best. 'Because of the position I was in I dressed a little more outrageously than the norm.'

The boutiques were relatively successful and, after Best lost interest, Summerbee went on to run a bespoke tailoring business, selling handmade shirts to stars like Michael Caine and David Bowie. But not all footballing forays into fashion were so successful. Peter Osgood opened a boutique in Mitcham, South London in 1970, but it closed after 18 months 'due to lack of interest, especially mine'. Malcolm MacDonald opened a short-lived boutique catering for 'the exclusive man' in a Newcastle shopping precinct in 1974. Newspaper adverts for the boutique showed Supermac wearing a *Saturday Night Fever* -style white suit. He later said, 'My personal appearance does not concern me much. It wouldn't worry me if I found out I had been walking around all day with my flies undone.' Kevin Keegan, Terry Venables, Ruud Gullit, David Beckham and Vinnie Jones have all launched fashion ranges. Kenny Dalglish's store, called 'Dalglish', was a flop, and former Blackburn Rovers player Simon Garner had to close his boutique, Rococco, after it was regularly ram-raided by Burnley fans.

Footballers need very little help when it comes to looking stupid. Whether they're wearing a horrible kit, promoting a daft product, or letting something slip from their shorts, their idiocy is often topped off with a dodgy haircut. The perennial footballing favourite was always the perm, favoured by the likes of Kevin Keegan, Terry McDermott, Graeme Souness, German Rudi Voller and Austrian Toni Polster. The latter now inexplicably runs his own fashion label.

The mullet is a tragic haircut wherever it surfaces. An American trailerpark favourite, it has recently made something of a comeback among fashion victims who believe they are being stylishly ironic. On the football field it was championed by the likes of Chris Waddle, Barry Venison, Mark Lawrenson, Colin Hendry and Paul Walsh. 'People took the piss out of me hair,' Waddle told *FourFourTwo* magazine, 'but I ran out with that hairstyle one week at Newcastle, and at the next home game there were ten thousand Geordies sporting it.' Ten thousand Geordies replied, 'He lies.'

Other footballing haircuts that should have been left on the barber's floor include the bowl cut, as modelled by Peter Beardsley, the rock cut, as favoured by Alexi Lalas, the Bobby Charlton comb-over and the Jason Lee 'pineapple on his head'. David Seaman's plain silly ponytail made him look like some sort of coke-snorting 1980s stockbroker, and Glenn Hoddle will surely be punished in his next incarnation for his hideous backperm.

All of these fashion rejects have now retired. In the age of the hideously overpaid footballer, hideously outrageous haircuts are on the way out. Today's player drives a top of the range car, wears a bespoke suit and has his hair styled by a celebrity barber. Thank God, then, for the dodgy football strip that, for 90 minutes every week, makes highly paid professionals look like circus clowns. Be thankful, too, for the great football strips that capture the romance and nostalgia of football in one overpriced piece of polyester. Perhaps the famous brown Covee kit wasn't that bad after all.

8. NAMES

Bob Wilson's middle name was a secret held close to his chest for thirty years. When the goalkeeper signed for Arsenal, he did so on the condition that the full name on his contract would never be revealed to his colleagues. And it never was. Until a civil servant called Pete came across Mr Wilson's DHSS records. Pete was a Tottenham supporter, and in the late '60s he travelled to Highbury to see his team take on Wilson's Arsenal. At half-time, Wilson collected his goalkeeping gear from the back of the net and looked up into the crowd. Then Pete struck his mighty blow: 'Oi! Primrose!' The crowd gasped and Wilson recoiled in terror. The name he had spent his entire life concealing had suddenly been hurled into the public domain.

Of course, Bob Wilson isn't the only professional footballer with a hideously embarrassing middle name. Stand up Emile William Ivanhoe Heskey, Gary Winston Lineker, Paul Emerson Carlyle Ince, Titus Malachi Bramble, Martin Harcourt Chivers, Earl Delisser Barrett, Larry Valentine Lloyd, Luther Loide Blissett and Eric Lazenby Gates. And they may be foreign, but Peter Boleslaw Schmeichel and Nolberto Albino Solano still raise a smile. Other

BALLS

footballers hide their real first names. Former Crystal Palace star 'Andy' Gray is really called Kermit. And Charlton manager 'Alan' Curbishley's real name is Llewelyn. Of course, there is never an inopportune moment to mention the fact that the dad of Manchester United and England stars Gary and Phil Neville is called Neville Neville.

Between 1999 and 2003, the manager of German Bundesliga club VFL Wolfsburg was Wolfgang Wolf. And that is surely how it should have been. While we are in the realm of slightly humorous names, the following 16-man squad of genuine professional footballers is offered up for your delectation, along with the country in which they ply their trade:

1. Frank Awanka (Belgium)
2. Christian Sinner (Luxembourg)
3. Gregory Playfair (Netherlands)
4. Francisco Arce (Paraguay)
5. Frankie Shank (Luxembourg)
6. Gerry Slagboom (Netherlands)
7. Mirko Dickhaut (Germany)
8. Dean Windass (England)
9. Jan Vennegoor of Hesselink (Netherlands)
10. Itfar Shitrift (Israel)
11. Pablo Plak (Netherlands)
12. Norbert Pronk (Netherlands)
13. Geoffrey Van Ass (Netherlands)
14. Nico Funk (Luxembourg)
15. Norbert Whooer (Luxembourg)
16. Jermaine McSporran (England)
Manager: Cha Bum Kun (South Korea)

And that squad was safely assembled without the need to call on Uwe Fuchs of Germany, Argel Fucks of Portugal, Oliver Fukka of Austria, or, of course, the German Stefan Kuntz. Perhaps the above team could appropriate a club name from the foreign leagues. In Tonga there are sides called the Minje Brothers and the Puke Turtles. In Samoa, you can find the Micalatee Sewer Side. Or perhaps the team could look to Argentina, where there is a league side called The Morons, or to Peru and Club Deportivo Wanka. Of course, the team would play in Switzerland at the Wankdorf Stadium, home of the Young Boys of Berne.

But before we allow ourselves to laugh too much at foreign cultures and their humorously interpreted languages, perhaps we should turn the situation around. In the Netherlands they no doubt stifle sniggers every time Premiership football appears on TV, for a quick translation of English player names into Dutch reveals that Alan Shearer means Alan Woolly Jumper, and Rio Ferdinand means Rio Bad Hairdresser. Jamie Redknapp, meanwhile, translates into Jamie Sore Penis. Redknapp is married to the pop star Louise.

In 2002, *The Times* reported that an entire West Midlands football team shared the same surname. The Sikh Hunter New Boys play in the Birmingham Amateur Football Alliance, and every single player on the team's books is called Singh. 'It makes writing the team-sheet easy,' said the manager, of course called Nick Singh. 'You just put down one name and then ditto the rest.' Nick's assistant manager is also called Singh, as are most Sikh men. It means 'lion'. 'We have to operate on a nickname basis, you don't go around shouting out surnames,' says Nick. But the side's hilarious name-based shenanigans may be short-lived. 'I think the league is going to clamp down on us. I don't think they can distinguish between Singhs when one is booked.' That's nothing compared to the problems suffered by the organisers of a five-a-side competition held in Kettering in 1994. All 200 of the tournament's players were called Patel.

At least the Sikh Hunter New Boys stuck with their real names. In 2002, a player in the Italian league was suspended by FIFA after playing for six years under a made-up name. Brazilian midfielder

BALLS

Luciano played for Chievo under the name 'Eriberto'. The player's registration showed the name Eriberto Silva Da Conceicao and the year of birth as 1979. In fact, the player's real full name was Luciano Siqueria de Oliveira, and he was born in 1975. Luciano revealed he had concocted the false identity to extend his career, with clubs tricked into believing he was four years younger than he actually was. The scam worked at Palmeiras in Brazil and Bologna in Italy, and then at Chievo, until Italian league administrators discovered the con and FIFA intervened.

In 2000, Sunderland manager Peter Reid bought a player called Milton Nunez for £1.6 million. Unfortunately, it was the wrong Milton Nunez. Confusion continues to surround the deal. The player Reid got was a 5 ft 5 in. Honduran international striker called Milton Omar 'Tyson' Nunez. The player he wanted, according to reports at the time, was a 6 ft Uruguayan called Milton Nunez. Twenty-eight-year-old 'Tyson' was signed from Greek club PAOK Salonika, but he had previously played for Uruguay's Nacional, where he had a decent goal-scoring record. Indeed, the transfer fee went to Nacional, which would suggest Reid did buy the correct player, but was just confused about his nationality, height and ability. Nunez made only a couple of brief and woeful substitute appearances before being shipped back to Honduras.

Peter Reid's transfer acumen took another knock at Leeds United in 2003 when *The Observer* reported he had invited a player called Ernest Gund for a trial. The story also ran in the *Yorkshire Post* and on the Planet Football website. Gund, they reported, was an Austrian Under-21 international striker and top scorer with his side DSV Loeben. He was also reported to be Austria's sexiest sports personality, and a host of websites dedicated to the player illustrated his popularity. One site, Gundweb, stated: 'Gund today landed in Manchester Airport, England, to start a week's trial with English Premier League team Leeds United. His agent Fritz Woll has apparently invited other English clubs to watch Gund while at Leeds.' Unfortunately for Peter Reid, and for the journalists who ran the story, Ernest Gund doesn't exist. He is actually a character in popular football computer game *Championship Manager*, and the websites listing his statistics, likes and dislikes and diary arrangements are hoaxes, initiated by an Everton fan called Neil Clegg.

The Times made a similar error when they announced Liverpool's Gerard Houllier was set to sign French under-21 international Didier Baptiste for £3.5 million. Baptiste was a fictional character from the Sky One soap opera *Dream Team*, where he plays for made-up team Harchester United.

In 1996, Southampton manager Graeme Souness received a call from Liberian legend George Weah. The caller recommended that Souness take a look at his former Paris Saint-Germain teammate, a Senegalese international footballer called Ali Dia. Only the caller wasn't George Weah, and Ali Dia wasn't a footballer. But Souness fell for the scam and invited Dia over for a week-long trial. Dia was registered to play, but missed a chance to impress in a reserve game against Arsenal when it was postponed. With the trial coming to an end, Souness decided to put Dia on the bench for a Premiership clash with Leeds. After an hour, an injury forced Souness to make a substitution. Ali Dia got his chance.

Unfortunately, it soon became clear that Dia was not a real footballer. A thoroughly unimpressed Souness subbed his sub ten minutes later. Dia was kicked out of Southampton and joined non-Leaguers Gateshead. But even the rigours of the Unibond League were too much for Dia. He was transfer listed within weeks and disappeared from English football's radar forever. It turned out that the caller impersonating George Weah had been Dia's agent. Dia did achieve his aim of playing in the Premiership, if only for ten minutes. As for Graeme Souness, he refused to be red-faced. 'I don't feel duped in the slightest,' he said. 'That's just the way the world is these days.'

In South America it is common for teams to take names that don't relate to their geographical location, like Vasco da Gama,

Racing Club and Colo Colo. In England there are several teams that aren't named after the place they come from. Queens Park Rangers are located in West London, but are named after a place in North London. Port Vale can be found in Burslem in Stoke-on-Trent, having moved from the Middleport, or 'Vale', area of the city. Grimsby Town are actually based in Cleethorpes. And many Manchester City fans would no doubt argue that Manchester United's Old Trafford ground is located in Salford, a city distinct from Manchester itself.

Only one professional English side, however, is not named after any geographical location. Arsenal began life as the team of a royal armament factory in the Woolwich area of South East London and were originally called Dial Square, after a sundial that hung over the entrance to the factory. The name was changed to Royal Arsenal and then, in 1891, to Woolwich Arsenal. For 23 years the team did have a geographical location in its name. In 1914, though, the club moved to Highbury in North London, and the 'Woolwich' part was dropped. Arsenal became Arsenal. Even the local tube station had its name changed from Gillespie Road to Arsenal.

In Scotland, it's common for team names to pay no due to the town they represent. Hibernian are in Edinburgh, St Johnstone are in Perth, Raith are in Kirkcaldy, Queen of the South hail from Dumfries and the marvellously monikered Albion Rovers are based in Coatbridge (Albion is an ancient word for Britain). Then there are Glasgow's Old Firm clubs. Neither Rangers nor Celtic have the word 'Glasgow' in their official names. Both sides were simply given 'fighting' names intended to give pride to those who played for them. As for the phrase 'Old Firm', arguments rage over its origin and whether it stems from the age of the clubs, or the dominance they hold over Scottish football. What is known for sure is that 'Old Firm' is a registered trademark, held jointly by both Rangers and Celtic.

AC Milan hail from the Italian city of 'Milano', in the native tongue. They use the Anglicised version of the city's name because they were formed by Englishman Alfred Edwards in 1899. Similarly, Italy's oldest club is called Genoa, despite being based in a city known to Italians as Genova. In Argentina, the club based in the city of Rio de la Plata are called River Plate. The name was chosen after the Anglicised name was spotted on a shipping container at the city's docks. And Brazilian side Corinthians, of Sao Paulo, were named after the English amateur side that visited the country in the early 1900s.

Other club names are far more straightforward. The German city of Essen boasts two sides – Rot-Weiss Essen and Schwarz-Weiss Essen. Rot-Weiss Essen translates to Red and White Essen. The club plays in red and white and is located in Essen. Schwarz-Weiss Essen translates to Black and White Essen. You can work that one out for yourself. Other examples of logical German naming include the Berlin trio of Rot-Weiss Berlin, Schwarz-Weiss Berlin and Blau-Weiss Berlin. This sensible practice also occurs in Austria, Switzerland and the Netherlands (where you can find Blauw-Wit Amsterdam).

Most British clubs have fairly straightforward nicknames. Many are named after the colour of their strips, like the Sky Blues (Coventry City) and the Reds (Liverpool). Others are named after trades associated with the area, such as the Cobblers (Northampton Town) and the Blades (Sheffield United). There is also the strange habit of naming clubs after birds. Some are so called because the bird shares the team's colours, like the Canaries (Norwich City) or the Bluebirds (Cardiff City), while others are named because of associations over place, like the Owls (Sheffield Wednesday) who reside in the Owlerton district of Sheffield, or the Seagulls (Brighton and Hove Albion) who are based by the seaside.

On top of this are some genuine oddities. Charlton Athletic are known as the Addicks because their players used to enjoy haddock fish suppers after games. Dundee United are known as the Arabs because they had a notoriously sandy pitch. Sunderland, who play in red and white, are now known as the Black Cats (following a fans' vote in 2000) in a tenuous reference to a pair of Napoleonic cannons which once protected the River Wear. That choice followed hot on the heels of the club's decision to steal the name of their new ground, the Stadium of Light, from Benfica of Portugal.

Peterborough United's nickname, The Posh, dates back to the early 1900s, when the then amateur club were known as Fletton United. The club's captain, Fred Taylor, was a former Chelsea skipper, and he was used to the airs and graces of the professional game. Not for him the amateur practice of rarely washing kits. Instead, Taylor insisted that Fletton's kits were washed and ironed before every game. As a result, the immaculate Fletton United stood out when they visited other sides, and they became known as 'the posh team'. Fletton's manager even announced he was looking for 'posh players for a posh team'. On one away trip to Kettering, the team were introduced as 'The Posh'. The name stuck, and was retained when the club became Peterborough United.

Not that footballer's wife Victoria Beckham cared a jot about any of that. In 2002, she blocked Peterborough's attempt to register the name as a trademark. Mrs Beckham, wife of David, had been known as 'Posh Spice' during her time with popular girl-pop combo the Spice Girls. 'The name "Posh" is inexorably associated with Victoria Beckham in the public's mind,' read a statement from her publicity company, 'and the concern from her team is that the public would think she had in some way endorsed products she had no knowledge of.' It seemed a football fan buying a Peterborough United scarf with the word 'Posh' on it would be very disappointed when he discovered Mrs Beckham had not officially endorsed the item.

Peterborough's Chief Executive Geoff Davey responded with disbelief: 'I was absolutely stunned when I got the letter,' he said. 'One reason was that our claim to the use of the name "Posh" should be challenged. The second reason was that someone as big as Victoria Beckham would want to raise this particular challenge. The name is part of the club's history and tradition.'

What made Victoria Beckham's move particularly unsavoury was her husband's high standing in the football world. The England captain was at the time on the verge of a high-profile move to Real Madrid that would make him the biggest name in sport. Yet his wife was trying to rob a relatively small football club of the nickname that had officially belonged to Peterborough United for 68 years and even predated the formation of the club in 1934. Three months later, after unfavourable media coverage, Geoff Davey reported that Victoria Beckham's position on the matter had 'moderated significantly'. Peterborough United would continue to be known as 'The Posh'.

Ironically, Victoria Beckham is about as posh as a tin of Spam. The stick-thin pop star speaks in a broad Essex accent and is well known for her bad taste, including famously sitting astride a hideous throne at her wedding. She was once asked by TV's Ali G, 'So Vic, is you really as posh as you say you is? Cos me mate Dave says he knew you when you was at school, an he said you was rougher than him.'

Victoria replied, 'Actually, Posh is just my nickname. I'm just your average Essex girl really.'

Derby County are known as the Rams because, apparently, a giant sheep was once spotted in the city. A traditional song, 'The Derby Ram', tells of one encounter: 'As I was going to Derby, Upon a market day, I met the finest tup, sir, That ever was fed on hay, Fay lay, fay lay, laddie falairy lay.' The ditty was converted into a play, *The Derby Tup*, which is still performed in Derbyshire to this day.

And of course there is Hartlepool United: official nickname – The Pool; favoured nickname – The Monkeyhangers. This handle originates from a story dating back to the Napoleonic Wars. A French ship was wrecked off the coast of Old Hartlepool. The only survivor was a small hairy creature, who washed ashore wearing a French sailor's uniform. The little fellow was swiftly apprehended by local fishermen, who interrogated him but couldn't understand his gibbering answers. He was, the Hartlepudlians sensibly decided, speaking French. The chap was found guilty of being a French spy and was sentenced to death by hanging. Of course, the prisoner was a monkey, probably kept on board the French ship for entertainment value. Nevertheless, the fishermen marched the simian down to the fish sands below the old town wall and strung him up over a gibbet. After something of a struggle, the locals finally succeeded in hanging the poor monkey and thus obtained their fantastic nickname.

The moniker was initially regarded as something of an insult by the residents of Hartlepool but has recently been embraced. Hartlepool United's mascot is H'Angus the Monkey. The popular ape was even elected mayor of the town in 2002. His winning campaign slogan was 'free bananas for schoolchildren'.

The man inside the costume, 28-year-old Stuart Drummond, landed the £53,000-a-year job despite having been criticised for the sometimes over-enthusiastic mascot tomfoolery which had seen him thrown out of football grounds – at Scunthorpe for simulating sex with a female steward and at Blackpool for posing with a blow-up sex doll. Within months of his election, provincial politics was shaken to its very core with another H'Angus-related sex scandal – Drummond was spotted watching a lesbian strip show at the Church pub. 'I did go to the pub,' he admitted, 'but I was not taking any great interest in what was happening on stage.'

That's a shame because, as the *Hartlepool Mail* reported, the show featured 19-year-old 'buxom blonde' Keri Mockler stripping and kissing with another girl. 'I wouldn't have thought a man of his standing would have turned up at a place like that,' said a clearly disgusted Keri.

'It was an error of judgement,' said Drummond, 'and I apologise if I offended anyone.'

Spanish club nicknames are often eccentric. Real Madrid are known as the Merengues or Meringues, after the speciality egg-white desserts served up in the city. Rivals Athletico Madrid are called the Mattress Makers, because their red and white stripes are said to resemble mattresses. Deckchair Makers would surely be more appropriate. Espanyol are the Parakeets. Scores of the long-tailed parrots had to be cleared from the fields where the club's first stadium was built.

Over in Italy, Turin club Juventus are known as La Vecchia Signora – the Old Lady. Ironically the club was founded by young students, and 'Juventus' means youth. There are various explanations for the Old Lady tag. Some say an old lady regularly watched the fledgling side play and it became known as 'the team of the old lady'. Others say that because the side suffered a bad run of results in the 1920s, their performances were likened by one journalist to those of an old lady, and the name stuck. Another, perhaps more plausible, explanation is that Juventus is the oldest of the so-called 'seven sisters' – the original giants of Italian football (Juventus, Fiorentina, Inter, Lazio, Milan, Parma and Roma).

Back in Scotland, Clyde are known as the Bully Wee. Again there are contrasting explanations. One says they are named after a group of little bully boys who terrorised the local area in the early years. Another claims the term was coined after a group of French businessmen visited the club somewhere around the year 1900. After a goal was disallowed, one of the visitors asked something along the lines of, 'But, il y a, oui?' meaning, 'It is a goal, yes?' Apparently, this French phrase was somehow interpreted as 'Bully Wee', and the name stuck with supporters. Another theory says 'Bully' was a term of approval, and 'Wee' means little, so Clyde supporters, cheering a small club, became the Bully Wee.

Another romantic Scottish nickname is the Hi-Hi. Unfortunately, the club to which the name belonged no longer exists. Third Lanark were a proud Glasgow club, formed by the Third Lanarkshire Volunteers. In its formative years, the club won the Scottish League and twice won the Scottish Cup. In season 1964–65, however, the club suffered a humiliating First Division campaign, losing 30 out of 34 matches and winning only 7 points. Third Lanark were relegated and money problems began to mount. Two years later the club was declared bankrupt, ejected from the League and dissolved by the receivers. The club's last match was a 1967 2–2 draw at Stranraer. The club's supporters blamed boardroom corruption and tried desperately to save their club, but it was to no avail. All that remains now of Third Lanark is a section of ruined terracing of the former club's Cathkin Park ground, situated high on a hill overlooking Glasgow. It was this towering location that gave Third Lanark the nickname the Hi-Hi.

Another name that has been lost from football's radar is Bradford Park Avenue. The club was formed in 1907 and played in the Football League for 63 years. Between 1914 and 1921, Avenue graced the First Division. They also reached the FA Cup quarter-finals three times – in 1913, 1920 and 1946. The great Len Shackleton played for Avenue between 1940 and 1946, scoring 171 goals before being transferred to Newcastle United. (He scored six goals on his debut for the Magpies.) By the late '60s, however, the club was in severe decline. After Avenue finished bottom of the Football League on three consecutive occasions – in 1968, 1969 and 1970 – they were relegated into the northern division and replaced by Cambridge United. Financial problems quickly surfaced. Park Avenue, the club's ground, was sold to property developers and Avenue moved to Valley Parade to ground-share with Bradford City. On 3 May 1974, after 698 supporters had watched Bradford Park Avenue beat Great Harwood 1–0, the club was liquidated, with debts of £57,652. However, on this occasion the club's supporters were able to do something about it. They registered the club's name as a company and started all over again, playing in the Bradford Amateur Sunday League Division Four. After 30 hard years, the club have worked their way up to the Premier Division of the Unibond League and are just a few steps away from a dramatic return to the Football League.

Back in the day, *Shoot* magazine presented readers with press-out cardboard League ladders at the beginning of every season. Team names were presented on tabs that could be slotted into the ladders. Every Saturday night, the ladders could be updated to reflect the current League standings. Far more excitingly, the team name tabs could be removed, shuffled and used to perform a fake FA Cup-style draw. Surely nothing could match the childhood excitement of pulling a plum draw from the proverbial hat: 'Barnet will play . . . Manchester United!' When the World Cup finals rolled around, the football magazines would offer a similar cardboard chart. Again, the team names could be used to perform a pant-wettingly thrilling draw: 'The Faroe Islands will play . . . Brazil!'

Even today, with simple childhood pleasures no more than a distant memory, football names retain the ability to excite. Whether familiar, intimidating, humorous, romantic, or just great to say, football names have a magical hold over football fans. For this is a world where, on a Saturday afternoon at 4.55, the classified football scores announcer can say, as he did in the 1963–64 season when the perfect result occurred: 'Forfar five, East Fife four.'

9. GOALKEEPERS

The goalkeeper is perhaps the most important – but least rewarded – player on the team, constantly treading the thin line between heroism and villainy. Standing alone in the penalty area, far from the action and near to the baying opposition fans, the goalkeeper is expected to fearlessly repel wave upon wave of attacks without error. What breed of man would choose to be a goalkeeper? A mad one.

The name 'Bruce Grobbelaar' is oddly synonymous with the phrase 'mad goalkeeper'. The former Liverpool goalie was renowned as much for his clown antics as his shot stopping. The Zimbabwe international would regularly pull comedy faces at fans and TV cameras, perform funny walks and hilariously twist his baseball cap backwards, much to the delight of slapstick fans up and down the country. A true eccentric, Grobbelaar would stray way out of his area, dawdle with the ball at his feet and come dangerously far off his line to catch crosses. It followed that Grobbelaar became associated with a number of high-profile goalkeeping cock-ups. He was also accused of letting in some goals less than accidentally when he was named in a match-fixing exposé involving a Malaysian betting syndicate.

Another clearly bonkers goalkeeper who had a brush with the

law was John Burridge. 'Budgie' played in goal for the likes of Aston Villa, Wolves, Southampton and Newcastle United over a 30-year playing career. He played for Manchester City at the age of 44 and continued to play into his late 40s, eventually becoming player–manager at Blyth Spartans. Budgie was as mad as a felt cap maker. He boasted of watching *Match of the Day* with his full kit and goalkeeper gloves on and sleeping with a football beside him. His pre-match warm-up routine comprised a series of flips and contortions more akin to a circus acrobat than a footballer.

While managing Blyth, Budgie would scare the players by running up and down the team bus completely naked. He also kitted out the Blyth team with sportswear from his sporting goods store, The Subs Bench. Unfortunately the gear was knocked off, and Budgie was convicted of dealing in counterfeit leisurewear, with the prosecution showing the court fairly conclusive evidence in the shape of video footage of Blyth players wearing the dodgy kit during a training session. Budgie pleaded poverty and legged it to Oman, where he still lives in a house by the beach and earns a crust by coaching the national side's goalkeepers.

Former Brentford goalkeeper Chic Brodie was known as 'Unlucky Chic – the one-man natural disaster'. Most goalkeepers have abuse and toilet rolls lobbed at them by away fans. On 6 November 1965, at Brentford's Griffin Park, a visiting Millwall fan threw something slightly more sinister at Chic Brodie – a Second World War hand grenade. Brodie nonchalantly picked up the grenade and threw it into the back of his net. Then he realised just what he had tossed into the rigging and promptly legged it for the safety of the touchline. 'I bloody scarpered!' he later recalled. Police officer Pat O'Connell was called from the crowd, and the PC calmly picked up the grenade and placed it into a bucket of sand. It was taken to a local police station and revealed to be a harmless dummy. Brodie returned to the pitch, and the match played on without further incident, although the next day's newspaper headlines, such as 'Hand Grenade Shames Football' and 'Soccer

Marches to War', helped ensure the incident went down in footballing history.

Brodie was later pole-axed by a falling crossbar in a game against Lincoln City and was also stretchered off against Oxford United with his side losing 1–0, only to see his ten goalkeeper-less teammates (in the days before substitutes) fight back to win 5–1 without him. His most infamous moment, however, occurred on 28 November 1970. In a televised match against Colchester, Brodie's career was tragically ended in the most bizarre of circumstances. In an animal–football incident that was not uncommon at the time, a small white dog ran onto the pitch. Several players and the ground staff desperately tried to catch the pooch, to no avail. The referee refused to stop play and Brentford defender Peter Gelson played a backpass to Brodie, which was swiftly chased by the yapping mutt. The goalkeeper kept his eye on the ball and attempted to gather it up, but tripped over the dog and fell to the floor. The ball went out for a corner. The crowd thoroughly enjoyed their hero's calamity, until he was stretchered off and the full extent of the incident was revealed. Brodie had severely injured his knee. 'The dog might have been a small one,' he later said, 'but it just happened to be a solid one.' Brodie never played professional football ever again.

In 1973 Brodie was interviewed by *The Sun*, which described him as 'a walking mishap, a one-man casualty station, a multiple accident statistic'. Typically, he was five hours late for the interview due to another trip to hospital. Brodie worked as a London taxi driver following his retirement and was once involved in a car crash. His cab collided with a top of the range Jaguar. Out of all the cars in London, Brodie had managed to hit the one being driven by World Cup winner Geoff Hurst. Charles Thomas George Brodie died in 2000, but remains fondly remembered by Brentford supporters as a fine, if unfortunate, goalkeeper and a great man who always had time for his fans.

Brodie was by no means the only goalkeeper to obtain a bizarre injury on the field of play. In a 1975 match between Manchester United and Birmingham City, United goalkeeper Alex Stepney screamed so hard at his defenders that he dislocated his jaw and had to be carried from the pitch. And former Middlesbrough goalkeeper Mark Crossley missed several matches in 1997 after falling heavily on his backside during a pre-season match in Finland.

In 2000, former Derby County goalkeeper Mart Poom was unable to play due to a freak injury obtained in a 'bad tempered' and seemingly unlikely charity match against heavy metal band Iron Maiden. The match, in Tallin, Estonia, had been organised by Poom's former club FC Flora to raise money for underprivileged kids. Playing to the crowd, the goalkeeper ran into the Iron Maiden penalty area to attack a corner. Not only did he get his head to the ball and score, he also got a punch in the head from the Iron Maiden goalkeeper and ended up in hospital with concussion, a broken cheekbone and a black eye. Poom also returned home with a bruised ego – Derby boss Jim Smith fined him for playing in the charity match without permission. For the record, FC Flora beat Iron Maiden 7–1.

England goalkeeper Ray Clemence had to be led from the pitch during the 1980 Nations Cup match against Belgium in Turin after being overcome by tear gas. The Italian police were using the gas to control the crowd amid fears of hooliganism, but a cloud of gas drifted onto the pitch and rendered Clemence useless. Eventually all of the players were taken from the field, returning once the cloud had dissipated to play out a 1–1 draw.

Former Welsh international goalkeeper Andy Dibble suffered a horrific and bizarre injury while playing for Barry Town at Carmarthen Town in December 1998. The *Barry & District News* match report described Carmarthen's council-maintained pitch as resembling 'a farmer's field'. After sliding about on the turf, Dibble noticed a burning sensation on his skin. When he removed his shirt after the game he found a severe burn scar four inches wide extending from his shoulder to his hip. The goalkeeper was hospitalised and underwent skin grafts. Richmond Park was closed, and investigations revealed that hydrated lime had been used to mark the pitch. Dibble was scarred for life, but did eventually make a return to football. He was awarded £20,000 in compensation for pain, suffering and loss of earnings.

Many goalkeeping injuries take place away from the football field. Former Arsenal goalkeeper David Seaman missed much of the 1996–97 season after damaging knee ligaments while reaching for his TV remote control. He also once badly injured his shoulder while fishing. Seaman made his England debut in 1988 only after first choice goalkeeper Chris Woods was ruled out after slicing open his finger while trying to free himself of the cord on his tracksuit bottoms using a penknife.

Tottenham Hotspur goalkeeper Kasey Keller, then of Leicester City, knocked out his own front teeth in 1998 with the golf clubs he was lifting out of the boot of his car. And Spanish goalkeeper Santiago Canizares missed the 2002 World Cup finals in Japan and Korea after dropping a bottle of aftershave on his foot at the team's training camp. The bottle smashed, and shards of glass severed an artery and caused tendon damage.

In 1995, Liverpool goalkeeper Michael Stensgaard dislocated a shoulder while trying to erect an ironing board. The *Sunday People* reported the story under the headline, 'Ironing Board Ruined my Life'. Stensgaard was out of action for six months and never played for Liverpool again. Everton goalkeeper Richard Wright also injured his shoulder, and missed the start of the 2003–04 season, after falling out of his loft.

Dave Beasant, the 6 ft 4 in. former Wimbledon goalkeeper, was out for two months in 1992 after dropping a bottle of salad cream on his foot while making a sandwich. Beasant was the first goalkeeper to save a penalty in an FA Cup final, the first goalkeeper to captain an FA Cup-winning side and the first FA Cup-winning goalkeeper to accidentally flash his nether regions at a legendary TV sitcom actress.

It was 1988, and Beasant's Wimbledon were rank outsiders at the Wembley final against Liverpool. Against all the odds, Wimbledon stifled Liverpool and eventually took the lead through a Lawrie Sanchez header. On the hour, however, Liverpool were awarded a penalty. John Aldridge stepped up and blasted the kick low to Beasant's left, but the big curly-haired goalkeeper dived full length to save it. Wimbledon held on to win 1–0 and Beasant led his team up to the royal box to collect the FA Cup. After the match, Wimbledon fanatic and grand old lady of British comedy June Whitfield, then 63, burst into the team's dressing room, only to be confronted by the very lanky and very nude figure of Dave Beasant, who had just come out of the shower. Cue the theme from *Terry and June* . . .

Legendary World Cup-winning goalkeeper Gordon Banks missed England's World Cup quarter-final match against West Germany in 1970 after drinking a bottle of 'dodgy' lager. By the end of his career, Banks only had one good eye. He lost the sight in the other in 1972 when his Ford Granada crashed into a van, but that didn't stop him from playing a full season in the North American Soccer League. Depth perception is overrated anyway.

Many goalkeepers have played on through similar adversity. West Bromwich Albion hero John Osborne played in goal when the club won the FA and League Cups in the 1960s. He once kept 22 clean sheets in one season. This despite the fact that he had a plastic knuckle. Osborne injured his hand during a Charity Shield match against Manchester City and had the replacement knuckle fitted to allow him to continue his career. Even more impressively, Hungarian international goalkeeper Karoly Zsak played for his country 30 times in the 1920s despite having only nine fingers following an amputation. And Welsh international goalkeeper Dr Bob Mills-Roberts put his medical training to good use in 1897 when he passed himself fit to play for his country against England. Perhaps Wales should have looked for a second opinion – the good doctor had splints on both arms following an accident and could barely move. Unsurprisingly, England won 4–0.

Former Reading goalkeeper Borislav 'Bobby' Mihaylov was completely bald. That shouldn't necessarily have put him at a disadvantage when it came to keeping goal, but the Bulgarian international shocked fans when he turned up at the USA '94 World Cup finals with a full head of hair. Mihaylov had decided to wear a wig to promote his Bulgarian toupee company. The result was less than flattering, particularly in Bulgaria's quarter-final match against Mexico. Mihaylov's rug slipped and had to be swiftly adjusted under a towel, in front of a live TV audience of millions. Mihaylov continues to run the rug company, and a Bulgarian website, www.borsa.bol.bg, carries the following small ad: 'Our company is looking to find long human hair for sale. We wish to purchase many kilos.'

Manchester United goalkeeper Tim Howard has Tourette Syndrome, which can cause involuntary physical and vocal ticks. One newspaper reported that Howard suffers from 'the cursing disease'. In fact, the involuntary swearing often associated with Tourette's is called Coprolalia, and Howard is unlikely to do any more swearing than the average footballer. 'As I have said many times, I consider myself a great example of why Tourette Syndrome should only be a speed bump, not an obstacle, in one's life,' he said. 'It should not hold anyone back from achieving anything they dream of.' Too chuffing right.

Adversity regularly stalks goalkeepers, and many of them lack the common sense to deal with it. In 2003, goalie Richard Siddall played on alone for ten full minutes after his match had been abandoned due to fog. Siddall could not see beyond his penalty area, so didn't know that the referee had called time on the match between Stocksbridge Steels and Witton Albion. 'I didn't have a clue,' Siddall told the *Daily Star*. 'I just stood there waiting for a player to come through the mist.'

The same thing happened to Charlton Athletic goalkeeper Sam Bartram on Christmas Day 1937. Charlton were playing at

Chelsea's Stamford Bridge when fog caused the match to be abandoned. Five minutes after returning to their dressing room the Charlton players were sent out onto the pitch to locate Bartram, who had been playing on unaware. The eccentric Bartram was also involved in many daft incidents of his own making. He once got married on a Saturday morning, played for Charlton in a 1–0 victory over Middlesbrough in the afternoon (entering the pitch to the sound of 'The Wedding March') and hurried back to his wedding reception in the evening. In 1938 he was hit with a house brick and had his goal nets set on fire while playing Portsmouth. Later he was beaten by a penalty kick, with the ball soaring through the netless goal into the crowd. Pretending the penalty had been missed, he calmly retrieved the ball and took a goal kick. The referee was fooled and the goal didn't count, much to the chagrin of the Pompey fans.

Perhaps the most famous goalkeeping error in British footballing history was scored by calamitous Leeds United goalkeeper Gary Sprake in a 1967 League match against Liverpool at Anfield. Just before half-time on a wet December afternoon, Sprake gathered the ball in front of the Kop and shaped to throw it out to Leeds full-back Willie Bell. But, with Liverpool's Ian Callaghan moving to close Bell down, Sprake seemed to half-change his mind. He didn't release the ball, instead swinging all the way around and flinging it into his net. Liverpool's Kop couldn't have had a better view of Sprake's moment of madness. At half-time the Anfield DJ played hit record 'Careless Hands' by Des O'Connor over the PA. When the players returned to the pitch, the Kop regaled Sprake with a rendition of the song, 'You need hands . . .', and did so every subsequent time he returned to Anfield.

Unfortunately for Sprake, that wasn't his only high-profile error. In 1970, he inexplicably dropped the ball into the net while playing Crystal Palace at Selhurst Park. Then, in the 1970 FA Cup final against Chelsea, Sprake famously dived lamely over Peter

Houseman's weak shot which duly ended up in the back of the net. Television footage of the aftermath of the goal showed Sprake's teammate Jackie Charlton saying something to the stricken goalkeeper. It wasn't entirely clear what Charlton said, but it certainly began with an 'f'.

And what of Oliver Kahn? The legendary Germany and Bayern Munich goalkeeper appeared to suffer some sort of mid-life crisis after a mistake in the 2002 World Cup final. Kahn uncharacteristically spilled the ball at the feet of Ronaldo, allowing the Brazilian to score. To his credit, he refused to blame the mistake on two injured fingers. 'That had nothing to do with it,' he said. 'There is no consolation. I have to live with this mistake myself. Because of it, everything is lost.'

The goalkeeper then seemed to slide off the rails. In the 2002–03 season he was involved in a number of violent incidents and began to refer to himself in the third person. After being criticised for ferociously grabbing Bayer Leverkusen striker Thomas Brdaric around the neck, the goalie said, 'That's Kahn. Those are my emotions. I will not let the moralists take anything from me.'

Kahn then left his pregnant wife for a 21-year-old blonde. He was also spotted smoking and drinking in a nightclub until 5 a.m. while sidelined through injury. Despite being fined by Bayern, Kahn continued to frequent discos, a conspicuous figure with his scantily dressed dolly bird at his side, a cigarette in one hand and a bottle of champagne in the other. And just in case anyone failed to recognise the German superstar, on at least one occasion he turned up at the nightclub wearing a Bayern Munich T-shirt.

Kahn made another high-profile error in March 2004 when he allowed a Roberto Carlos free kick to slip under his body in a Champions League match against Real Madrid. 'It was one you could have saved with no arms or legs,' Kahn wailed. Again he was crucified in the press. 'I need to look inside myself, ask questions and find out what it all means,' he said. 'Maybe I have to ask myself if it's all worth it.'

The goalkeeper was thoroughly depressed until, at Bayern's next match, a young fan brought along a banner reading, 'OLI, WE'VE FORGOTTEN REAL'. Kahn was deeply moved. 'I imagined him carefully making the banner with marker pens,' he said. 'It was one of those moments in a sportsman's life that really moves you.'

In the run up to Euro 2004, Kahn became embroiled in a war of words with Arsenal goalkeeper Jens Lehmann – a rival for the national jersey. 'If there is any justice, I will be playing,' said Lehmann. 'The Germany coach Rudi Voller once said, "Good players attract attention through good performances over a long time and not through scandals off the pitch or talk". My goal is to play.'

Kahn, who declared his intention to reform his ways, reacted surprisingly calmly. 'It is my intention to withdraw from the public eye and apply myself to the national team,' he said. 'I would like to concentrate on the things that make me happy, which are soccer games. I am at the age where I don't need to respond to his comments. That would bring me down to kindergarten level.'

If Lehmann is unlikely to take Kahn's place in the national team, there is a strong possibility he may yet become Germany's maddest goalkeeper. 'I am an arrogant soccer player,' he once said. 'A difficult player, whom one does not like very much. That is me and so be it. Thus one is not a fan's favourite.'

But Lehmann has a long way to go, and a lot of pies to eat, if he is to match the crazy antics of William 'Fatty' Foulke. Fatty spent his turn of the century career playing for Sheffield United, Chelsea and Bradford City. He also spent a lot of time eating. The 6 ft 2 in. goalkeeper ballooned from 15 st. to 25 st. during his playing days, making him the heaviest footballer ever to play professional football, yet he remained remarkably agile and even played for England. Fatty, who wore a 24 in. collar shirt, once caused a game to be abandoned when he snapped his crossbar. On another occasion Fatty was injured, but the trainer's stretcher couldn't bear his weight, and six men had to drag him from the pitch.

'I don't mind what they call me,' he once said, 'as long as they don't call me late for lunch.' On one occasion, while playing for Chelsea, Fatty arrived very early indeed for lunch and proceeded to eat a full table of food laid out for the entire squad. Foulke was also notoriously bad-tempered, and his huge girth enabled him to pick up and toss around opposition players at will. He once picked up Liverpool striker George Allan, turned him upside down and stuck his head in the mud. In another game, against Burslem Port Vale, Fatty lifted up a Vale forward and chucked him into the back of the net.

Several South American goalkeepers have been christened 'El Loco' (the crazy one), but the original madcap South American goalkeeper was Ramon Quiroga of Peru. The goalie, who made his name in the 1978 World Cup finals, fancied himself as an outfield player and could regularly be found wandering out of his penalty area, often into the opposition's half. He would make tackles on his halfway line, surge forward to create attacks and play keepy-uppy when pressurised by opposition players. He also pioneered the penalty-saving technique of jumping forward off his line before diving – revolutionary at the time, but later adopted by other eccentrics like Bruce Grobbelaar.

And then there is Rene Higuita, the mullet-haired Colombian custodian who, in a 1995 friendly match with England at Wembley, famously saved a goal-bound shot from Jamie Redknapp with what has become known as the 'scorpion kick'. The offside flag was up, and Redknapp's goal would not have counted, but did Higuita know that when he launched himself into the air, allowed the ball to go over his head, flipped forward and cleared the ball with his heels? It wasn't Higuita's first brush with madness. He spent seven months in prison in 1993 after being involved in a drug cartel kidnapping. Higuita acted as a go-between to secure the release of crime lord Carlos Molina Ypes' daughter. The goalkeeper delivered the ransom money to kidnapper Pablo Escobar, another famed drug baron. The girl was released, and Ypes rewarded Higuita with a reward of $64,000. The goalkeeper was promptly arrested and jailed for profiting from a kidnapping.

Another 'El Loco' is Velez Sarsfield's Jose Luis Chilavert. The goalkeeper, known for his brightly-coloured short-sleeved shirts, has an enviable goal-scoring record. The flamboyant Paraguayan regularly scores from penalties and free kicks, notably curling a free kick home in a 1998 international match against Argentina. He is also the only goalkeeper to have ever scored a hat-trick, that being in a 1999 match against Ferro Carril Oeste. He once scored a 60-yard free kick for Velez against River Plate, having spotted Argentinean international goalkeeper German Burgos off his line. Chilavert publicly mocked Burgos after the goal and boasted that he would score again when Paraguay met Argentina in a forthcoming World Cup qualifier. Paraguay were duly awarded a free kick in that game, 25 yards from goal. Chilavert stepped up to the ball, and photographers behind the net saw Burgos tremble with fear. But this time Burgos was not going to be caught off his line. Chilavert whacked the free kick over the wall, but Burgos managed to get behind the shot and placed two hands on the ball – only to somehow let it slip from his grasp and drop over the line for a sensational goal that made Chilavert a living legend in his home country.

Chilavert has never scored from a drop kick though, unlike Pat Jennings, who famously scored for Spurs in the 1967 Charity Shield against Manchester United. His kick was caught by a gust of wind and blew past United goalkeeper Alex Stepney. The match finished 3–3, and the trophy was shared. Stepney himself was no stranger to goal-scoring. At Christmas 1973 he was Manchester United's top goal-scorer, albeit with just two goals, both scored from the penalty spot.

Up until 1912, goalkeepers were allowed to handle the ball

anywhere up to the halfway line, and in those days it was quite common for a goalkeeper to score from a drop kick. In 1910, the goalkeepers of Third Lanark and Motherwell both scored in the same match. In the modern era, Peter Shilton has scored from a drop kick, for Leicester against Southampton in 1967. Ray Cashley of Bristol City did likewise against Hull in 1973, as did Steve Sherwood for Watford against Coventry in 1983. And, in 1986, Steve Ogrizovic put a drop kick past Martin Hodge to score for Coventry City against Sheffield Wednesday.

Many other goalkeepers have scored from closer range. Bruce Grobbelaar, Ray Clemence, Peter Schmeichel, Kevin Pressman and Andy Goram have all scored goals for their sides. In September 2003, Mart Poom of Sunderland and Paul Robinson of Leeds both scored match-saving headers in the final minutes of crucial games. When thoughts turn to goal-scoring goalkeepers, though, one particular goalie and his amazing *Boys' Own* story very much stands out. On 8 May 1999, on-loan goalkeeper Jimmy Glass scored a legendary 95th-minute goal in the last game of the season that kept Carlisle United in the Football League. Drawing at 1–1 in injury time, Carlisle had won a last-gasp corner, and Glass's manager waved him upfield. As the corner kick floated over, the goalkeeper swung his right boot at the ball and belted it towards the goal. He struck it perfectly, and the ball shot into the back of the net. Glass wheeled away, gloved hands clenched above his head. Teammates and fans mobbed him. Amid the jubilant scenes, the referee blew the final whistle. Carlisle had won 2–1, leapfrogged Scarborough and famously avoided relegation.

And then we come to the ultimate act of footballing madness, and a story so loopy and heroic it could only realistically involve a goalkeeper. In September 2002, 18-year-old goalkeeper Tom Janssens was training with his Belgian side Veerle Sport FC of Laakdal. As the session progressed, a hot air balloon passed overhead, some 100 feet in the air. The Veerle coach turned to Janssens and said, 'I bet you can't kick a ball as high as that balloon.'

'Without replying to that remark, I took a ball and kicked it right into the basket,' Janssens told *Het Laatste Nieuws*. 'Everyone on the field was very surprised because they thought it was impossible. The two ladies in the basket just had time to dive out of the way. They weren't mad about it and were kind enough to throw us back the ball.'

10. BOSSES

Football managers and chairmen are football's big daddies. They act as moral examples to their players and set the standard for footballing behaviour – which is unfortunate, as a good number of them are completely bonkers. If a manager can slap a player across the face with a dead pigeon, and if a chairman can sack his entire squad halfway through the season, what chance is there that the rest of the footballing community can turn out anything other than quite mad?

Brian Clough's pedigree as a manager is undoubted. As the man himself once commented, 'I wouldn't say I was the best manager in the business. But I was in the top one.' However, he was equally well known for his eccentricities as for his footballing successes. 'Old Big 'Ead', perennially kitted out in a sloppy green sweatshirt, ordered his players to search hedgerows for mushrooms during training sessions and organised competitions to see how many players could be squeezed into a five-a-side net. Something of a boozer himself, Clough encouraged his players to drink before big matches. Before one European Cup second leg tie at Anfield in 1978, his Nottingham Forest players drank bottles of Chablis at lunchtime, slept it off in the afternoon and qualified for the next round in the evening.

But Clough was also a strict disciplinarian. He paid £1 million for Trevor Francis, then forced him to clean the entire squad's boots and play in the third team to stop the transfer fee from going to his head. He had little time for errant supporters either. During the pitch invasion that followed Forest's Littlewoods Cup win over QPR in 1989, Clough ran onto the field and clipped two fans around the ear. He later apologised by kissing the pair in front of local television cameras. But the incident didn't stop Clough dishing out his own brand of punishment to his players. 'If I had an argument with a player we would sit down for twenty minutes, talk about it and then decide I was right!' he explained. He once punched striker Nigel Jemson for playing badly in a reserve game and even whacked former boxer Roy Keane, knocking him to the floor after a defeat. 'I only ever hit Roy the once,' said Clough. 'He got up, so I couldn't have hit him very hard.'

On 15 February 2003, a tabloid sensation erupted when football's best manager drew blood from football's biggest player. Manchester United had just lost 2–0 to Arsenal at Old Trafford in the FA Cup. Sir Alex Ferguson was furious, and it was reported that he blamed star David Beckham for Arsenal's second goal. While unleashing his trademark 'hairdryer' rant in the dressing room, Ferguson kicked out at a football boot, which flew across the room and struck Beckham above the eye. Cue a press frenzy. Ferguson was reluctant to comment. 'It was an incident which was freakish,' he said. 'First and foremost you have to stress that in 29 years as a coach whatever happens in the dressing room is sacrosanct.'

Beckham didn't agree. He hired Tom 'Lofty out of *EastEnders*' Watt to ghost-write an autobiography that was later serialised in *The Sun*. 'I went for the gaffer,' he revealed. 'I don't know if I've ever lost control like that before. A couple of the lads stood up. Suddenly it was like some mad scene out of a gangster film with them holding me back as I tried to get to the gaffer.' Beckham spent the next few days flashing his patched-up head to the paparazzi. Within months he'd jumped ship to join Real Madrid.

BALLS

But Beckham should think himself lucky that he was only hit with a flying boot. Former Partick Thistle manager John Lambie once slapped a player in the face with a dead bird. 'I did once hit a player in the jaw with a dead pigeon,' admitted Lambie. 'His name was Declan Roche and he was talking back to me, so I got these dead pigeons out of a box and slapped him round the face with one. He was certainly surprised, but it couldn't have improved him much because I got rid of him soon afterwards.' Lambie, a keen pigeon fancier, brought the birds into his office after they died of an unspecified disease. 'I was going to bury them, so I put them in a box and took them to the ground,' he explained. 'It was a bit of fun really.'

Former Grimsby Town manager Brian Laws has also hit a player over the head with a dead bird – albeit a cooked one. After the Mariners lost 3–2 at Luton Town in February 1996, Laws raged at his players in the dressing room and chucked a plate of chicken wings at midfielder Ivan Bonetti. The Italian received the plate full in the face and ended up flat on the floor with a broken cheekbone. Both Laws and Bonetti (who had apparently 'started it') were forced to make public apologies.

Other managers shun bird-related thuggery in favour of good old-fashioned fisticuffs. Former Southampton manager Lawrie McMenemy once launched a stinging post-defeat attack on central defender Mark Wright. Wright refused to take his criticism and shoved the manager into the showers where the pair proceeded to knock seven bells out of each other until spoilsport teammates intervened.

Cambridge manager John Beck didn't even wait for the sanctity of the dressing room before throwing haymakers at his star striker Steve Claridge. Cambridge were riding high in the old Second Division and heading for promotion to the inaugural Premier League. But a mid-game dispute between Beck and Claridge resulted in a full-scale touchline boxing match, and every punch thrown damaged Cambridge's dreams of top-flight football.

Claridge was sold within the week, and Cambridge lost in the promotion play-offs before slipping back into lower league obscurity.

Trevor Francis obviously learned a thing or two from his harsh treatment at the hands of Brian Clough. As manager of Crystal Palace, Francis took offence after spotting reserve goalkeeper Alex Kolinko laughing when Palace conceded a goal to Bradford City. Francis turned around in the dugout and cuffed Kolinko around the head. The grin was successfully removed from Kolinko's face, but Francis was fined by Palace and by the FA.

Old school managers like Brian Clough are extremely quotable, but the king of the football quotes is undoubtedly Queens Park Rangers manager Ian Holloway. His post-match press conferences are little comedy gems, stuffed with the most unlikely metaphors. There is nothing more interesting that can be said about the man than what he has said himself, so here, for your delectation, are Ian Holloway's top ten football quotes, in ascending order of madness:

10. 'This is the people's club and everybody can have a piece of that pie – a pie that's already smelling beautifully.'

9. 'If the club was a chocolate bar, it would have licked itself.'

8. 'I used to keep parakeets and I never counted every egg thinking I would get all eight birds. You just hoped they came out of the nest box looking all right.'

7. 'Do you believe everything you read in *The Sun*? They've got some nice tits in that paper.'

6. 'My day didn't start very well. The Holloway household was very sad this morning. We had to have our dog put down, unfortunately, but that's life. I've just said to the lads – you're born and you die on a date, you've got to work on the dash in the middle.'

5. 'I always say that scoring goals is like driving a car.

BALLS

When the striker is going for goal, he's pushing down that accelerator, so the rest of the team has to come down off that clutch. If the clutch and the accelerator are down at the same time, then you are going to have an accident.'

4. 'It's all very well having a great pianist playing but it's no good if you haven't got anyone to get the piano on the stage in the first place, otherwise the pianist would be standing there with no bloody piano to play.'

3. 'You can say that strikers are very much like postmen – they have to get in and out as quick as they can before the dog starts to have a go.'

2. 'I am a football manager, I can't see into the future. Last year I thought I was going to Cornwall on my holidays but I ended up going to Lyme Regis.'

1. 'To put it in gentleman's terms, if you've been out for a night and you're looking for a young lady and you pull one, you've done what you set out to do. We didn't look our best today but we've pulled. Some weeks the lady is good looking and some weeks they're not. Our performance today would have been not the best looking bird but at least we got her in the taxi. She may not have been the best looking lady we ended up taking home but it was still very pleasant and very nice, so thanks very much and let's have coffee.'

Barry Fry is another very quotable manager. Unfortunately, most of his quotes contain profanities. To be fair, Fry has had his patience tested by a succession of odious chairmen. He began his managerial career at Dunstable under Lamborghini-driving chairman Keith Cheeseman. Fry was only 28, and was led astray by Cheeseman, who conned him into delivering suitcases full of embezzled money around the country. Eventually Cheeseman fled to Miami, where he took refuge with

Frank Sinatra. Fry remembers him as 'the greatest conman I've ever known'.

Fry moved to Barnet and there found himself working under Stan Flashman, the self-styled 'King of the Ticket Touts'. Flashman sold overpriced tickets, passed counterfeit money to players, argued over team line-ups, insisted his son play in goal and sacked Fry 20 times. Fry ignored his chairman and turned up for work as normal. Flashman then told Fry he would bury him in concrete under the M25. After being sacked by Flashman for a final time, Fry said, 'I'm absolutely gutted. I'm devastated. The man is a complete and utter shit.'

Another king of the post-match interview is former Southampton manager Gordon Strachan. He was once asked, 'This might sound like a daft question, but you'll be happy to get your first win under your belt, won't you?' to which he replied, 'You're right. It is a daft question. I'm not even going to bother answering that one. It is a daft question, you're spot on there.'

In another post-match interview, a reporter said, 'Bang, there goes your unbeaten run. Can you take it?' Strachan replied, 'No, I'm just going to crumble like a wreck. I'll go home, sit in a darkened room, become an alcoholic and maybe jump off a bridge. Umm, I think I can take it, yeah.'

In November 2001, a pagan witch was called in to bless Southampton's St Mary's Stadium. The club had failed to win a game at the new stadium, which was built on an old pagan burial site. Forty bodies were removed during the building of the £30 million stadium, and experts claimed the site was cursed, so Cerridwen 'Dragonoak' Connelly turned up in her purple robe and performed a Celtic ceremony. 'The Saxons loved gatherings and competitions and I am sure they were the kind of people who would be delighted for a stadium like this to be built over their remains,' she explained. 'Saxons, it is good to have you here and the players want to celebrate this and accept that this is also your home. I predict Saints will beat Charlton.' Sure enough, Southampton won 1–0.

BALLS

'I didn't know the witch had been there,' said Gordon Strachan, 'but she can take training for the next two weeks so I can practise my golf.'

Former Leeds United boss Don Revie was famously superstitious, insisting on wearing the same clothes when his side went on a winning run. When Revie was told that Elland Road had been built on the site of an old gypsy camp, he decided that the ground was cursed, so he enlisted the dependable skills of a genuine gypsy fortune-teller from Scarborough seafront. The fortune-teller did sense an evil presence, contained within something brown. Eventually, she managed to locate the cursed source of the trouble – Revie's brown suede overcoat. She instructed Revie to get rid of the coat, but it had to be lost, not thrown away. Revie immediately drove out to a motorway service station, took lunch and left, leaving his overcoat hanging on a restaurant cloak peg.

Portsmouth boss Jack Tinn was equally superstitious. He managed Pompey from 1927 to 1947 and led the club to three FA Cup finals. He attributed all of his success to a pair of fortunate white spats. The lucky leggings were fixed to his ankles before every match by the same Portsmouth player, winger Fred Worrall (who himself always carried a lucky sixpence and horseshoe during matches). But, in the 1939 Cup final against Wolverhampton Wanderers, Tinn came up against a manager with equally outlandish beliefs.

Wolves manager Major Frank Buckley was a decorated First World War hero and a strict disciplinarian. His tough training methods were said to be more like those of an army platoon than a football club. A footballing pioneer, Buckley employed a football psychologist, insisted his players wear numbers on their shirts and virtually invented stadium restaurants and hospitality facilities. He also gave his players 'mystery injections' to boost performances. It was eventually revealed that the shots were monkey gland injections, containing fluid extracted from monkeys' testicles. Buckley forced his players to have the injections and angrily confronted worried parents with foul-mouthed tirades. The side were mocked in the press and were pictured in cartoons swinging from goalposts like chimpanzees. They were also said to play games with glazed expressions on their faces. Whether or not this was the case, they were undeniably successful. They powered their way to the so-called Monkey Gland Final in 1939, but then came unstuck. Jack Tinn's lucky spats proved more powerful than Frank Buckley's monkey gland injections, and Portsmouth beat Wolves 4–1. Questions were nevertheless asked in Parliament about the dangers and legality of Buckley's simian shots, but the Health Minister decided that no investigation was necessary.

Former Sunderland manager Johnny Cochrane didn't give his players monkey gland injections or, for that matter, a team talk or any sort of pre-match preparation whatsoever. Cochrane, who managed Sunderland between 1928 and 1939, would turn up five minutes before kick-off, smoking a cigar and cradling a glass of whiskey. 'Who are we playing today, boys?' he asked. 'Manchester United,' the players replied. Cochrane sipped his whiskey, turned to leave and said, 'Oh, we'll piss that lot.'

Len Shackleton, the former Newcastle and Sunderland forward, included a chapter in his autobiography entitled 'What the average soccer director knows about the game.' The chapter comprised two blank pages. That may have been a little generous, as the following examples illustrate.

Cruz Azol chairman Guillermo Alvarez Cuevas sacked his manager and all of his players in 2003 after the Mexican club went four months without winning a game. Manager Mario Carrillo and his players were understandably distressed to be the first football team ever to be fired *en masse*. Then Cuevas realised Cruz Azol still had ten games to play, but no players to play them, so he offered his former charges a temporary contract until the end of the season. The players swallowed their pride and played out the season, before joining the dole queue.

BALLS

Daniele Carassai, manager of Italian side Gotico, received a text message from club chairman Andrea Pollastri after a 2003 defeat reading, 'You're sacked'. Pollastri explained he decided to dismiss his manager by text because he thought it was a friendly way to break the news. Carassai didn't think so. 'At first I thought it was a joke,' he said. 'It's not exactly the best way to find out you've lost your job.'

In 2004, Marius Lacatus was sacked as manager of Romanian first division side Stiinta Craiova after just eight hours. Former Romanian international Lacatus had spent 20 years at rivals Steaua Bucharest, and Stiinta fans were extremely unhappy at his appointment. Lacatus arrived at the club to find over 100 masked men waiting for him. The police stepped in to protect him, and a battle ensued which saw five of the masked men end up in hospital. Stiinta Craiova's owner, Dinel Staicu, was also intimidated by fans, who telephoned him and threatened to set the club on fire. Lacatus and Staicu shared a panicked phone call and quickly decided that Lacatus should leave. 'I cannot coach under these conditions,' the outgoing manager said. 'Having the supporters against me would be like sitting on dynamite.'

In January 1997, the president of Romanian club Sadcom FC, Aurel Rusu, appointed his six-month-old son as team manager. Sadcom are based in the village of Caragele and play in Romanian football's lowest league. Still, you would expect the rigours of football management at any level to be beyond the abilities of someone who struggles with potty training. Nevertheless, Rusu threw his baby son into the deep end. Apparently, he desperately wanted his boy to be a footballer, so decided to give him an early start in the game.

Saudi Arabian millionaire Saleh Aisawi liked Faversham Town so much he bought the team. The former Saudi international paid £250,000 in 1996 for the club, which sat bottom of the Winstonlead Kent League and boasted an average attendance of 33. He declared himself to be a devoted fan of the club and revealed that his 14-year-old son Karim played for the youth team. Aisawi made sweeping changes. When the Faversham squad turned up for the start of the 1996–97 season, they walked into the dressing room to find Aisawi had brought in an entire team of London-based players to replace them. The old boys walked out, and the new boys crashed to a 3–0 defeat.

Dundee United chief executive Jim McLean once responded to questioning over manager Alex Smith's future by punching out the interviewer. BBC Sport reporter John Barnes (not *that* John Barnes) asked McLean, 'How long do you give Alex Smith to get it right on the park?'

'You think I'm going to answer a stupid question like that?' replied McLean.

'I'm only asking,' said Barnes.

'I told you before I wouldn't be fucking answering it,' said McLean. 'And make sure that's cut. And I'll tell you something else [whacks Barnes on the nose]: don't ever fucking offer me that again.'

In 1989, property tycoon Michael Knighton announced he had bought Manchester United for £20 million and celebrated by juggling a football on the pitch at Old Trafford in front of his adoring new subjects. However, he was being a little presumptuous. The deal had not yet been signed, and it eventually fell through when the financial backers pulled out. Knighton bought Carlisle United instead. In 1996, Knighton attended a UFO conference in Carlisle organised by The Aetherius Society, a group of alien mentalists who communicate with UFOs via yoga. It was here that he revealed a remarkable story.

It was 1977, and Knighton was driving along the M62 with his wife Rosemary when he saw a light in the sky. 'The bright dot became a triangle and shot down from the sky at an incredible speed,' Knighton allegedly said. 'It then turned into a glowing disc which hovered above a petrol station at about the height of

Nelson's Column.' Then the disc spoke to him, via some sort of space-age telepathy.

'Don't be afraid, Michael,' said the strange voice inside his head.

The disc hovered above him for thirty minutes and performed 'impossible aerogymnastics' before speeding off. 'I was so excited,' said Knighton. 'It was just the most incredible experience. For seven years after that I spent time UFO spotting. I just wish I could come in contact again.' After his story appeared in the *Carlisle News & Star* under the headline 'Knighton: Aliens Spoke to Me', the chairman claimed his comments had been misinterpreted and threatened to resign. Unfortunately for Carlisle fans, Knighton decided to stay on and helm the club to the very brink of extinction instead.

And then there is Knighton's very good friend George Reynolds. The former smuggler, safe cracker and bare-knuckle boxer claimed to be worth £260 million when he bought Third Division Darlington Football Club in May 1999, declaring, 'We will bring a new dawn to Darlington and give fans a real reason to celebrate. They won't have to wait long before we are knocking on the door of the Premiership.' He did build a multi-million pound Premiership stadium, modestly called the Reynolds Arena, but he neglected to build a Premiership team. Darlington fans' new hopes were soon dashed, and their relationship with their new chairman quickly soured. 'I never listen to the fans or manager because they never get it right,' he said.

Reynolds managed to alienate his players as well. In 2000, he accused them of being greedy and published details of their wages in *The Northern Echo* (Neil Heaney was the top earner with £139,251 per year including bonuses). Then Reynolds' wife attended a fans' forum where she made an ill-advised speech in which she accused the players of throwing games. 'It isn't unknown for games to be thrown,' she said. Fans gasped, and the entire Darlington squad stood up and left in disgust.

Reynolds didn't take criticism lightly. He was well known for turning up on detractors' doorsteps. 'People are all right in groups until you knock on their front doors at twenty past two in the morning,' he told the BBC. 'They don't like that. Nobody has a go at me. I find out where they live and I go and knock on their door.' Then Reynolds likened 16-year-old fanzine editor David MacLean to Joseph Goebbels. 'Hitler would have been proud of Mr MacLean and awarded him the Iron Cross,' he said. And when local resident Jan Mazurk protested against Reynolds' plan to build a new stadium, the chairman responded by placing an advertising hoarding at the side of Darlington's pitch reading, 'Can *The Northern Echo* stop Jan Mazurk's dog from crapping here?' Reynolds compared himself to Robin Hood and Dick Turpin, saying, 'Sometimes I find that the bad guys are the good guys.'

Then Reynolds announced he had pulled off a sensational transfer coup and was seen on national television with Colombian superstar Faustino Asprilla. Tino did agree terms with his new pal Reynolds, but then had second thoughts and disappeared, never to be seen in Darlington ever again. Darlington went into administration two days before Christmas 2003, and Reynolds resigned a few weeks later. 'If I turn the clock back, I probably should have looked into getting Sunderland instead of Darlington,' said Reynolds. 'But there again, I took Darlington because it was a lame duck.'

Jesus Gil was president and owner of Atletico Madrid for 17 years and went through 39 managers before he retired in 2003: 26 of them were sacked, and 13 – including Ron Atkinson – walked away in despair at Gil's control freakery. A colourful character, Gil was jailed in 1969 when a building erected by his shoddy contractors collapsed killing 58 people. He then became mayor of crime haven Marbella and was involved in over 80 court cases involving corruption and the transferring of public funds to Atletico's bank account. He was eventually banned from public office in 2002.

BALLS

As a football president, he punched other presidents, insulted other managers and lambasted his own players. He threatened to machine-gun his own team, told them to swim home after a defeat on the Canary Islands and called Hugo Sanchez 'as welcome as a piranha in a bidet'. The final straw came when Gil came out of hospital after having a pacemaker fitted only to see Atletico lose 4–3 to Villareal. 'There's too many bloody passengers!' Gil said in an interview. 'They're not going to laugh at this shirt any longer. They are not going to make fun of me. Carreras, Santi and Orero are not good enough. I feel like not paying them. And anyone who does not like it can die.' At this point the interviewer pointed out that, as he had just had a pacemaker fitted, he should perhaps calm down. 'I'm sick of people telling me to relax,' Gil replied. 'They can stick my heart up their arses.'

Gil, whom *El Mundo* called a 'sinister clown', retired and put all of his energy into a television show in which he sat in a jacuzzi alongside scantily-clad models and delivered controversial tirades while wearing swimming trunks and chunky necklaces. Gil died in May 2004, aged 71, after suffering a stroke.

And then there is Wimbledon FC and Charles Koppel. The club had risen from the Southern League to the Premiership in just two decades, and its 'Crazy Gang' side famously won the FA Cup in 1988. Wimbledon's problems began in 1991, though, when eccentric owner Sam Hammam controversially moved the club from its traditional Plough Lane ground. Hammam said he planned to build the club a new stadium in the London borough of Merton. In the meantime Wimbledon groundshared with Crystal Palace at Selhurst Park and the proceeds from the sale of Plough Lane to Safeway remained unspent. Then Hammam came up with an outlandish plan to move Wimbledon to Dublin. The Irish city was full of fans of English football, he reasoned, and there was huge potential in moving there. But Wimbledon's fans were furious. Surely a British football club could not be franchised, as is common in US sports, and moved lock, stock and barrel to another city?

Hammam eventually abandoned his plan and instead sold the club to a pair of Norwegian millionaires, Bjorn Rune Gjelsten and Kjell Inge Rokke, for £28 million. The club was homeless and had no assets other than a handful of players. In essence, all the pair had really bought was a name. The Norwegians asked South African Charles Koppel to take over the running of the club. Koppel, a former speedboat racing team manager, had never been to a football match in his life. His decisions were ham-fisted from the start. He sold top players to raise cash, severely weakening the side in the process. Then he sacked backroom staff, getting rid of the scouts and coaches who had spotted and nurtured the succession of young players who had been the club's lifeblood.

Then Koppel turned his attention to the groundshare. The Merton development, he decided, was a no-goer. Then he met Pete Winkleman, formerly a 1980s pop svengali responsible for such stellar acts as the Thompson Twins. Winkelman was now head of the Milton Keynes Stadium Consortium, and he wanted a football club. Milton Keynes, with the fastest growing economy in the UK and a huge potential audience, was crying out for a team, Winkleman explained. He had already been turned down by Barnet and Queens Park Rangers. But Charles Koppel saw the offer as a godsend. Wimbledon would get a share in the new stadium, and financial security would surely follow. So, it was announced, Wimbledon Football Club would move 90 miles north to Milton Keynes.

The Wimbledon Independent Supporters Association (WISA) immediately launched the biggest fans' protest in football history. Fans from other clubs united behind WISA's campaign, and the Dons Trust, a charitable organisation, was set up to raise funds. But Koppel ignored fans' protests and pressed ahead. He was now convinced he could fill the Milton Keynes stadium with that town's locals and didn't need Wimbledon's faithful fans. WISA pressed the football authorities but, in May 2000, the FA officially decided that Koppel could move the club to Milton Keynes.

BALLS

Wimbledon supporters were left devastated, but the fight was far from over. In a daring move, a group of fans decided to form their own club. AFC Wimbledon was born. The AFC stands for 'A Fans' Club'. Within a month the new team had been entered into the Seagrave Haulage Combined Counties League (six steps below the Premiership), secured a sponsorship deal worth £100,000 and arranged to groundshare with Kingstonian, located just a mile away from Merton. An open player trial on Wimbledon Common attracted 230 footballers, and a relatively high-calibre team was assembled under the management of former Wimbledon player Terry Eames.

For AFC Wimbledon's first match, 4,168 fans turned up. The club sold 1,500 season tickets and 2,500 replica shirts and boasted an average home gate of over 3,000. Wimbledon FC, meanwhile, were in turmoil. The club had averaged crowds of 6,000 before the move to Milton Keynes had been ratified. Now, abandoned by the vast majority of its fans, attendance at their matches at the 26,000-capacity Selhurst Park dwindled to an average of only several hundred. The official attendance at the first home match of the 2002–03 First Division season was given as a pathetic 2,476. But the WISA, who had members outside protesting and counting, claimed that the real figure was nearer 1,000.

Later that week, just 21 Wimbledon FC fans travelled to Grimsby. *The Mirror* named each and every one of them and revealed that several were players' family members. Soon, with more fans deserting the club for AFC Wimbledon and with away fans staying away in protest, the club's official attendance had fallen below the 1,000 mark.

Wimbledon FC managed to finish the season tenth in the First Division, but financial problems saw the club forced into administration. In September 2003, the club finally moved to Milton Keynes, playing at the National Hockey Stadium. But the move coincided with a slump in form. By January 2004, Wimbledon FC were rock bottom of the First Division and heading for relegation, having won just 5 matches out of 24.

AFC Wimbledon finished their inaugural season third in the Seagrave Haulage Combined Counties League with a mighty 111 points. They scored 52 goals in their last 16 games, but just missed out on promotion in a strong league. WISA announced plans to buy the Kingsmeadow ground from Kingstonian, offering the K's a favourable tenancy deal as part of the package. They also declared their intent to force Wimbledon FC to abandon the Wimbledon name. The name 'MK Dons' had been linked with the Milton Keynes club, but the FA had rejected it. The next goal for AFC Wimbledon is to rise up the leagues and overtake the team that abandoned them – the dwindling Wimbledon FC. If that happens, AFC Wimbledon fans will have scored a huge victory.

11. COMMENTATORS

The world of football commentary is littered with banal statements, mixed metaphors and plain stupidity. But the men with the mikes harbour many secrets. This sweep through football broadcasting uncovers a football commentator who doesn't like football, rucks with Alex Ferguson, a bus called 'Des Lynam', the 'outing' of Mark Lawrenson, Dougie Donnelly's sheepskin museum piece, a language called 'Ronglish', the wit and wisdom of Stuart Hall and the greatest piece of football commentary of all time (and it's not from Kenneth Wolstenholme).

Football broadcasters are supposed to be impartial, but, like any fan, they all have their favourites. It's time to nail their colours to the (television) mast:

Gary Lineker, the BBC's jug-eared anchorman, went to the same Leicester school as Liverpool and England striker Emile Heskey and followed Leicester City home and away before playing for them. He claims to be more enthusiastic about the club than ever since retiring, although fails to explain why he allowed his eldest son, George, to become a Manchester United supporter. It should come as no surprise that Lineker has risen to the top at BBC Sport. As a player, he offered such nuggets as,

'There's no in-between – you're either good or bad. We were in-between.'

Top BBC summariser Alan Hansen played for Liverpool for fourteen years, winning three European Cups, seven League championships, two FA Cups and four League Cups. He also has a soft spot for Partick Thistle, but it is no secret that he loves Liverpool. Just as it is no secret, following his on-air World Cup 2002 outburst, that he dislikes 'the fucking Krauts'.

BBC icon John 'Motty' Motson joined the *Barnet Press* newspaper as a junior reporter at the age of 18. His devotion to non-Leaguers Barnet has continued, and he is president of the Barnet Sunday Football League. Football's favourite commentator has also lent his support, if not his sheepskin, to the ongoing 'Keep Barnet Alive' campaign. He once perceptively told viewers, 'The match was settled either side of half-time.'

Motty caused no end of trouble for himself when asked in a 1998 radio interview about the difficulty in telling players apart. 'There are teams where you have got players who, from a distance, look almost identical,' said Motty. 'And of course, with more black players coming into the game, they would not mind me saying that that can be very confusing.' To be fair to Motson, he does support the Football Against Racism campaign, and he was backed by his black colleague Garth Crooks. But Motty's attempt at an apology only made things worse. 'I am just saying that if there are five or six black players in the team, and several of them are going for the ball, it can be difficult,' he said, while digging a very deep hole for himself.

Barry Davies is the BBC's longest-serving football commentator, but claims not to have a favourite team as he 'doesn't really like footy'. However, the broadcaster with fingers in many sporting pies, from tennis to ice-skating, is not as impartial as he claims. He revealed on Tottenham fan Simon Mayo's BBC radio show that he collects Spurs memorabilia. His knowledge of the game he doesn't love is perfectly illustrated by his famous line, 'If it had gone in, it would have been a goal.'

Ray Stubbs, the BBC's lad-friendly perennially Ben Sherman-clad *Football Focus* man, supports Tranmere Rovers, a side he played with for five years. Or rather, he didn't. Because, much like the way he is perennially left studio-bound by the BBC while his colleagues swan off to exotic international climes, the full-back was permanently confined to the Tranny reserves.

Alan Green, BBC Radio Five Live's outspoken commentator, has often been accused of supporting whoever Manchester United are playing. In fact, a resident of Macclesfield, Green supports his local side, Macclesfield Town. However, he does state in his autobiography, 'I intensely dislike Alex Ferguson and I wouldn't be surprised if the feeling was mutual. For me, it's become almost a badge of honour.' Green is known for his forthright comments, such as, 'That Dion Dublin – he's a big awkward sod, isn't he?'

Excitable Radio Five Live and sometime Channel Five man Jonathan Pearce turned to commentary after his hopes of becoming a professional footballer were dashed by a leg injury and his love of pies. He began his career at Bristol's Radio West and has been a life-long Bristol City fan. Pearce once made an unlikely appearance in top US TV show *The Sopranos*. One episode saw Mafia boss Tony Soprano asking his sister to turn off her TV, which was loudly broadcasting Pearce's nerd-friendly *Robot Wars*.

'Dishy' Des Lynam moved to Brighton from County Clare at the age of six. The fact that he has been a Seagull ever since is just about the only snippet of personal information the 'housewives' favourite' has ever revealed, excluding unsubstantiated tabloid disclosures. He even has a Brighton & Hove bus named after him.

Clive Tyldesley, ITV's number one commentator, is famously unable to get through a single Champions League match without referring in glowing terms to Manchester United's 1999 European triumph. He first visited Old Trafford in 1960 and barely missed a match for 15 years before commentating commitments, including covering rivals Liverpool for many years at Merseyside's Radio City, intervened.

Gabby Logan joined Newcastle United's Toon Army while studying law at Durham University. ITV's golden girl put on a posh dress at the end of the 2001–02 season to present Alan Shearer with his North-east Player of the Year award. Unfortunately she looked slightly out of place, as the event was held in the back room of a brewery.

Alan Parry supports Wycombe Wanderers. Although retaining a soft spot for his boyhood heroes Liverpool, Parry is a club director at Wycombe and is not averse to charging onto the pitch and kissing the players to celebrate Wanderers' occasional triumphs, as he did following the 2001 FA Cup win over Leicester.

Gorilla-like Sky presenter Richard Keys declared his love for Coventry City as a youngster, writing to the *Coventry Evening Telegraph* every week to correct their mistakes. The editor asked him to stop pestering them, but Sky Blues chairman Jimmy Hill, who Keysie also badgered, advised him to try the *Wolverhampton Chronicle*, which eventually took him on.

Andy Gray supports Everton, but, when he was offered the vacant managerial job at the club, he turned it down, preferring not to put his money where his mouth was. And that's a lot of money, as Sky have made their star man football's highest paid pundit. Gray has declared his love for Aston Villa, but remains a die-hard Evertonian.

Despite claiming complete impartiality, Sky's Martin Tyler co-wrote *The Official Illustrated History of Arsenal* and is name-checked in Nick Hornby's Highbury bible *Fever Pitch*. If that wasn't enough, Tyler's cover was completely blown when he turned up to commentate on an Arsenal–Chelsea cup tie wearing a Gunners tie.

Jeff Stelling, Sky's smooth *Soccer Saturday* host – the statistic-loaded daddy of football broadcasting – is a well-known supporter of Hartlepool United. Stelling began his career at his local

BALLS

Hartlepool newspaper and remains a proud 'monkeyhanger' to this day.

Football's favourite fire-eating belle Helen Chamberlain is the co-presenter of Sky's anarchic *TISWAS*-with-goals Saturday morning show *Soccer AM*. She travels to virtually every Torquay United game, usually carrying a large drum. In her quest to race from the Sky studios to Torquay's Plainmoor in time for the matches, she has been known to slightly exceed the speed limit and has, in the past, been banned from driving.

Tim Lovejoy, *Soccer AM*'s producer, creator, writer and presenter, supports both Chelsea ('The Mighty Blues') and Watford ('The Glory Hornet Boys'). The self-styled 'Golden Drifter' captains *Soccer AM*'s Badgers team, but is renowned for regularly 'having a 'mare', now known throughout the footballing world as 'having a Lovejoy'. At the 2002 FA Cup final between Chelsea and Arsenal, Lovejoy was allowed to do Sky's *Fanzone* commentary. At one point, he remarked of an Arsenal attack, 'They're through . . . Oh it's all right, it's only Ray Parlour.' Parlour raked the ball into the back of the net, Chelsea lost, and Lovejoy's embarrassment was complete.

The broadcasting career of Mark Lawrenson, the former Liverpool star, cannot be so neatly summarised in a paragraph. A veritable failure as a football manager, Lawrenson was sacked by Oxford United after just seven months and lasted just over a year at Peterborough. He was then recruited as a defensive coach by Newcastle United, whose defence proceeded to leak goals with new-found gusto. But what Lawro lacks in expertise, he makes up for in personality. His on-air comments are often incredible. He once said of a shot that flew over the crossbar, 'That was a real half-pound of bacon shot – lean back.' Another cringeworthy effort was, 'Arsenal are having a real Gene Hackman day – *The French Connection*.' The comment was made even worse by the fact that it was so obviously scripted, as was this attempt at a joke: 'What have Rangers got in common with a total eclipse of the sun? Both only last for two minutes in Europe!'

The man who once described a Paul Scholes goal as 'deliciously bent' has an undeniably camp voice. Although it should be stated that Mark Lawrenson is not at all gay (not that there would be anything wrong with that), at times it appears that there is something of a game being played between Lawro's BBC colleagues to portray the pundit in an effeminate light. Five Live commentator Mike Ingham once responded to Lawro's mention of smoking with, 'You're obsessed with fags.' And after a *Football Focus* feature on father and son footballers, Ray Stubbs remarked of his studio guest, 'Mark Lawrenson's son: Now that would be something!'

Lawro joins a real motley crew at BBC Sport. Do they really merit a low-quality display at Hampden Park's football museum, where a row of mannequins wear clothes donated by BBC folk (the star attraction is a sheepskin coat once owned by Dougie Donnelly)?

What of the mysterious Garth Crooks? It is difficult to tell whether Crooks is uncomfortable in front of the cameras to the point of madness, or is in fact deliriously overconfident. Whenever he makes a statement, he lifts his head, his eyes bulge and he turns away as if to say, 'Point proved. Move on.'

However, the BBC can boast a true genius of football broadcasting on its payroll. It's just after five o'clock on a Saturday afternoon. BBC Radio Five has broadcast the football classifieds and is now taking reports from around the grounds. Former *It's A Knockout* stalwart Stuart Hall (he of the incessant laugh and chunky jewellery) is on hand to cover a mid-table First Division clash. And so begins his report: '*A Winter's Tale* – a tragedy for Norwich. *Much Ado About Nothing* – a farce for theatre-goers . . .' As governing bodies, referees, greedy TV companies and unscrupulous boards do their best to ruin football, Stuart Hall stands as a beacon of light. At just after five on a Saturday afternoon football is great again.

BALLS

Hall, a Manchester City fan (with a soft spot for Everton), references everything from Shakespeare, through Greek tragedy, to classical music in his reports. In 1999, after struggling Everton had managed to scrape a 2–1 win over Coventry, Hall summarised, 'Ah, but 'twas serendipity at the School Of Science . . .' He has even described Everton's football as being as smooth and creamy as Sharon Stone's thighs. Below are some pearls from five of Hall's most memorable match reports:

1. Blackburn Rovers 3–1 Wimbledon (20 March 1999): 'It was like watching Vanessa Feltz, struggling in a basque, lapdancing.'

2. Sheffield Wednesday 1–2 Coventry City (3 April 1999): 'This match didn't have the taint of the drop, it had the stench.'

3. Manchester City 2–0 Blackburn Rovers (23 October 1999): 'At 3 p.m., the distant brooding Pennines ghouled in the autumn sun.'

4. Stoke City 2–2 Burnley (29 January 2000): 'Stoke, owned by Iceland, fielded a kipper. Frode Kippe. Their mascot is a hippopotamus. Don't ask me why.'

5. Derby County 3–2 Liverpool (13 March 1999): 'A record audience leaned forward like a string section under Bernstein's baton.'

Football eccentrics are not confined to the BBC. Ron Atkinson took his co-commentary position with ITV Sport so seriously that he went to the extreme of inventing his own language. It has become known as 'Ronglish', and, as befits the man who once said, 'I'm going to make a prediction – it could go either way,' it is improbably brilliant. The following eight phrases are Ronglish essentials, offered with a definition and an example of common usage. Note that Ronglish lines are almost always followed by a reference to Big Ron's regular commentary partner Clive Tyldesley.

Lollipop: Step over ('He's given it about 20 lollipops there, Clive.')

Spotter's badge: Award for perceptive pass ('Spotter's badge to Beckham for the through ball.')

Early doors: Early in the game ('They've taken the lead early doors, Clive.')

Little eyebrows: Flicked header ('He's given it little eyebrows at the front post and it's past the goalkeeper.')

Locker: Well of ability ('What a comeback – they've pulled this one out of the locker, Clive.')

Full gun: Hard ('He hit that shot full gun, Clive.')

Second post: Far goalpost ('He was completely unmarked at the second post.')

Wide Awake Club: TV-am kids' breakfast show hosted by Timmy Mallet ('The defence were caught out – they need to get in the Wide Awake Club, Clive.')

Big Ron was forced to resign from ITV in April 2004 after he unleashed a racist foul-mouthed rant during a Champions League match between Chelsea and Monaco. UK viewers did not hear the incredible outburst, but it was transmitted via the ITV feed to up to 80 million people across the world. 'Bigot Ron', as *The Sun* labelled him, also lost his job as a columnist for *The Guardian* and a valuable sponsorship deal with Britvic. 'I must have rocks for brains,' said Ron.

A less inflammatory, but still eccentric, ITV co-commentator is Kevin Keegan. Often sounding alarmingly like Mark Lawrenson, Keegan once commented on Borussia Dortmund's horrific fluorescent yellow strip, saying, 'I tell you what, Brian, I love the colour of those shirts! I've never seen a colour like it!' He also once confusingly observed, 'I don't think there's anyone bigger or smaller than Maradona.' Keegan quit as England manager after a short and unsuccessful reign and has so far failed to win any major prizes in club management. That's hard to believe, because his tactical knowledge seems sound. 'The good news for Nigeria is that they're two–nil down very early in the game,' he once offered. On another occasion, Kev summarised, 'Chile have three options – they could win or they could lose.' The great thing about Keegan, as proved when he fell off his bike on the TV show *Superstars*, is that he makes mistakes but gets back up, dusts himself down and jumps right back into the saddle.

David Pleat is another ITV co-commentator, notable for his simple love of the English language. During a Champions League match between Arsenal and Bayer Leverkusen he remarked, 'The referee has got to decide whether the player is trying to disguise an injury.' After a thoughtful pause, he added, 'Lovely word that, isn't it? *Disguise*.'

Another former ITV football broadcaster is Nick Owen, best known for his work as a TV-am anchorman and as co-presenter of TV's *Anne & Nick* housewives' magazine show. A long-standing fan of Luton Town, Owen was honoured by the club when at the peak of his televisual fame – Luton's powers that be named the club bar after their star supporter. The 'Nick Owen' bar remains to this day, even though the star himself has somewhat slipped from the limelight, now fronting provincial news magazine *BBC Midlands Today*. Owen's fall from grace was tragically illustrated in 2002 when the presenter was prevented from entering the bar that bears his name by bouncers. 'Do you know who I am?' asked Owen. 'No,' replied a bouncer. The situation was only resolved when a fellow supporter told the bouncer, 'His name is above your head in big letters!' 'It was a very funny moment,' reflected Owen. Yeah, right.

For an outrageously outspoken commentator, look no further than Ahmet Cakar. The star of Turkish television's *Telegol*, Cakar is a former referee who regularly offends the Turkish football community. He quit refereeing at the age of 35 because he was sick of corruption, and he once caused an uproar when he announced, 'Turks may not be well educated, but they are capable of understanding that most of the people who appear to be at the top of Turkish football are worthless men.' Cakar was asked if he feared the consequences of his outspoken tirades. 'The worst they can do is kill me,' he replied. 'Whoever dares can come and try and take my life. He who has the guts to shut me up, the heart and the courage to do it, bring him on. But my flesh is thick.' Within days, Cakar was recovering in hospital after being shot five times at point blank range. A gunman approached Cakar and shot him in the groin and stomach with a gun hidden in a bouquet of flowers. Cakar said there were several suspects, but he refused to name names. 'If I speak this would cause outrage in Turkey,' he said. 'There are four or five scenarios, but I don't even dare to consider some of them.'

While English football fans may hold Kenneth Wolstenholme's, 'They think it's all over . . . It is now!' line close to their hearts, the prize for the very best piece of football commentary must nevertheless go elsewhere. Wolstenholme himself was much more proud of another of his lines from the 1966 World Cup final. As Bobby Moore lifted the Jules Rimet trophy, Ken offered, 'It is only twelve inches high . . . It is solid gold . . . And it undeniably means England are the champions of the world.' But even that timeless classic is bettered by another piece of commentary, actually describing one of English football's darkest days.

In September 1981, England travelled to Oslo to play Norway in a crucial World Cup qualifier. Ron Greenwood's side lost 2–1, and Norwegian radio commentator Bjørge Lillelien was on hand to offer tea and sympathy. Or possibly not. Lillelien allowed his commentator's hat to slip and let passion overtake professionalism. Reverting to the role of a delighted fan, he unleashed the following hilariously bizarre rant in both Norwegian and English:

'We're the best in the world! We're the best in the world! We have defeated England 2–1 at football! It's completely unbelievable! We have defeated England! England, the nation of giants! Lord Nelson! Lord Beaverbrook! Sir Winston Churchill! Sir Anthony Eden! Clement Attlee! Henry Cooper! Lady Diana! We have defeated them all! We have defeated them all! Maggie Thatcher! Can you hear me? Maggie Thatcher! I have a message for you in the middle of your election campaign! I have a message for you! We have knocked England out of the World Cup! Maggie Thatcher! As they say in your language in the boxing bars around Madison Square Garden in New York – your boys took a hell of a beating! Your boys took a hell of a beating! Maggie Thatcher! Norway has defeated England at football! Maggie Thatcher! Norway has defeated England at football! We're the best in the world!'

12. REFEREES

Who's the bastard in the black? In the 1878 FA Cup final the answer to that question was Segar Richard Bastard. Mr Bastard officiated the match between Wanderers and Royal Engineers aged just 24. Wanderers won 3–1, with Bastard controversially disallowing what would have been an Engineers equaliser at 2–1. Throughout the years, the referee, like the game, has changed. Indeed, the 'bastard in the black' rarely even wears black any more, and some referees could not, under any circumstances, be considered bastards (think of assistant referee Wendy Toms, the UK's first female match official). But the referee remains the man all football fans love to hate, and the game just wouldn't be the same without a healthy dose of refereeing nincompoopery.

The fastest ever booking in British football was issued to big shot film star Vinnie Jones in 1992. The lightning-quick yellow card came just three seconds into a game between Jones's Chelsea and Sheffield United. Jones clattered Dane Whitehouse straight from the kick-off and found his name in the ref's notebook, and in the football record book. 'I must have been too high, too wild, too strong, or too early,' says the Hollywood hardman in his autobiography, 'because after three seconds I could hardly have been too bloody late!' The second fastest ever booking in British football came five seconds into a 1992 game between Wimbledon and Manchester City. Niall Quinn was the player scythed down. The player who was shown the yellow card was, surprise, surprise, Vinnie Jones.

The fastest ever sending off in British football happened in a 2002 match between Sheffield Wednesday and Wolverhampton Wanderers. Just 13 seconds into the game, Wednesday goalkeeper Kevin Pressman came blundering out of his box and handled a shot from Wolves striker Temuri Ketsbaia. Pressman was shown the red card, and took the record from Darlington's Mark Smith, who had been sent off against Crewe in 1994 after 19 seconds.

The record for the quickest sending off in the World Cup finals is held by Uruguay's Jose Batista. He was shown the red card after hacking down Gordon Strachan 56 seconds into a 0–0 draw with Scotland at Mexico '86. Incidentally, the first player to be sent off in the World Cup finals was Peru captain Mario de Las Casas in 1930. But those were the days before the introduction of cards, so the first player to be shown a red card in the World Cup finals was Chile's Carlos Caszely in 1974.

The fastest sending off in world football occurred in Italy in 1990, when Bologna's Guiseppe Lorenzo was sent off after ten seconds against Parma. Or did it? Popular legend has it that the fastest sending off actually took place in British non-League football. An unnamed hungover footballer was startled by the referee's shrill starting whistle. 'Fuck me, that was loud,' he exclaimed, before being shown the red card for using foul and abusive language.

Occasionally, the red card is produced with such speed and frequency that the referee resembles a Wild West gunslinger. There have been several British matches in which a mighty five players have been dismissed. In November 2002, five players were sent off in injury time as Cambridge beat Exeter 2–1. First Exeter goalkeeper Kevin Miller was sent off for tripping Cambridge striker Dave Kitson. Then a mass brawl saw Exeter's Glenn Cronin and Gareth Sheldon and Cambridge's Shane Tudor and Tom Youngs join Miller in a not particularly early bath.

In 1997, five players were sent off in two separate matches. In February, five were sent off in the Second Division match between Chesterfield and Plymouth following a last-minute ruckus. And in December, five were given their marching orders before half-time in a match between Bristol Rovers and Wigan Athletic.

As all refereeing course alumni know, a team must have a minimum of seven players to participate in a football match. Therefore, if five players from the same team are sent off in a game, the match must be abandoned. Millwall were the first British team to have four players sent off in one match, in the 1992–93 season, but no British team has ever had five players sent off. However, such an occasion has arisen in world football, occurring once in an African Nations Cup tie. In June 2003, a group match between Cape Verde and Mauritania was abandoned after Mauritania had five players sent off amid violent scenes. The referee was forced to call off the match, despite the fact that Cape Verde were leading 3–0, as Mauritania were left fielding just six players. In the interests of fairness, the match was not replayed, and Cape Verde were awarded the three points.

Such shows of handbags are nothing compared to the ruck that referee William Weiler had to deal with in 1993. In a Paraguayan Second Division match between Sport Ameliano and General Caballero, he sent off 20 footballers, including all 11 home players. With Caballero leading 2–0, Weiler sent off 2 Ameliano players. The ensuing argument became a ten-minute free-for-all scrap. Once the hair-pulling had subsided, Weiler sent off all nine remaining Ameliano players, plus nine Caballero players. The match was, unsurprisingly, abandoned.

Paraguay in 1993 was perhaps not the best place to be a referee. That year's national championship was abandoned after several dodgy doings. Olimpia were on top of the league and going into the championship final, having gone 27 games unbeaten, when bitter rivals Cerro Porteno obtained a court injunction to stop the competition. They cited various irregularities. First, Porteno's pitch had been sabotaged, with individuals alleged to be connected to Olimpia digging holes all over the field. Then Sport Colombia had points deducted, allowing Cerro Cora to overtake them and move into third place in the league. The side in second place, Presidente Hayes, disputed this decision and refused to play in the championship final against Olimpia. Cora were then allowed to take Presidente's place in the final. Porteno's court order claimed that this was against the league rules.

The Paraguayan sports council investigated the claims and found further irregularities relating to rules, player registrations, TV deals and ticket sales. Every official of the Paraguayan FA resigned, and FIFA threatened the country with international suspension if the matter was not resolved. A meeting of club presidents voted against resuming the championships and instead named Olimpia as champions. Footballing controversy of the highest order.

Nothing, not a penalty, not a goal, not a final whistle, gets such a unanimously appreciative cheer in a football ground as a referee being hit by the ball. Occasionally, referees are hit by an implement other than a ball – such as a fist. In 2002, in a heated game between Nantwich Town and Winsford United, Town's Glenn Attequayefio and United's Wes Wilkinson became embroiled in a scuffle. Ref Billy Smallwood quickly stepped in, only to be knocked clean out by an Attequayefio punch. After five minutes of treatment, Smallwood was revived. With a split lip and a broken tooth, the ref couldn't remember who had taken a swing at him, so he booked both Attequayefio and Wilkinson and restarted the game.

Also in 2002, Welsh referee Terry Lowrie was punched in the face twice by a 15-year-old footballer. After a controversial local derby match between Aberaeron and Newcastle Emlyn in the South Ceredigion Junior Football League, the six-foot schoolboy ran the length of the field and smacked Lowrie, first on the cheek and then on the jaw. The incensed teenager had been one of three Aberaeron players sent off in a 5–2 defeat for the team. The badly dazed ref was taken to hospital and treated for bruising. The boy was banned from playing football for life, with his family calling the Welsh FA's ban, which means he cannot play competitive football anywhere in the world ever again, 'absolutely ludicrous'.

Refereeing knockouts aren't confined to the lower leagues. In 2003, Paul Danson was knocked unconscious while refereeing a match between Crystal Palace and West Brom. Stepping in to stop two players from squaring up to each other, he accidentally collided with Michael Hughes. The ref lay motionless on the grass for six minutes, while medical staff offered treatment, before being stretchered from the pitch wearing a spinal board and an oxygen mask. Supporters realised the incident could be serious and generously applauded him from the pitch. Danson needed eight stitches in his mouth, but recovered within a few days.

Referees do occasionally get their own back. In 2003, a Premiership match between Newcastle United and Birmingham City saw referee Matt Messias knock out Blues fans' favourite Robbie Savage. St James' Park erupted in laughter as Messias raised his arm to signal a free kick, only to smack Savage in the nose. The girly-haired midfielder crumpled to the floor and required lengthy medical attention. Newcastle's Alan Shearer took the ref's red card and flashed it at Messias. Both Messias and Savage stayed on the pitch to complete the game. 'It was just one of those incidents, and Alan Shearer helped everyone to see the funny side,' said Messias. 'It just goes to show that we are human after all.'

Of course, the referee's most commonly used weapon of revenge is his notebook. Red and yellow cards were invented by Ken Aston during the 1966 World Cup finals, after the match between England and Argentina at Wembley. Argentinean captain Antonio Rattin was sent off for dissent by the game's German referee, but refused to leave. Acting FIFA official Aston promptly walked onto the pitch, took Rattin by the arm and gently escorted him from the field. On his way home, Aston considered whether Rattin had indeed refused to leave the pitch, or whether he had in fact not understood the German referee and simply did not know he had been dismissed. Stopping at a set of traffic lights, Aston watched their sequence turn from green to amber to red. In that moment he came up with a simple method of giving players their marching orders, and red and yellow cards were born. Aston, a headmaster, also used his cards outside of football, using them to discipline naughty school kids.

Red and yellow cards, and a referee's whistle, however, are not always available. Take the 1990s non-League match between Pinewood and St Cass in Manchester. The allocated referee didn't turn up, so, as tends to happen on these occasions, one of Pinewood's substitutes was delegated the task. Unfortunately, he didn't have a whistle. Kitbags were raided, and one footballer produced the solution – a harmonica. The story was related on a football phone-in show, and listeners learned that the match was successfully officiated with the mouth organ.

Radio phone-in archives reveal a veritable cornucopia of impromptu refereeing paraphernalia. One afternoon, Wiltshire referee Mark Tesler left his whistle at home and, being unable to muster a whistle through his lips, he procured a squeaky pork chop, a rubber toy offered up by a passing dogwalker. Unfortunately, the chop's pathetic squeak was not loud enough to be used in lieu of a whistle. Instead, Tesler popped into a local pub and borrowed a wooden spoon and a tin tray, proceeding to beat out his decisions with a loud clang. Red and yellow cards are perhaps even harder to come by. When one non-League referee had his cards stolen, he responded by snipping replacements from Weetabix and cornflakes packets.

Another caller brought to the table the story of the referee who parked his car on the halfway line and, refusing to get out, flashed the vehicle's headlights to signal his decisions. The Reading

TALES FROM FOOTBALL'S NETHER REGIONS

Referees' Association website features a similar tale of a teacher who refereed school games by driving up and down the touchline in his car, winding down the window to issue blasts of the whistle. The Reading site also tells the story of referee Gordon Crutchfield, who showed bravery beyond the call of duty in rescuing King's Meadow's only match ball. When an errant clearance landed the ball in an adjacent river, Crutchfield quickly stripped to his vest and dived into the water to retrieve it. He returned to the riverbank, ball under arm, and was met with unanimous applause from both sets of relieved players.

Not all referees are cut from such cloth as Mr Crutchfield. Some just aren't up to the job. Ref Arthur Holland may not be technically colour-blind, but, in a match between Coventry City and Southend United, it did take him three full minutes to spot the fact that both sides were playing in indistinguishable blue and white strips.

Belgian ref Marc Gevaert ended a 2002 league match early because he felt sorry for the losers. FC Wiftschate were losing 16–0 to Vladslo when Gevaert blew his whistle to end their agony. 'After an hour, with the score at 11–0, the players of Wiftschate came to me to beg me to end the game,' he said. 'Near the end, when the score was 16–0, they became frustrated and began to kick the Vladslo players for nothing and play tricks on them. I felt sorry for them. I didn't want to send the boys off, so that's why I ended the game early.' But Wiftschate, with the worst record in Belgian football having conceded 132 goals in 15 games, were used to losing and declared themselves unhappy with the ref's decision. 'All our players are farm boys who are too busy working and studying,' a spokesman explained. 'We don't have sponsors, and therefore no money for better players. But that doesn't give the referee the right to end the game early.'

Another Belgian ref, Jacky Temmerman, vowed never to officiate ever again after an unsavoury incident at a 2004 match between Young Stars Eelko and FC Zelzate. Part way through the game, a fan ran onto the pitch and pulled down Mr Temmerman's shorts and underpants. 'That looked very nice in front of a few hundred supporters,' Temmerman fumed. 'That man made a fool of me. I will never dare show up for another match. They can look for another idiot who is prepared to stand and bare his naked ass for 20 euros a game.'

According to the coach of Young Stars Eelko, Marnix Speekaerts, pitch incursions are not uncommon in the league. Still, Speekaerts was shocked. 'Sometimes supporters spit at the referee but we have never had a fan come onto the pitch and do something like that,' he said. 'I hope he is severely punished.'

The pitch invader turned out to be the 20-year-old player–coach of another league side, KFC Eelko. 'I don't know what came over me,' the unnamed underpants-grabber was quoted as saying.

In Cumbria in 2003, a match between Askam United and Furness Rovers was delayed for 15 minutes when two referees turned up and couldn't decide who should take charge. Both Jimmy Hunter and Dick Green refused to move from the centre circle and stood arguing and blowing whistles at each other for a quarter of an hour. Eventually, the players found another ref to take over. Hunter and Green refused to leave the pitch, so were allowed to run the line. 'It was my match,' said Hunter, 'he had no right to muscle in.' 'If he had asked politely to take charge of the game I would have let him,' countered Green, 'but it became a point of principle.'

Amateur ref Wayne Millin from Gloucestershire was sacked from his job at a printing firm after booking his boss. The trouble started when Millin awarded a throw-in to Ebley in a match against King's Stanley in the Stroud League. King's Stanley manager, and Millin's boss, Robert Smith shouted, 'You're a wanker, ref!' Millin marched over to Smith, booked him and told him he would be reported to the FA. Millin also booked a King's Stanley player, another colleague, who he said later attacked him and sprayed him with cleaning fluid. On his return to work, Millin was sacked. 'I should never have been sacked,' he said. 'I was only doing my job as a ref. It was only over a throw-in.' Millin was eventually awarded £6,000 compensation at tribunal. His boss, Mr Smith, was fined seven quid by the FA.

Spare a thought, too, for Per Arne Brataas. The Norwegian fourth division referee revealed in 2003 that he didn't show red or yellow cards because he suffers from dyslexia. 'I was reluctant to give red cards,' he said. 'I didn't give yellow cards either, so I could avoid having to write reports.'

Another Norwegian referee, officiating at a 2003 Norwegian junior football match in Sunndal, had to be replaced because he was pissed. 'He was clearly drunk and unable to judge the match,' said a tournament organiser. He was replaced at half-time. A spokesman for Sunndal referees admitted the whole event had been rather embarrassing.

Despite these Nordic indiscretions, referees remain so well respected in Norway that, in 2003, the Norwegian postal service put a ref on a stamp. Unfortunately the stamp, celebrating the Norwegian Soccer Federation's centenary year, was printed with a picture of the wrong referee. The 1.3 million stamps issued into circulation were supposed to show 27-year-old FIFA ref Lars Johan Hammer in whistle-blowing action. 'I was really looking forward to it,' Hammer admitted. 'I had told all my relations about the big event.' But confusion replaced excitement when Hammer and his eager relatives first saw the stamp. 'I don't have glasses or a beard,' he said, scratching his head, 'and I must say I was stunned to see this strange referee on the stamps.'

A postal service spokeswoman described the mix-up as 'unfortunate'. The 'strange referee' was eventually tracked down by the postal service, after a full page wanted poster was printed in a Norwegian newspaper and an appeal was launched on an Oslo radio station. He turned out to be a German, Peter Hertel, who had presided over a Norwegian Junior Cup match way back in

1997. Unlike Hammer, Hertel is not a FIFA ref and officiates in the lowly German seventh division. Hertel was amused by the mix-up and had no objection to the back of his head being licked by 1.3 million Norwegians.

Hammer, meanwhile, took the disappointment in his stride, saying, 'It is only human to make mistakes.' As a referee he should know that better than most.

It's highly unlikely that any British referee will ever end up on a stamp, but our top refs still attract a certain level of celebrity, or perhaps notoriety. A rare insight into the world of refereeing was offered by a 1980s television experiment in which well-known ref David Elleray, who once appeared in an advertising campaign for Holland's pies, was miked for sound at a match between Millwall and Arsenal. As a boy, Elleray, who grew up to become a Harrow schoolmaster ('the best job in the world'), collected newspaper clippings about referees, such was his odd devotion to footballing officialdom. The TV experiment crumbled into hilarity after Elleray disallowed a clear Arsenal goal, incorrectly deciding that the ball had not crossed the line.

'You're a fucking cheat!' Arsenal's Tony Adams told Elleray.

'You may call me useless,' replied football's poshest ref, 'but I am not a cheat.'

Adams was not booked for that indiscretion, although he was later shown the yellow card for again spitting the word 'cheat' at the ref. 'I was very emotional, wasn't I?' Adams later explained. 'But it did fucking cross the line, didn't it?'

Switzerland's Kurt Roethlisberger is one referee who can't object to being called a cheat. Although he did send Manchester United's Eric Cantona off in a 1993 match against Galatasaray for doing just that. Cantona later claimed the ref had been bought. Hindsight suggests the Frenchman may have been right. In 1994, Roethlisberger was sent home from the World Cup finals after failing to award Belgium a clear-cut penalty in a match against Germany which they lost 3–2, knocking them out of the tournament. Then, in 1995, he was suspended for three months for posing in his referee uniform with a political slogan over his FIFA badge in an attempt to win a seat in the Swiss parliament. Finally, Roethlisberger attempted to fix a 1997 Champions League match between Zurich Grasshoppers and Auxerre. Roethlisberger approached Grasshoppers manager Erich Vogel and told him he could buy the match referee, Vadim Zhuk of Belarus, for £50,000. Vogel declined the offer and reported the matter to UEFA, who suspended Zhuk and banned Roethlisberger for life. The schoolteacher appealed against the decision, but lost. 'The Board of Appeals found the statements made by Roethlisberger to be inconsistent and not convincing,' said UEFA's Markus Studer. 'At first he denied everything and then later admitted wrongdoing. Mr Roethlisberger has seriously abused his role and damaged the image of his profession.'

In March 1997, the coach of Brazilian club Itaperuna protested at a bad refereeing performance by streaking across the pitch. Paulo Mata was so angry when the ref sent off three of his players and allowed a dubious late goal against his team that he tore off his shirt and ran onto the field. Two policemen tackled him before he could flash his tackle in front of a live television audience. But Mata had the last laugh. Standing in front of a camera during a post-match interview, he turned his back, dropped his trousers and mooned millions of shocked viewers. 'I went naked because I'm tired of working honestly only to be scandalously robbed,' said Mata. 'Football in Rio de Janeiro is a disgrace.'

Football's most famous ref is undoubtedly Pierluigi Collina. The striking Italian, with goggle eyes and hairless head, looks uncannily like the actor Michael Berryman who played the cannibalistic mutant Pluto in Wes Craven's 1978 horror film *The Hills Have Eyes*. Born in 1960, Collina was 24 when he lost his hair to the disease alopecia. It disappeared within the space of 15 days over Christmas. 'I don't know what happened,' he recalled. 'I don't remember anything particular.' But even FIFA's number one referee is not above criticism. He is regularly accused by Serie A coaches of bias and is thought by many Italian football fans to be too big for his refereeing boots. He's also not above taking a gigantic strop. In October 2002, Collina appeared on an Italian TV show to receive a 'Sport Oscar'. But when the show's presenters made a joke about 'Collina Hair Lotion', the ref stormed off, smashing his award to pieces as he went. 'My bald head is not a fashion gag,' he complained. 'It's not nice to be teased because of an illness.'

Collina is not the only referee to have felt the satirical wrath of Italian TV. Ecuadorian ref Byron Moreno became the most hated man in Italy after the 2002 World Cup. Italy were knocked out after losing a match against South Korea, in which Moreno awarded a dubious penalty to the Koreans, wrongly disallowed an equaliser for the Italians and sent off Italian captain Francesco Totti. First a Sicilian holiday resort named its public toilets after him. 'We look at this as an outstanding opportunity for locals and tourists to remember Moreno's performance at the World Cup,' said a spokesman at the ceremony to affix a brass plate bearing Moreno's name to the toilet door. Then Moreno guested on an Italian TV show called *Hotel Stupido*. The controversial appearance saw the ref stand in front of a baying audience while being soaked under gallons of water. Italian politicians and footballers complained that Moreno was benefiting from his biased performance and was corrupt. Moreno said his conscience was clear.

Moreno found himself in trouble again while refereeing an Ecuadorian league match in September 2002. He saw fit to add a massive 22 minutes of injury time in the game between Barcelona de Guayaquil and LDU Quito. Quito were losing 2–1 at 90 minutes, but the added time allowed them to equalise after 99 minutes and score the winner on 112 minutes. After the winning goal, Moreno immediately blew his whistle to end the game, causing aggrieved Guayaquil fans to riot. Could Moreno's ridiculous amount of added time have had anything to do with the fact that he was at the time standing for election to Quito city council? Most Ecuadorians thought so, and even the national referees' association admitted that Moreno had been 'mistaken' to add the 22 minutes. Guayaquil's president, Leonardo Bohrer said, 'This man's handling of that game was an insult to Ecuadorian football.'

The widely held belief that referees are inherently biased was given credence by the results of a 2003 scientific study. Austrian researchers Matthias Sutter and Martin Kocher proved beyond doubt that referees favour the home team over the away side. They analysed every match from the 2000–01 Bundesliga season, and their findings were conclusive. Referees were found to be twice as likely to award a penalty to a home team as to an away team. They were also twice as likely to send off an away player as a home player. And they were likely to add more injury time if the home side was behind after 90 minutes of play. But the study ruled out deliberate bias on behalf of referees. The researchers claimed that accurate refereeing decisions were made extremely difficult by shouting crowds. A plainly rubbish excuse.

13. FANATICS

Fans are football's lifeblood. Professional football would not exist if supporters did not pony up the dough to watch it. And footballers would not have expensive mansions, sports cars and celebrity girlfriends without the generosity of their fans. Yet footballers and football clubs regularly forget this. The relationship between fan and club is a strange one. Fans will go to incredible lengths to follow their clubs, and supporters' loyalty to their teams is extreme. But the relationship walks a fine line between love and hate, depending on whether the team wins or loses. When that fine line is crossed, all manner of madness surely follows.

It is now considered fashionable to be a football fan, with everyone from pop stars to politicians expressing a hitherto hidden love for the beautiful game. Tony Blair claims to be a Newcastle United fan and has famously recalled sitting on St James' Park's Gallowgate End watching Jackie Milburn play. However, Milburn retired long before Blair was old enough to attend football matches, and the Gallowgate End he so fondly remembers sitting on was a standing section until the 1990s (and West End lyricist Sir Tim Rice claims Blair once confessed to him to being a 'Sunderland devotee'.)

TALES FROM FOOTBALL'S NETHER REGIONS

Fidel Castro, Osama bin Laden and Kevin Costner all support Arsenal. Bertie Aherne, Roger Moore and Mick Hucknall (hence 'Simply Red') support Manchester United. Henry Kissinger, Michael Caine and Sir Richard Attenborough support Chelsea. Michael Jackson is an honorary supporter and director of Exeter City, courtesy of his relationship with spoon-bender Uri Geller. Bill Clinton is a football fan. Prince William supports Aston Villa. And Mikhail Gorbachev is said to support Wigan Athletic.

Pop star Robbie Williams supports Port Vale, but hit the headlines in 2003 when it was claimed he had abandoned his side to spend £10 million on executive boxes at Roman Abramovich's Chelsea. Williams acted quickly to quell the anger of Vale fans. In fact, he had bought a £50,000 box as a gift for his manager. 'The papers can talk about my personal life or whatever,' he told the *Stoke Sentinel*, 'but don't mess with me and the Vale.' Even Arsenal devotee and *Fever Pitch* author Nick Hornby has had mixed loyalties. He abandoned the Gunners when he went to university in the late '70s and instead supported Cambridge United.

Conversely, some real football fans have become celebrities in their own right. Helen 'The Bell' Turner is in her 80s, yet continues to spur on her beloved Manchester City by ringing her famous bell. City fans afforded her a standing ovation after the club's last ever game at Maine Road. Paul Gregory is a big, bald Sheffield Wednesday supporter who became known as 'Tango Man' when he eccentrically stripped to the waist and painted himself orange in tribute to the star of the popular 1990s Tango fizzy pop commercials.

Newcastle United fan Keith Roberts is known on the terraces as 'Beefy'. The 26-stone fan became a legend after stripping to the waist to display the huge NUFC tattoo on his ample belly. Beefy revealed his strict match day feeding routine to the Newcastle *Evening Chronicle*: 'I get up early and have a full fry-up with all the trimmings. On the way to the match, I keep going on a couple of cold saveloys, and nothing beats a steak pie. During the game there's only one food that will do, and that's a good old-fashioned pastie – you can't beat them. After that it's just rubbish – burgers, chicken, that kind of stuff. But there's got to be room for the beer. And I always save the best until I get home and my wife fixes me up a curry – no match day is complete without one.'

Beefy would no doubt be interested in Jane Aukim's ingenious match pie holder. The Coventry University design student created the device in 2003 to help fans eat the notoriously dangerous snackfood – a steaming pastry-load of unidentifiable abattoir run-off swimming in molten gravy. Jane came up with the idea after seeing a man accidentally dripping gravy on a little girl's head during a Wolves match. Her round plastic invention will seem like a godsend for anyone who has ever suffered burnt fingers while struggling to control a pie using only a tin foil tray and a cheap napkin.

Some football fans choose to avoid the perils of the match pie in favour of a bag of chips from the local chippie. But the United Fisheries chip shop, near Leeds United's Elland Road, ran into problems in 2003 when fans boycotted their red chip forks. 'I kept putting out these boxes of plastic forks,' owner Mick Bailey told the *Yorkshire Evening Post*, 'and on match days the white and yellow ones would go really quickly, but the red ones were always left over. Basically they won't touch them because red is associated with Manchester United, and they would rather eat with their fingers than pick one up.'

Leeds fan Gareth Hemingway summed up the problem. 'I won't eat tomato ketchup on match days,' he said, 'so a red fork is out of the question.'

'It's got to the point where I've had to throw all the red forks out and start using wooden forks because they're a neutral colour,' said Mick. 'It's unbelievable.'

Other chip-eating football fans aren't always so loyal to their local team. David Miller ran a promotion at his Sunderland chippie offering a free bag of chips to every customer who wore their football colours in the shop for the first time. Sunderland fan Rod Latherick duly turned up wearing his Sunderland shirt and claimed his free chips. The next day, Rod returned to the chippie wearing the shirt of arch rivals Newcastle and shamelessly claimed more free chips – which proves that some people will do literally anything for a bag of chips.

In 2003, Berwick Rangers fans took several bags of celery into their club's Shielfield Park before the visit of Stranraer in the Scottish Second Division. But it wasn't part of some crackpot match food diet. At the match at Stranraer, Berwick fans had been pelted with coins. At the return match, Berwick fans responded with a non-violent 'satirical' protest. Two fans carried the bags around the pitch at half-time and proceeded to pelt the visitors with celery. The pair were ejected by stewards, but escaped police attention. 'I drove 200 miles to watch the game,' said a disgruntled Stranraer fan, 'only for some fat bearded git to bombard me with celery.'

He should think himself lucky. If he had been visiting Steaua Nicolae Balcescu he would have been more likely to have some fat bearded git bombard him with bricks, bottles and fireworks. Fans of the Romanian Fourth Division club have an unrivalled reputation for crowd violence and, in 2003, the club was threatened with expulsion from the league after repeated violent pitch invasions. But the club had a devious plan to stop such incidents ever happening again. They would, they decided, build a moat around the pitch and fill it with crocodiles. 'This is not a joke,' said club chairman Alexandra Cringus. 'We can get crocodiles easily enough and feed them on meat from the local abattoir. The moat will be wide enough so that no one could manage to jump over it. Anyone who attempted to do so would have to deal with the crocs.' The proposed moat would be electrically heated to prevent the crocs from freezing to death and would be far enough from the touchlines to prevent players from falling in. The idea had to be ratified by the local authorities, but Cringus was convinced he was onto a winner, saying, 'I think that the problem of fans running onto the pitch will be solved once and for all.'

Unfortunately, even a crocodile-infested moat is unlikely to be sufficient to prevent notoriously bad-tempered Romanian football fans from venting their anger. In September 2003 the Romanian national side drew 2–2 with Denmark in a Euro 2004 qualifier and effectively crashed out of the championships. (Romania had lost their previous qualifier against Denmark 5–2. On that occasion, Romanians forsook bacon sandwiches and boycotted Danish livestock.) Romania needed to win to qualify, but the controversial match saw Denmark score a disputed penalty, Romania take a 2–1 lead and Denmark equalise in the fifth minute of injury time. Seconds after the final whistle, police were called to investigate five 'small explosions' in the streets of Iasi. They discovered five broken television sets that had been ripped from walls and thrown out of windows. One of the sets belonged to Marian Mire, who said, 'Goodbye Portugal! Goodbye my TV set!'

The defeat was blamed almost entirely on Swiss referee Urs Meier. Top lawyer Catalin Dancu lobbied the Romanian government to have Meier declared an 'undesirable'. 'I think if the government cares for the people then this referee will never set foot in this country,' Dancu said. 'He humiliated us all.'

Meanwhile, a coven of Romanian witches attempted to put a curse on Meier. 'Romania won but the referee took our victory,' said a woman called Mother Maria. 'I talked to some witches and asked them to curse the man and get him fired from his job.'

Romanian football is steeped in superstition. Players always step onto the field with their right foot, team coaches are not allowed to reverse, and women are not allowed to travel with football squads. In 2003, female reporter Gabriela Arsenie of the *Gazeta Sporturilor* was kicked off the Romanian international team's plane before a trip to the Ukraine because it was feared she would bring bad luck.

Peterborough United fan John Magee is something of a propitious talisman for his side due to his remarkably lucky underpants. The Posh have never lost when Magee has worn the blue and white briefs. 'I bought these pants seven years ago, and they've not failed me yet,' he told the *Peterborough Evening Telegraph*. 'Everyone considers me a lucky omen.' Peterborough fans can only hope Magee wears his lucky pants to matches more often.

In March 1994, disgruntled Dorchester Town supporter David Green put a curse on the Beazer Homes League team's Avenue Stadium. Green, a white witch, was unimpressed by the club's decision to move to a new home after supermarket Tesco purchased the old ground. He duly cursed the brand new £2.3 million stadium, and Dorchester accordingly began to lose home games. In the 1993–94 season, the side won only four out of 21 home games. Club officials were worried enough to turn up on BBC TV chat show *Esther* to express their concerns. But club chaplain Reverend David Fayle had a solution. He performed an exorcism to remove the curse. Dorchester played Nuneaton at home on the following day, and won 1–0.

In 2003, one Brazilian football fan protested at his team's bad form in a unique manner. Corinthians supporter Roberto climbed into a tree outside the club's stadium, tied himself to it and refused to come down until the team agreed to change its line-up and tactics. The club refused to bow to Roberto's demands and left the fan living in the tree, eating bananas and throwing the skins at the stadium doors. Roberto told reporters he had no plans to come down.

Some footballers find it hard to take criticism from their fans. In 2003 the Swaziland national team played out a disappointing 1–1 draw in a World Cup qualifier against Cape Verde. As the team bus left the Somhlolo Stadium in Mbabane, it was surrounded by a group of supporters who began to taunt the players. Swaziland were without a manager, as Mandla Dlamini had resigned earlier in the month after being pelted with rotten vegetables following a 3–0 friendly defeat to Botswana. Without an authority figure on the bus, the players decided to take action. They ordered the driver to stop and piled off the bus brandishing sticks. 'In a scene reminiscent of an action-packed film, one fan ran as if he had a third lung as the players moved menacingly towards him,' reported the *Swaziland Times*. Luckily for that fan, the police were on hand to step in and put a stop to the aggressive hi-jinks.

Other players treat their fans with a little more respect. Take SV Hamburg forward Naohiro Takahara. After scoring his first goal for the club, an injury-time header past Oliver Kahn that gave his side a 1–1 draw with Bayern Munich, the Japanese player celebrated by handing out 500 pints of beer to fans. He distributed the drinks at the AOL Arena before Hamburg's following league game against VFL Wolfsburg. An extra 200 pints were held back for Takahara's lucky teammates.

Handing out free beer is a great way to create a good atmosphere in a football stadium, but fans rarely need much encouragement to get excited at the sight of 22 men running around a field. There is no more renowned display of soccer excitement than the Mexican Wave, or La Ola. First recognised at the World Cup finals in Mexico in 1986, the celebration sees groups of fans stand up and sit down in succession to create a rippling wave effect across the crowd. In 2002, Hungarian biological physicist Dr Tamas Vicsek determined the science of the Mexican Wave. He found that the waves usually move in a clockwise direction at around 12 metres – or 20 seats – per second. How much Dr Vicsek was paid for this Earth-shattering piece of research is completely unknown.

Other fans go to greater lengths when excited. During Scarborough's debut League match against Wolverhampton Wanderers in 1987, several Wolves fans clambered onto the roof of one of the old stands. One particular fan began to chant and stamp up and down as TV cameras around the ground zoomed in on him. Then he stamped a hole through the roof and fell to the ground. Miraculously, he was not seriously injured and discharged himself later that afternoon, before any Scarborough fans had a chance to deliver a get well soon card.

A much worse injury occurred at Villa Park in December 1998 when Aston Villa decided to lay on some spectacular Christmas entertainment at half-time during a League match with Arsenal. The plan was for a series of skydivers to parachute down onto the centre circle. All went well, until final skydiver Nigel Rogoff, who was dressed as Father Christmas, misjudged his descent. He crashed into the roof of the Trinity Road Stand at 70 miles per hour and then toppled 70 feet to the ground. Rogoff lost a leg, but survived, and fell in love with the nurse who looked after him during his many months of recuperation.

Football clubs often forget that football fans go to football matches primarily to watch football. They believe that supporters will lose interest unless they supply pre-match and half-time cabaret shows involving mascots, cheerleaders, flags, balloons and fireworks. In Sky Sports' formative years, live Premiership matches were preceded by cheerleading and firework displays, with tinpot pop acts dragged out to mime badly in the centre circle. The whole sorry affair had less razzmatazz than a blue rinse and was quickly scrapped. Yet some Premiership clubs failed to learn from that debacle. The likes of Arsenal and Middlesbrough have 'flag days' where fans are encouraged to bring flags to the match and, presumably, wave them in an attempt to improve the match-going experience. Bolton Wanderers offer their supporters a mascot, cheerleaders and two men waving giant flags. Blackburn Rovers fans, meanwhile, are treated to a half-time jumbotron TV show that has been known to feature the expert football analysis of *Bullseye*'s Jim Bowen.

Things finally came to a head with a shambolic fireworks

display at Molineux in 2003. As Wolves and Newcastle players ran onto the pitch to start the match they were greeted by an array of rockets, one of which errantly shot straight at them. Newcastle's Jonathan Woodgate was forced to dive for cover as the firework whistled past his ear. It flew into the crowd and hit a female Wolves fan in the face, just missing her eye but nevertheless causing serious injury. Wolves were quick to announce that there would be no further firework displays at Molineux.

The first football fanzine was almost certainly *Off The Ball*, which was founded in Birmingham in 1985. It was written by Aston Villa fan Adrian Goldberg, who later became best known as Anne Robinson's bespectacled sidekick on TV complainathon *Watchdog*. Three separate publications claim to have been Scotland's first football fanzine. It's a toss-up between *Sick as a Parrot*, *The Absolute Game* and *Meadowbank Review*. Then came the daddy of all football fanzines – *When Saturday Comes* – a national publication for football fans that was first produced in 1986 and is still going strong today.

The fanzine explosion proved that football fans had a valid voice and something interesting to say. Radio soon woke up to this fact, and football phone-ins were born. Usually broadcast after the day's games, shows like BBC Radio Five Live's *606* (going out at 6.06 p.m. on a Saturday evening) invited fans to call up and vent their spleen, express their delight and indulge in transfer gossip. Phone-ins grew immensely popular, but the quality of the shows depended on the quality of the calls, and endless calls from Manchester United fans debating team line-ups soon grew boring.

In the mid-'90s, *606* presenter Danny Baker began to encourage calls of a more offbeat nature. Consequently, there were calls about football lookalikes, tramps on the terraces, bribing turnstile operators and all manner of other absurdities related to being a football fan. Baker's halcyon football phone-in days saw him teamed up with Danny Kelly. 'It was apparent straight away that the two combined superbly,' says Andrew Gee, webmaster of the *Danny Baker Internet Treehouse*. 'To those like myself, brought up on the traditional fare of football phone-ins, their radio programmes were a breath of fresh air. Their speed of recall and ability to wring 15 minutes of top class radio from even the most pedestrian of calls marked them out as something very special in the normally sterile world of sports broadcasting.'

The pair became known as 'The Two Dans' and helmed shows on Five Live and TalkSport. Baker was sacked from Five Live after slamming an incompetent referee, insulting a caller and arguing on air with his producer. He was then removed from TalkSport after an elaborate hoax involving an audiotape allegedly containing a frank England dressing room exchange between Alan Shearer and Glenn Hoddle (Shearer to Hoddle: 'Have you ever thought it could be *you*?'). Baker and Kelly briefly returned to Five Live, before controllers eventually snuffed out the show for good, but the Baker and Kelly phone-ins left us with a plump legacy of fantastic football stories.

One such tale is that of the wooden bow tie. Dundee United fan Gordon was nine years old when he asked his dad to make him a United bow tie. It was the 1960s, and football memorabilia such as hats, scarves and rattles were commonplace on the terraces. But Gordon wanted something out of the ordinary. Gordon's dad duly obliged, creating a black bow tie with 'UNITED' written across the middle. 'But,' said Gordon, dropping his bombshell, 'it was made out of plywood. It was two-feet wide, and it was tied around my neck with a big leather strap. It weighed about a stone and a half.' Clearly, young Gordon's unique plywood accessory was too heavy for the lad to carry around his neck, and, on its debut outing, he spent the match hunched over 'like Quasimodo'. Gordon's handy dad had a solution. He produced an eight-foot pole, to which the bow tie was strapped 'like a Roman standard'. Gordon's dad also made him a football rattle. Of course, Gordon's dad being Gordon's dad, the rattle was made out of cast iron.

Other notable tales involved a Nazi mother, bogus Standard

BALLS

Liege scouts, illegal Sky Sports broadcasts, fake classified results and a crazy bet involving a Celtic strip and the Shankhill Road. Many of the stories were mind boggling, but none were as outrageous as Steven Marks of Coventry's macabre tale of football and death. 'Four of us travelled down from Coventry for the FA Cup final in 1987,' he said. 'Just before we pulled off the M1, my dad's friend's father had a seizure and died. Not wanting to miss the only opportunity we would probably ever have of seeing Coventry in a Cup final, we left the corpse in a sleeping pose in the car park of Stanmore Tube Station. Even as we talk about it today, we still think we made the right decision.'

The most talked about Baker and Kelly story came from a piece of correspondence labelled by Danny Kelly 'the best letter ever'. The letter was written by one Jay Schitto, a ranger from Wilnuna, Western Australia. The full startling story is presented here with permission from the sender:

> The school at Wilnuna has only one football. The kids use it for Aussie rules, basketball, volleyball and football. A local nuisance, Kepto – an Aborigine alcoholic – was arrested for breaking into the school and stealing the television and the football. I, being the local ranger, had to escort Kepto to the nearest courthouse. With Kepto handcuffed to my seatbelt, we set off for the six hundred mile journey. After a few hours I felt a bit sorry for the prisoner and released his handcuffs. A big mistake. Travelling at 60 over the rough desert, Kepto grabbed the football from behind his seat, opened the door and threw himself out of the speeding car. I slammed on the brakes and brought the vehicle to a halt, half expecting Kepto to be a pile of broken bones at the trackside, only to find that he was a quarter of a mile behind, kicking the football in front of him. Like an idiot, instead of getting back into the truck and driving after him, I set off in foot

pursuit. Being 19 stone I soon slowed down in the 100°
sun. The only feature in the vicinity were two Bulobo
bushes about 800 yards ahead. He must be hiding there,
surely. A little closer to the bushes I could smell him but
I could not see him. Then I felt something tug at my belt.
I spun around, and there was Kepto – with my gun in one
hand and the football in the other. Although he had not
spoken a word during our trip from Wilnuna, it now
became apparent that we were now playing by his rules.
He pointed the gun at my face, grinned like a madman
and said a single word – 'Maradona'. This trigger-happy
Aboriginal absconder wanted to play football. He had my
gun. Who was I to argue? For the next three hours I had
to act as goalkeeper, using the Bulobo bushes as
goalposts, while he took pot shots at me. If I made a save
he would shout, 'Moolango!' and point the gun at me. By
this time I was absolutely exhausted and decided a bit of
psychology might get me out of my predicament. 'Hey
Maradona. I think you deserve a drink. I have some beer
in the car,' I shouted. At which point he took one last
shot and collapsed on the ground. I approached him
cautiously, then kicked the gun out of his hand. He was
stone dead. There is no punchline, I'm afraid, except,
perhaps, that he died a happy man, playing football.

The story was swapped on terraces and posted on the internet,
and Jay Schitto became something of a cult hero. Unfortunately,
he didn't exist. Baker and Kelly, and their legion of listeners, had
been conned. 'Jay Schitto' was, in fact, a pseudonym of Mick
McSorley, known as the Clairvoyant Barber, who was dubbed by
Danny Baker 'the greatest phone-in contributor in the history of
the world'. *Kepto and Gun*, as the story became known, was an
elaborate and brilliant fake. 'It began life as a short story,' says
Mick, 'but I happened to be listening to Baker and Kelly on the

radio as I was writing it. It was faxed to the show and was coming out of the speakers within one hour of being fabricated.'

Another of the very best Baker and Kelly moments came from Mick's pen, and this time it was true. It involved Leeds United's historic 7–0 humiliation of Southampton from 1972. In a story involving a rifle, a mad dog and a suspected assassination attempt, Mick claimed to have personally damaged the Southampton players' confidence that afternoon. As Mick explained, 'On that fateful day, I was Lee Harvey Oswald.' The 13-year-old Mick had just bought a second-hand air rifle with which to shoot rats and was innocently returning home to his house on Elland Road when he was approached by two match-day police officers. The first officer dived 'theatrically' onto the weapon, while the second 'performed origami' on Mick's left arm. Mick's dog promptly bit that officer on the thigh. Mick was then escorted away by half a dozen officers. One officer held the weapon triumphantly above his head, drawing much pointing and gasping from the general public. Then the Southampton team coach arrived. So the first thing the visitors saw was a Leeds fan being led away with a rifle above his head. Mick then noted: 'I made accidental eye contact with keeper Eric Martin. He looked anxious.' One freak result later, Mick found himself in the local nick. The sum total of that was: 'Received a police caution and was encouraged to join a boys' club.'

'The rifle story is 100 per cent genuine,' says Mick. 'One positive thing to emerge from that fateful day was that I instantly gained a certain kudos amongst my peers. Although my intentions on the day were purely honourable, I gained a temporary reputation as a total nutcase who would be willing to shoot First Division footballers "for a laugh". For a few glorious weeks, bullies and hardcases stepped aside and girls in hotpants lent me "clackers" on demand.'

14. LAW AND ORDER

Footballers are notoriously badly behaved. There are incidents of fisticuffs and unsporting behaviour at football grounds across the country every week. But what happens when a footballer does something really bad? What happens when a footballer commits armed robbery, murders someone, or becomes a suicide bomber? And was an FA Cup-winning former Everton and Spurs player really hung for stealing an Australian sheep? Remember, the chances of you being involved in a football-related crime are small. So, please, don't have nightmares.

Three international footballers are known to have killed someone, although in one case it was an accident. Netherlands and Barcelona striker Patrick Kluivert narrowly escaped a jail sentence after being convicted of vehicular homicide in 1996. Kluivert slammed a borrowed BMW into another car, killing the driver. He was sentenced to 240 hours of community service.

Turkish midfielder Emre also killed a man while driving. However, the verdict in that case was 'accident'. Emre was driving at 90 mph in the middle lane of Turkey's E5 motorway when Kadir Cetin walked in front of the car. The accident occurred at 5.30

a.m., and questions were asked about why the footballer, who was recovering from injury at the time, was driving at that time of night.

In 1999, Brazilian striker Edmundo, known as 'The Animal', killed three pedestrians while driving in his jeep. He was found guilty of speeding and sentenced to four years in prison. He appealed and only spent one night in jail, but was sacked by his club Vasco da Gama anyway. Just a few months later, Edmundo was lambasted by animal welfare groups after being pictured pouring beer down a chimpanzee's neck. He had hired the chimp, Pedrinho, for his daughter's first birthday party.

Edmundo scored a record 29 goals for Vasco in 1997, despite being sent off seven times that season. He moved to Fiorentina after being sacked, but was kicked out after leaving to attend the Rio carnival. The striker was later sacked by Cruzeira after deliberately missing a penalty against Vasco. He got into further trouble for fighting and smashing a TV camera and was then named in a paternity suit by a Brazilian TV star. And trouble ran in his family. Edmundo's brother Luis Carlos Alves de Souza was involved in drug trafficking and rioting and once burgled Edmundo's house. Luis Carlos disappeared in Rio in 2002 and was found several days later in the boot of a car with a bullet in his head.

Then there are the footballers who dabble in international terrorism. Two days after the terrorist attacks in America on 11 September 2001, Tunisian footballer Nizar Trabelsi was arrested in Belgium. Trabelsi played professionally in Germany for Wuppertaler Sport Verein before heading to Afghanistan to meet FBI 'most wanted' terrorist leader Osama bin Laden. After offering himself up as a suicide bomber, Trabelsi began to organise a network of Islamic radicals across Europe. The judge at his trial said, 'While bin Laden was preparing for attacks on the United States, Trabelsi and others were preparing and looking for explosives in Europe.'

Phone and credit card records confirmed his involvement, and Trabelsi admitted to plotting to blow up the US military base in Belgium. The Kleine Brogel base accommodates 100 US troops and is said to house nuclear weapons. Trabelsi had planned to drive a car bomb into the base canteen. He denied he was also plotting to blow up the US embassy in Paris. In the absence of any specific Belgian anti-terrorism laws, Trabelsi was convicted of attempting to destroy public property, illegal arms possession and membership of a private militia. He was sentenced to ten years in prison.

Of course, bin Laden himself is actually a keen Arsenal fan. The beardy cave-dweller spent three months in London in 1994 recruiting followers and financial support for his terrorist activities. During his visit, he went to see Arsenal play four times and bought replica home shirts for his sons. He was said to have told friends he had never seen passion like that of football fans. Then, when plans were announced to extradite him to Saudi Arabia, bin Laden fled to the Sudan. (Arsenal officials wisely eliminated the possibility of bin Laden popping back to England to catch an Arsenal home match later on, by issuing a statement saying that the terrorist would no longer be welcome at Highbury.)

Four years later, bin Laden was involved in a plot to massacre the England and US football squads during the World Cup finals in France. An al-Qaeda cell planned to assassinate the English players on the pitch during their match against Tunisia in Marseille on 15 June 1998 and simultaneously murder the American team in their hotel as they watched the game on television. Six weeks before the planned attack Belgian police arrested over 100 suspects and foiled the plot. In August 1998 al-Qaeda bombed the US embassies in Kenya and Tanzania killing 224 people. According to bin Laden's biographer, Yossef Bodansky, this act was planned because of 'the failure of the primary operation – an attack on the soccer World Cup'.

Then there is the tale of Sandy Young. The former Everton and sometime Tottenham Hotspur striker was rumoured to have been hung in Australia in the early 1900s for stealing a sheep. Others claimed the player had gone mad and died in an Edinburgh mental hospital. In fact, neither story is quite true. Scotsman Alex 'Sandy' Young (not to be confused with the Toffees' Alex 'The Golden Vision' Young of the 1960s) joined Everton in 1901. The *Liverpool Echo* said of him: 'The centre-forward is a variable sort of man who plays one good game in three on average. He takes the bumps a centre-forward must inevitably expect smilingly, and determination makes up for his lack of skill at times.'

The editor of the Everton match programme said: 'I think Young distinctly dirty. He may not intend to be dirty, but he is dirty and the sooner he amends his methods the better. He is undoubtedly clever, possibly the best centre-forward we have today, but I have no hesitation in describing him as unfair.'

Nevertheless, Young scored 124 goals in 314 games, including the winner in the 1906 FA Cup final against Newcastle United. Fans sang of their hero: 'Sandy Young he has won the Cup, And the Cup to Everton was brought up!' The Scottish international was Everton's all-time top scorer until the great Dixie Dean eclipsed him.

Young was sold to Tottenham in 1911 and scored three goals in his first two games. But, when he failed to find the net in the next two games, Young was dropped. He immediately requested a transfer and was duly sent to Manchester City, where he remained for a short period before moving to amateur side South Liverpool. Young retired in 1914 and emigrated to Australia. Here his tale becomes slightly unclear but undeniably disturbing.

What is known is that, in December of the following year, Young was charged with the wilful murder of his brother. At his trial in June 1916 the English FA submitted evidence showing that Young had suffered from bouts of insanity during his football career. As a result, Young was cleared of murder on the grounds of diminished responsibility, and therefore he avoided the mandatory death penalty. He was, however, convicted of manslaughter and sentenced to three years in a mental institution. At the end of his sentence Young was found still to be mentally unstable and was not released. He spent several further years in the institution. It is known that he returned to Edinburgh and died in Portobello in 1959 aged 79.

Prisoners have a lot of time on their hands, and football is a popular prison pastime. Prison football is the same as normal football, only without any away fixtures. Author Chris Hulme spent an entire season with HMP Kingston's Kingston Arrows team while writing his book, *Manslaughter United*. Goalkeeper Luke revealed that he had ended up in prison after reacting badly to his wife leaving him for a friend. 'On the morning of the offence I just totally lost it,' he explained. 'I hit her with a hammer a number of times. And she died.' Makes Harald Schumacher look like Gary Lineker.

In 2002, the inaugural Thailand Klong Prem Central Prison World Cup took place. The competition was the brainchild of the Thai director general of corrections Siwa Saengmanee. An attempt to boost morale, the competition was staged in tandem with the real World Cup in Japan and Korea. The notorious prison is home to a multinational population of over 7,000 prisoners from 56 countries, so Siwa was able to assemble teams to represent England, France, Germany, Italy, Japan, Nigeria, Thailand and the USA. Only inmates with good behavioural records were considered for selection.

Invited reporters were conscious that the last time the media had been invited into a Thai prison, to Bang Kwang – the 'Bangkok Hilton' – in 2000, it had been to witness a dozen drug runners get shot in the head as a warning to wannabe dealers.

However what the visitors found was a bona fide international football competition, complete with overblown opening ceremony. On a pitch ringed by M16-carrying guards, over 1,000 inmates took part in a fancy dress carnival of flags, balloons and bunting.

BALLS

The ceremony, sponsored by Coca-Cola, saw each team led out by a genuine Thai ladyboy dressed in appropriate national dress. The English ladyboy wore a Queen Elizabeth-style robe and crown.

As the matches got under way, it became apparent that there would be no *Escape To Victory*-style breakout. The watching inmates were extremely well behaved, partly because of the guards and the guns, but also because they had been bribed with the chance to watch the real World Cup on TV if they complied. Still, inmates chanted, 'We want to go home!' throughout the first match, which saw Nigeria beat Japan 6–1. England's first match, against Thailand, received no press coverage as it was played outside of the prison's official visiting hours.

Meanwhile, on the Indonesian island of Sumatra, 48 prisoners escaped from the Pekanbaru prison during the real World Cup match between Belgium and Brazil. The inmates overpowered the prison's guards, who were distracted while watching the match on a portable television. 'The guards should not have been watching the game,' the prison manager said, 'but it's understandable.' Of the escapees, 16 were rounded up, but 32, understandably, remain at large.

Back in Thailand, France won the Prison World Cup, beating Nigeria 7–6 on penalties in the final. The French captain was presented by the Thai interior minister Purachai Piumsombun with a wooden replica of the World Cup, crafted in the prison's workshop. The victorious skipper gratefully thanked the prison authorities. Crawler.

Former Coventry City goalkeeper Steve Ogrizovic is imprisoned in Kazakhstan. Or is he? An organisation calling themselves the Free Steve Ogrizovic Group distributed a petition in 2003 calling for the release of the popular net-minder. Apparently, Oggy had been working for a charity called Over the Bar, attempting to raise money by travelling around the world on public transport. Oggy was forced to walk across Kazakhstan due to a lack of buses, but he accidentally strayed onto military land and was arrested on charges of spying.

'Here is our petition to Tony Blair and the Kazakhstani government demanding the release of footballing legend Steve Ogrizovic and protesting his innocence,' said the petition. 'Please sign the petition and help bring forward the release of Steve Ogrizovic.' Over 600 people did sign the petition, adding comments like, 'Please free Steve, as he's a bent-nosed hero to millions!' But Oggy's millions of fans were worrying for nothing. 'This is a complete hoax,' the Oggmeister told the *Coventry Evening Telegraph*. 'I haven't a clue where it has come from. I haven't made any trips to Kazakhstan of late – nor am I planning to. I can only assume that with the well-documented breakthroughs in science of late, I have obviously been cloned.'

So Steve Ogrizovic hasn't been in prison, but many of his fellow footballers have. Former Sunderland and Bradford City winger Jamie Lawrence was actually signed by Sunderland from Shanklin prison on the Isle of Wight. The club spotted him playing for the prison football team during a friendly match. Lawrence was serving three years for his part in an armed robbery.

Stocky Danish midfielder Stig Tofting, nicknamed 'The Little Lawnmower', was jailed in 2002 after assaulting two restaurant employees. The incident occurred at a party arranged to celebrate the Danish squad's return home from the World Cup in Japan and Korea. Fuelled by drink at Copenhagen's Café Ketchup, the former Bolton Wanderers player unwisely decided to head-butt a waiter and punch out the restaurant manager. The footballer was jailed for four months and his Bolton contract was cancelled.

Tofting was raised by his grandmother, after his father murdered his mother with a shotgun before turning the gun on himself. The 13-year-old Tofting discovered their bodies. The footballer, who has the words 'No Regrets' tattooed on his back, became involved with biker gangs, and this led to further trouble in 2004 when Tofting was probed by police after lending £90,000 to Danish Hell's Angels leader Jimmy Nissen. Police were looking into the biker boss's affairs after jailing him for tax evasion.

BALLS

Typically, Tofting had no regrets. 'It is no one's business,' he said. 'It is my money, and I will do what I want with it.'

Another Danish midfielder, Jan Molby, was jailed for reckless driving in 1988 after turning a car over outside a nightclub. His three-month sentence hampered Liverpool's League challenge, but fans were delighted to see the beefy midfielder return to the side looking slimmer and fitter after regular workouts in the prison gym.

Mickey Thomas, the former Manchester United, Leeds United, Chelsea, Everton and Wrexham midfielder, spent ten months in jail over a counterfeit money scam. Famed for his hard drinking during a long career, Thomas hit the headlines twice in 1992 – first when he scored a great free kick for Wrexham that knocked Arsenal out of the FA Cup, and second when he was stabbed in the backside with a screwdriver by his wife's brother after being caught having sex with that brother's wife in the back of a car down a country lane.

Then, in 1993, he was caught passing fake £10 and £20 notes to Wrexham trainees. Thomas didn't expect to get sent down and even joked, 'Anyone got change of a tenner for the phone?' during his day in court. Judge Gareth Edwards made an example of the footballer, but Thomas's stay in prison wasn't too bad – once he got rid of the cellmate who confessed to him he had killed two people then cut off their heads. The *News of the World* pictured Thomas the prisoner supping from a champagne bottle, calling it a photo that would 'enrage every law abiding Briton'.

Upon his release Thomas played upon his notoriety at football talk-ins, where he entertained crowds with gags such as: 'Roy Keane's on 50 grand a week. Mind you, so was I until the police found my printing machine!'

For sheer variety of illegal escapades, look no further than former England international and Arsenal Double-winning team stalwart Peter Storey. A notorious boozer and womaniser during his playing days, he turned to criminal activities after hanging up his boots in 1977. Within two years of his retirement Storey had been found guilty of running a brothel in East London. He was fined £700 and given a six-month suspended sentence. In 1980 he was jailed for three years for financing a plot to produce counterfeit gold coins. He didn't see out that sentence, and two years later he was given two six-month sentences for car theft. In 1990 Storey was jailed for 28 days for smuggling 20 pornographic videos into the country from Europe. The mucky tapes were hidden in his spare tyre. Finally, Storey received a 28-day suspended sentence in 1991 for swearing at a traffic warden.

Former Soviet Union and Torpedo Moscow striker Eduard Streltsov was imprisoned in a Siberian labour camp for a crime he almost certainly didn't commit. The footballing legend was accused of rape and arrested in 1958. Two other men were suspected of committing the crime, but it was Streltsov who was banged up for seven years. The so-called 'Russian Pelé' had earlier been coveted by both the KGB-affiliated Dinamo Moscow and the Red Army team CSKA Moscow. Streltsov, however, had turned down the offers and stayed at Torpedo, much to the chagrin of the Russian authorities. He was axed from the Soviet national side and then charged with the rape. Many observers felt the charge was a fit-up. After doing his time in the labour camp, Streltsov returned to Torpedo, leading them to the Russian championship. He also returned to the national side, although he had missed the 1958 and 1962 World Cups due to his incarceration and also missed the 1966 tournament as he was still forbidden from travelling abroad.

Manchester City legend Bert Trautmann came to England as a prisoner of war in 1944 and was interned at Camp 50 in Ashton-in-Makerfield until the end of the war. Bernard Carl Trautmann is most famous for his heroic display in Man City's 1956 FA Cup win over Birmingham. The German goalkeeper famously played out the game with a broken neck. He became the first foreign player to win the Player of the Year award later that year. All this despite the fact he was a dedicated Nazi.

BALLS

Trautmann joined the Hitler Youth when he was ten years old and volunteered to fight in the Second World War at 16. He fought at Arnhem, the Ardennes and Normandy and won the Iron Cross. Trautmann was captured by the Russians and by the Free French, but escaped on both occasions. He was also buried in a collapsed cellar for three days and court martialled for sabotage, before deserting the army to walk home. During his trek he was captured by American soldiers, but was allowed to run away. He fled, and ran straight into a British patrol. The Brits greeted Trautmann with the line, 'Hello Fritz, fancy a cup of tea?'

This time Trautmann wouldn't escape, and he was imprisoned as a high-level POW, labelled 'Category C' as a committed Nazi. He played football in the POW camp and began to keep goal after an injury prevented him from playing outfield. After the war, Trautmann stayed in England, working in bomb disposal. He also played football for St Helens Town and was eventually spotted and signed by Man City in 1949. Despite initial reservations over his background, Trautmann established himself as a fans' favourite and kept goal for the club for 14 years. At his testimonial, 60,000 fans turned up to show their support. The former Nazi is now regarded as one of the greatest players ever to play for City and one of the greatest goalkeepers of all time.

15. SCANDALS

Football, like politics, has seen more than its fair share of shady deals, dodgy characters and wicked scandals. But people seem to expect corruption in politics. Football, on the other hand, is supposed to be pure and untainted, with millions of fans across the world pinning their hopes on the outcome of individual matches. So controversial fixtures, match-fixing, bribery and betting scams have the ability to rock the sport to its very foundations. When England players give Nazi salutes, when Sir Matt Busby's Manchester United throw games in a betting scam, when an international side fields foreign ringers, when the entire German Bundesliga is crippled by match-fixing and when Marseille bribe their way to winning five consecutive league championships and the European Cup, the game so many love so dearly is flipped completely bum over breast.

Many football scandals have evolved from controversial fixtures. In 1938, England played a friendly against Germany in Berlin. It was the first sporting meeting between the two nations since the 1936 Olympics, when a huge diplomatic row erupted after British athletes refused to give the Nazi salute. This time, the FA promised, the England players would perform the salute. Indeed, the FA actually forced the likes of Stanley Matthews and Cliff Bastin to salute Nazi party representatives Goebbels, Goering, Hess and von Ribbentrop (Hitler wasn't a big football fan – he only ever attended one match, which Germany lost to Norway, and the Fuhrer left early in a huff). The humiliated English players had the last laugh on the pitch, though – they thrashed the Germans 6–3.

Fate threw a rather large spanner into the works during the draw for the 1974 World Cup finals when hosts West Germany were paired with East Germany. The uncomfortable neighbours were separated by the Berlin wall, and fans from East Germany were banned from attending the match in Hamburg, lest they take the opportunity to defect. In fact, many East Germans supported West German clubs and the West German national team, having decided their loyalties before the building of the wall in 1961. Many persecuted Hertha Berlin fans would stand on the Eastern side of the wall on match days, listening to the crowd noise from the stadium just a few hundred yards away. These fans were labelled 'dissenters', and border guards soon put a stop to their Saturday afternoon gatherings. They were instead encouraged to support Dynamo Berlin, the team controlled by the secret police. The dissenters called Dynamo 'The Eleven Pigs' and pledged their allegiance to the West Germans.

The East German league was corrupt and unpopular, and many footballers were 'persuaded' by the government to take up other sports. As a result, the East German national team was decidedly weak. The World Cup match should have been a walkover for their neighbours from the West, but a goal from Jürgen Sparwasser gave East Germany a shock 1–0 win. Sparwasser, however, was by no means a hero when he returned home. He was shunned by his fellow East Germans for scoring against their favourite side. West Germany picked themselves up and went on to win the World

Cup. As for Sparwasser, he defected to the West.

In 1974 an unusual World Cup qualifying draw saw the Soviet Union matched with Chile. The Soviets were deeply unhappy about playing the two-legged match in the aftermath of General Pinochet's bloody military coup, in which the regime of Salvador Allende had been violently overthrown. When the venue for the second leg was announced as Santiago's National Stadium, where untold numbers of Allende supporters had been rounded up and executed, the situation became intolerable. After playing out a goalless first leg, the Soviets refused to travel to Chile for the return match. Chile turned up and kicked off anyway, and were awarded the points. The Soviets were booted out of the World Cup, and Chile went to the finals, where they were eliminated in the first round.

FIFA's decision to award the 1978 World Cup finals to Argentina was frowned upon by many, following the Videla regime's 1976 military coup. Johan Cruyff refused to travel with the Netherlands squad and retired from international football partly in protest against the Argentinean *junta*. The tournament descended into controversy. Argentina needed to win by more than three goals against a talented Peru to progress to the final, and they easily managed it, winning 6–0. Allegations of bribery quickly surfaced, and it was later suggested that the Argentinean *junta* had shipped food and weapons to Peru and credited the Peruvian government with millions of dollars in return for their side throwing the match. Argentina went to the final, where they beat the Cruyff-less Netherlands 3–1 to lift the World Cup.

In another controversial move, Libya withdrew from a 1990 World Cup qualifier against Algeria and forfeited the points to thank the Algerians for their support in the wake of the US bombing of the Libyan capital, Tripoli. The decision to forfeit the match was made so late in the day that Libyan fans were already in the stadium waiting for the kick-off. Algeria happily accepted the three points but still failed to qualify for the finals.

BALLS

In 1998, the USA's excitement at reaching the World Cup finals in France was tempered somewhat by the draw, which placed them in the same qualifying group as Iran. Such was the depth of feeling surrounding the much-anticipated 'Great Satan' versus 'Axis of Evil' clash that usually disinterested US sports fans began to take a keen interest in 'soccer'. Even President Clinton appeared on TV with a conciliatory message for the two nations, in which he notably broke rank by referring to the sport as 'football'. In the event, the US lost 2–1 and crashed out of the tournament.

And then there is match-fixing. Welshman Billy Meredith was regarded as the greatest player of his generation. He scored the winning goal for Manchester City in the 1904 FA Cup final and became a City legend. But, in 1905, his name became synonymous with an unprecedented betting scandal. City were involved in a tight title race with Newcastle United and, on 29 April 1905, they played a must-win match against Aston Villa. City were so desperate to win that they offered their players an illegal win bonus of £10. The bonus, however, was never paid. City lost 3–2 to Villa, and Newcastle won the title. This was despite the fact that Billy Meredith had bribed the Villa players to throw the match. Meredith and 16 other players were sacked by City and banned from football for seven months. City's chairman and secretary were banned for life. After serving out his ban, Meredith resumed his career with Manchester United, and ten years later he was involved in another huge scandal.

On Good Friday, 2 April 1915, Manchester United faced Liverpool at Old Trafford. United were hanging on to the very coat tails of the First Division and desperately needed to win to avoid relegation. Liverpool were playing well, sat comfortably in the League, and were clear favourites. So it was something of a surprise when United won 2–0, not least because of the apathetic performance of their opponents. Liverpool had only one shot on goal, which hit the bar, after which the striker was chastised by his teammates for the audacity of attempting an effort at goal. Balls were regularly kicked into touch, and a penalty kick was blasted woefully high, wide and handsome. Even the referee noted that something peculiar was going on.

A few weeks later, a firm of bookmakers passed handbills around Manchester and Liverpool accusing the sides of match-fixing. The bookies had laid odds of 7–1 against United beating Liverpool 2–0 and had taken an unusually high number of bets. They refused to pay out, and the FA were forced to commission an enquiry. The investigation revealed that Jackie Sheldon, the Liverpool winger who had previously won the League with United, had conspired with teammates old and new to fix the match. He had recruited three United players (Turnbull, West and Whalley) and three Liverpool players (Fairfoul, Miller and Purcell) to help him organise the scam. In the end, all seven named players were suspended. Six admitted their involvement, but the other, Enoch West, loudly protested his innocence and brought a libel suit against the FA. He lost, but continued to claim his innocence until the day he died. Billy Meredith had played in the fixed match, but he was not charged with any misdemeanour and avoided an FA reprimand. He eventually returned to Manchester City after a dispute with United and played for the club until he was just days short of his 50th birthday.

In his 2002 autobiography *Harry's Game*, Harry Gregg, the former Manchester United goalkeeper and Munich air crash survivor, made a startling revelation. 'Yes, match-fixing went on at the biggest club in the world – Manchester United,' he said. 'It is an event in United's history that disgusts me because they should never have been allowed to tarnish such a great club.' Gregg claimed that United players fixed matches in the 1963–64 season in order to cash in on high-stakes fixed odds bets. According to Gregg, the unnamed stars colluded with players from other clubs to fix multiple scores across the League on the same day. 'They know who they are,' he said, 'and the shame will haunt them for the rest of their lives.' Incredibly, Gregg revealed that United manager Sir Matt Busby was well aware of the scam, but could do nothing about it. 'If he had blown the whistle everything he had stood for, and the work he had put into the club following the Munich air crash, would have been undone,' Gregg said. 'His instinct would have been to expose them, but he put the club first.'

In December 1962, Sheffield Wednesday players Peter Swan, David 'Bronco' Layne and Tony Kay won £100 each, betting that their side would lose 2–0 at Ipswich. Two years later, the trio were exposed on the front page of the *Sunday People*. The full scale of the betting scandal was uncovered, and it was revealed that over 60 players were involved, and matches between Lincoln and Brentford, and York and Oldham, had also been fixed on the same day. Ten players were imprisoned, including Swan, Layne and Kay. Swan and Kay had recently moved to Everton for £55,000. They were tipped to break into the England squad, but missed out on the 1966 World Cup due to their incarceration.

In 1971, the German Bundesliga was rocked by a huge match-fixing scandal, exposed after lowly Arminia Bielefeld beat high-flying Schalke 04 1–0 in suspicious circumstances. Gerd Roggensack scored the minnows' goal, but the celebrations were short-lived. An investigation found that the match had been rigged, with Schalke's players paid £800 each to throw the match. The scam, moreover, extended right across the Bundesliga. Dozens of league matches had been fixed, with around £10,000 paid as bribes. Fifty players, coaches and officials from Schalke, Bielefeld, Kickers Offenbach, Hertha Berlin and FC Koln were banned. Offenbach were suspended from German football for two years, and Bielefeld were relegated to the regional leagues. The Bundesliga as a whole suffered from this. Fans lost confidence in the game and stayed away from matches, and numerous continuing allegations cast a shadow over subsequent seasons. It took several years before German football properly recovered.

Italy's Serie A was similarly rocked by a scandal involving its biggest clubs in 1980. The controversy began with a 2–1 win for AC Milan over Lazio. The match had been fixed as part of a betting scandal, as had dozens of other games across the Italian leagues. Eleven Milan players, including goalkeeper and scam ringleader Enrico Albertosi, plus the club's president, Felice Colombo, were arrested. All were banned from football for life. Both Milan and Lazio were relegated to Serie B.

Many other players were indicted in the scandal, including Paulo Rossi, who had been on loan from Vicenza to Perugia at the time of the scam. The striker was accused of taking a bribe to fix a match between Perugia and Avellino. Interestingly, Rossi scored two goals in that 2–2 draw and protested his innocence. His suspension was reduced on appeal, but Rossi was still banned from football for two years. He returned in 1982, just in time to make the Italian World Cup squad. And he had clearly kept himself fit during his enforced sabbatical. Rossi was the tournament's star player, winning the Golden Boot and scoring in the final to help his side win the World Cup.

In 1982, Belgian football was mired in controversy with a scandal involving top club Standard Liege. Liege were on the verge of winning the league for the first time in eleven years, but first they needed to beat Belgian Cup-holders Waterschei. Liege captain Erik Gerets approached Waterschei's Roland Janssen and set up a scam. On behalf of his Liege teammates, Gerets offered the Waterschei players their winning bonuses if they threw the match. Waterschei agreed, and Liege won the match. Thirteen players were suspended, including Gerets, who had subsequently signed for AC Milan. He was forced to quit the Italian club to serve out his suspension. Liege received only the paltry punishment of a £75,000 fine and retained the league championship, although club chairman Roger Petit and manager Raymond Goethals were banned from Belgian football for life. Goethals wasn't out of a job for long, though. He soon found employment at Marseille under Bernard Tapie.

BALLS

The multi-talented Tapie is a French businessman, politician, film star, pop singer, TV presenter and tax fraudster. He was president of Olympique Marseille from 1986 to 1994, during which time the club won the French league title five times in a row and became the first French side to win the European Cup. The fact that Tapie had been fixing matches for much of his presidency had no small bearing upon this success. The scam was uncovered when Valenciennes player Jacques Glassmann revealed his side had been bribed by Tapie to throw a league match in April 1993. Glassmann's story gained credibility when £30,000 was found buried in his teammate's garden. Marseille were stripped of their European title plus banned from entering the competition in the following season and demoted to the second division. Two Marseille players and two Valenciennes players were banned for life. Tapie was charged with complicity of corruption and subornation of witnesses and was sentenced to two years in prison, of which he eventually served six months in 1997 after appeal. Meanwhile, whistle-blower Glassmann, regarded as 'football's honest man', became a virtual pariah. He was shunned by clubs across Europe and resorted to playing on Reunion Island, a French territory in the Indian Ocean, where he was constantly booed by Marseille fans. He eventually quit football altogether, returned to France and signed on to unemployment benefit. So much for honesty.

Scandals are not uncommon in Malaysian football, but one particularly notable match-fixing scam arose in 1994. Alarm bells began to ring when Penang conceded 12 goals in 2 games and were knocked out of the Malaysian Cup. The club accused four of its own players of taking bribes. The authorities investigated and suspended a whopping 120 players, plus coaches and officials from across the M-League. Several players, coaches and bookmakers were banished from the country. Malaysian officials also accused players from Singapore-based teams of corruption. Singapore responded by withdrawing its teams from the M-League, effectively bringing Malaysian football to its knees.

TALES FROM FOOTBALL'S NETHER REGIONS

Malaysian scammers were also involved in the most recent match-fixing scandal to hit British football. Bruce Grobbelaar, John Fashanu and Hans Segers were charged with throwing several matches at the insistence of Malaysian businessman Heng Suan Lim. The matches in question included Liverpool's 3–0 defeat at Newcastle in November 1993 and Wimbledon's 3–2 loss to Everton on the last day of the 1993–94 season. The latter result kept Everton in the Premier League after Wimbledon lost despite being 2–0 up, due partly to some atrocious goalkeeping from Segers. It was also claimed that Grobbelaar lost £125,000 when he accidentally pulled off a spectacular save in a 3–3 draw with Manchester United – a match he was trying to lose. It was found that Heng Suan Lim was acting as a go-between for a Malaysian betting syndicate, and the case went to court. One jury failed to reach a verdict, and a second cleared the defendants.

Following allegations of match-fixing in *The Sun*, Grobbelaar denied 'conspiring corruptly to give and accept gifts of money improperly to influence or attempt to influence the outcome of football matches or as rewards for having done so'. Grobbelaar was initially awarded £85,000 in damages in 1999 when a High Court jury decided that the goalkeeper had been libelled by the newspaper. But the damages award was taken away in 2001 when the Court of Appeal ruled that there had been a miscarriage of justice.

However, Grobbelaar took his case to the House of Lords in 2002. The Lords decided that Grobbelaar had accepted bribes, but had not deliberately let goals in. The original libel decision against *The Sun* was reinstated, but Grobbelaar's damages were reduced to just £1. Lord Bingham said Grobbelaar 'had acted in a way in which no decent or honest footballer would act and in a way which could, if not exposed and stamped upon, undermine the integrity of a game which earns the loyalty and respect of millions.' Grobbelaar walked away with his £1 compensation and a £1 million legal bill. You do the maths.

BALLS

George Graham was Arsenal's most successful ever manager, having won six trophies in eight years, when he was sacked for accepting brown envelopes stuffed full of cash. It was 1995, and Graham was found to have taken £425,000 worth of bungs from Norwegian agent Rune Hauge. The cash was skimmed from the transfers to Arsenal of Pal Lydersen from IK Start in 1991 and John Jensen from Brondby in 1992. Graham was banned for 12 months by the FA. He handed all the money back to Arsenal, plus interest, and then really smoothed things over with Arsenal fans by going on to manage local rivals Tottenham Hotspur.

At the World Cup finals in 1994, controversy surrounded the peculiar third place play-off match between Bulgaria and Sweden. According to Swedish football magazine *Offside*, Swedish players Thomas Brolin, Lars Eriksson, Klas Ingesson and Anders Limpar were approached by a Malaysian businessman on the day before the match and offered £15,000 each to throw the game. The four players refused, and Sweden thrashed Bulgaria 4–0. But the bizarre performance of their opponents raised speculation that the Bulgarians had accepted a bribe. Bulgaria had played brilliantly throughout the tournament, but here they offered up a pathetic performance, regarded by their fans as the country's worst ever. The Bulgarian players spent their time arguing with each other, and star player Hristo Stoichkov took particular umbrage with defender Trifon Ivanov. Stoichkov could have been the tournament's top scorer had he made any attempt to score a goal in this match. Instead, he took exception to a catalogue of mistakes by Ivanov, argued incessantly, and then demanded his teammate be substituted. So had the lacklustre Bulgarians been bribed to throw the match? Not according to Swedish newspapers at the time, who found witnesses who allegedly saw the Bulgarian squad drunkenly partying in a Las Vegas strip club just hours before the match. Apparently, they lost the game because they were seriously hungover. 'There was girls, booze, everything,' said one witness. 'Some were so hungover they couldn't run 20 metres.'

The most spectacularly obvious case of match-fixing occurred in February 2004 in the Indian state of Goa. Curtorim Gym and Wilfred Leisure were level on points at the top of the Goan Second Division as they went into the last match of the season, with Curtorim leading with a goal difference that was five better than Wilfred's. So Wilfred needed to beat Dona Paula by six goals to have a chance of winning the title. At half-time it was 6–0, and everything looked rosy. But news filtered through that Curtorim were leading Sangolda 1–0. Wilfred would have to score more. In the event, Wilfred scored 49 more. The final score was Wilfred Leisure 55 Dona Paula 1. So Wilfred won the league, right? Wrong. Because Curtorim managed to score 60 second-half goals. That's a goal every 45 seconds. Their final score was Curtorim Gym 61 Sangolda Lightning 1.

Curtorim won the league on goal difference, but their celebrations were short-lived. The ridiculous scorelines attracted the attention of the Goan FA. They found Curtorim had bribed Sangolda Lightning to throw the match. When Dona Paula found out about this they had agreed to throw their match against Wilfred to teach Curtorim a lesson. So, officials from both teams relayed scorelines back and forth as the teams desperately tried to outdo each other in the scoring stakes, sharing a mighty 118 goals. The game of silly beggars backfired, and all four teams were suspended from the league for a year and fined 5,000 rupees (a measly £60).

One scandal that is rarely reported in the British press is that of disappearing footballers, who vanish into the ether never to be seen again. Disappearing footballers have become a real problem in Pakistan, where travelling squads see trips abroad as an opportunity to flee the country.

In 2001, the Pakistani international side travelled to England to play Bury and Coventry. The British authorities were well aware of the penchant of Pakistani sportsmen to 'slip away', so the squad members were heavily guarded throughout their stay. The

BALLS

Pakistani authorities had also taken preventative steps, owing to the disappearance of some of their boxers, swimmers and two tae-kwando teams in previous months. They ordered the parents of each player to submit a surety bond of one million rupees, around £20,000, to be refunded upon their child's return. None of these measures worked.

During a press conference, Nasir Iqbal of the Khan Research Laboratories team asked to use the bathroom. He was escorted by two policemen but, after doing his business, he proceeded to leg it. The policemen chased him out of the building but Iqbal jumped into a waiting car and sped away, never to be seen again.

'You cannot believe the consequences of the incident,' said Pakistan's English coach John Layton. 'Our stay in England had been made terrible and all the players and team officials were heavily guarded from hotel to the stadium and also during the match. Sometimes we felt that the organisers might put us in chains.'

But Iqbal's flight pales when compared to the 1994 disappearance of an entire Pakistani Football Team, who vanished while visiting Japan. Crescent Mills Faisalabad were in Japan to play in the Asian Cup-Winner's Cup championship. As Pakistan's *News On Sunday* reported, 'Pakistan lost the match as well as all the 16 players.' The Japanese authorities managed to round up half of the missing squad, and the Asian Football Association sent investigators to grill the remaining players' families. They found that the team had decided to abscond because of decreasing opportunities for sportsmen in any game other than Pakistan's beloved cricket. At least one of the vanished eight footballers made good. He eventually returned to Pakistan as a millionaire, having set up a huge import/export business in England.

It's universally accepted that Americans don't like football, but that might not have been the case had a group of shady money-men not kneecapped the country's original football league. Contrary to popular belief, professional football (some say soccer) in the US dates way back to 1894, long before American football and basketball leagues were ever formed. The American League of Professional Football (ALPF) kicked off in October 1894, having been formed by the owners of six National League baseball teams. The Baltimore Orioles appointed Englishman AW Stewart as a player–coach who kept goal as well as picking the side. He brought in several players from England, including four players (Little, Calvey, Ferguson and Wallace) from Manchester City. After the Orioles thrashed the Washington Nationals 10–1, the Nationals complained to the league about the Orioles' use of foreign players. The Orioles attempted to deflect the blaze of controversy by claiming that the English players were, in fact, from Detroit.

Such was the ensuing furore, that the US government stepped in and declared its intention to investigate the Orioles. Meanwhile, rumours of a proposed rival national baseball league had the club owners on hot bricks. Suddenly, with their baseball franchises in danger, the prospect of running a football league seemed less enticing. There were also fears that the increasing popularity of the football league could damage the baseball league. So, on 20 October, just six games into the season, the plug was pulled on the ALPF. The decision was announced with a one-line notice in the press: 'The proposed professional game between the New Yorks and Brooklyns, at the Polo Grounds today, has been declared off.'

Incredibly, the league didn't see fit to inform all of its teams. Three days later, the seemingly unaware Orioles beat the Phillies 6–1 in perhaps the only league match ever to be played *after* its league had been abandoned.

Coincidentally, in 1994, exactly 100 years after the ALPF formed and disbanded, the US hosted its first World Cup. Instead of celebrating the centenary of the country's first professional football league, US soccer fans were left to look back at nothing more than a monumental cock-up. Controversial team selection, short-sighted organisation and cash-hungry owners who knew nothing about football combined to make the ALPF the shortest-lived professional league in footballing history.

Football, however, was not forgotten in the US. By the 1920s, the American Soccer League ('soccer' being an abbreviation of 'association football') had formed and become relatively successful, so much so that the US was invited by FIFA to send a team to the inaugural World Cup finals in Uruguay in 1930. The US put a team forward, and the story of its involvement in the competition is typically bizarre and controversial.

The US team trainer was Jock Coll from County Down, Northern Ireland. Coll moved to Scotland as a boy and grew up to coach football and train track athletes and boxers. After moving to the US in 1922, he coached the New York Football Club, Scullin Steel of St Louis, the New York Giants, the Chicago Bricklayers and the Brooklyn Wanderers, before being appointed to the national team. In 1930, the US side was picked up by World Cup boat the SS Munargo, which had already transported the participating European teams across the Atlantic, and Coll whipped his players into shape on deck during the journey south.

The US team played well, but Coll's defining moment came during the semi-final match against Argentina. During the second half, Coll ran onto the pitch to treat a player with a split lip. As he opened his bag, a bottle of chloroform fell out and smashed on the ground. Coll was almost immediately overcome by the fumes. He passed out and had to be carried from the pitch. The official match report, written by US manager Wilfred Cummings, does seem to mention the incident. 'Andy Auld had his lip ripped wide open,' wrote Cummings, 'and one of the players from across the La Platte River had knocked the smelling salts out of Trainer Coll's hand and into Andy's eyes, temporarily blinding one of the outstanding "little stars" of the World's Series.'

Perhaps suffering from the effects of the chloroform, the US were beaten 6–1 by Argentina, who reached the final where they lost to champions and hosts Uruguay. But the USA's impressive semi-final placing was sullied by controversial claims. It seemed the US side had contained no less than *six* ringers. All six had been born in Britain, and, it was claimed, they were former British professionals. Andy Auld (he of the split lip) was Scottish, as were James Brown (presumably not *that* James Brown), Jimmy Gallagher and Bart McGhee. None of these men had played professional football in Britain, but were, inescapably, British. George Moorhouse was a Liverpudlian who did play professionally in Britain, for Tranmere Rovers. And another Scot, Alexander Wood, returned to Britain after the World Cup, playing for Leicester City and Nottingham Forest. So the US achieved their best ever World Cup finals performance with over half a team of Brits. As an aside, 1930 was also the only year in which Scottish footballers have played in a World Cup semi-final.

On 27 June 1950, the USA achieved their greatest and most famous World Cup result. England, making their first appearance in the World Cup finals, lined up as 500–1 favourites to beat the lowly US at the Mineiro Stadium in Belo Horizonte, Brazil. So confident were the English that they rested Stanley Matthews. Nevertheless, the side still featured the likes of Alf Ramsey, Tom Finney, Wilf Mannion and Stan Mortensen.

The US side, by contrast, contained just one professional footballer and, in their third finals appearance, the US again utilised foreign players. Lining up alongside goalkeeper and D-Day veteran Frank Borghi, and inside-forward and former prisoner of war Frank Wallace, were three non-Americans. Half-back Ed McIlvenny was Scottish, full-back Joseph Maca was Belgian and centre-forward Joe Gaetjens, who would go on to have a key place in footballing history, was from Haiti.

The English players began the match with smiles on their faces, strolling about the pitch and shooting from ridiculous distances, but the Americans knuckled down and produced a gritty defensive display. On 37 minutes, to the amazement of the 10,000 spectators, the US scored. A shot from Ed McIlvenny was fumbled by English goalkeeper Bert Williams, and Joe Gaetjens dived full-length to head the rebound into the back of the net.

For the remaining 53 minutes, England pummelled the Americans. But several dodgy decisions and a bizarrely unpunished rugby tackle on a clear-on-goal Stan Mortensen, combined with a dogged American display, allowed the US to hold on. The final score was England 0 USA 1. The Brazilian crowd invaded the pitch and carried the US players off on their shoulders. They were heroes, for a short while. The US were knocked out of the competition in their next match by Chile. The side returned home, and never played together ever again.

One English newspaper editor believed that the wired result was a mistake and incorrectly reported the score as England 10 USA 1. When the correct score was finally ascertained, English newspapers published editions with black borders normally reserved for a death in the royal family. The *Daily Express* reported that England had been 'outplayed by American amateurs and semipros'. The English FA protested the result to FIFA, pointing out the fact that the US side had included three foreign players, but it was to no avail.

In subsequent years, England did its best to forget about the result, aided by the fact that only ten seconds of film footage from the match exists. The footage doesn't include the goal, and no photograph exists of the diving header. Only one US reporter attended the match – the brilliantly named Dent McSkimming from the *St Louis Post Dispatch*. The entire US squad was inducted into the US National Soccer Hall of Fame, but a lack of public interest, and the approaching Korean War, meant their feat was largely ignored. Walter Bahr, the captain of the US team, told the *Palm Beach Post*, 'I never even did an interview about that game for, I bet, 25 years.'

By the time the World Cup became a worldwide phenomenon and Americans recognised the achievement of their 1950 side, the Haitian goal-scoring hero, Joe Gaetjens, was dead. Gaetjens was 26 years old when he scored his famous goal. He had moved to the US to study at New York's Columbia University, and he worked as a restaurant dishwasher to pay his way. His dream, though, was to play football. 'If you play soccer the way you wash dishes, forget about it,' advised his restaurant boss, who nevertheless got him a place in a local team. A distinctive player, he wore his socks around his ankles and was renowned for his speed and style.

'Joe was a free spirit, and that's how he scored goals,' said Walter Bahr. 'He was always getting goals and you'd say, "How the heck did he get to that ball?" He would go around people, through people, over people, all the time.'

Joe returned to Haiti shortly after the 1950 World Cup and opened a dry cleaning business. In his spare time he trained local schoolkids and cultivated roses in his small garden. Early one morning in 1964, Joe said goodbye to his wife and set out to open up his shop. He was never seen again.

After years of searching, Joe's family discovered that he had been arrested by the Tontons Macoute, Haiti's secret police. It seemed that Joe's three brothers, living in the Dominican Republic, had declared their opposition to Haiti's dictator François 'Papa Doc' Duvalier. Although Joe himself had no political leanings, a major in the Tontons Macoute saw an opportunity to punish the Gaetjens family and appropriate the dry cleaning business for himself. Gaetjens was taken, with a gun to his head, to Papa Doc's Fort Dimanche prison.

Joe's family feared the worst. Fort Dimanche was notorious for its brutal midnight executions. Fifteen years later, in 1979, the Inter-American Commission on Human Rights published a report on Joe's disappearance. 'Joseph Nicolas Gaetjens was arrested in Port-au-Prince on 8 July 1964 at 10 a.m. by an armed, uniformed police officer, Lt Edouard Guillot and by two armed plain-clothes men in the presence of numerous people,' began the account. 'No proof has been shown that he was brought before competent authorities. The fact that Mr Gaetjens, a football player of international standing, has not been seen since his detention in 1964 leads to the conclusion that he is dead.'

The family later tracked down a friend who had been with Joe in Fort Dimanche. The friend was transferred to another prison within days and was told by a guard on his arrival at his new prison, 'You're lucky. Last night they killed everyone at Fort Dimanche.'

Joe's son, Richard, eventually traced his father's killer. Horrifically, just days after his arrest, Joe had been lined up against a wall in the prison courtyard and shot dead by one of his best friends. In 2000, the Haitian government issued a stamp with Joe's photograph on it. Not much of a tribute for a true footballing hero, whose contribution to the game and tragic demise have been largely forgotten.

16. DANGER

Football is a very dangerous game. As well as making and evading tough tackles, players must attempt to avoid gunshots, lightning strikes and plane crashes. Fans, meanwhile, must contend with riots, fires and collapsing stadiums. And, when a controversial World Cup qualifier causes a full-scale 'Soccer War', the shit really hits the fan.

The very fixtures and fittings of a football pitch can be highly dangerous. While playing for Scotland Under-21s in Bosnia, Everton's Gary Naysmith fell down a manhole. 'I was taking a long throw when I stood on a drain cover and it disappeared under my feet,' he said. 'You don't expect that sort of thing to happen in international football.'

In May 2000, Arsenal's Thierry Henry celebrated scoring his second goal against Chelsea in front of Highbury's North Bank by running to the corner flag, gripping it like a rock star's microphone stand and swinging it away from himself as he stood proud in front of his adoring public. Unfortunately the flag snapped back upright and smacked Henry in the face. He required treatment from the Arsenal physio and missed the restart of the game, although he did recover in time to play out the remainder of his side's 2–1 win. Modern corner flags have springs built into them to prevent them snapping, and this increases the chances of being hit while celebrating. But Italy's Marco Tardelli managed to injure himself in similar style using a good old-fashioned corner flag while celebrating a goal at the 1982 World Cup finals.

In 2003, Manchester City's Shaun Goater injured his foot when he kicked an advertising hoarding in celebration of teammate Nicolas Anelka's goal against Birmingham City. The daft striker had to be substituted.

When Arsenal's Steve Morrow scored the winning goal in the 1993 League Cup final against Sheffield Wednesday, his teammates celebrated by severely injuring him. In the post-match celebrations, Arsenal skipper Tony Adams attempted to hoist the match-winner onto his shoulders. Unfortunately Morrow flew up in the air, shot over Adams' shoulder and landed with a bump, breaking his arm.

Other bizarre football injuries have occurred away from the pitch. Rio Ferdinand missed three matches after picking up an injury while watching TV with his feet up. 'He was watching television and had his foot up on the coffee table,' explained his manager David O'Leary. 'He had it there in a certain position for a number of hours and strained the tendon behind his knee.' Experts have long been saying television is bad for your health. Another former Leeds player, Robbie Keane, once damaged his ankle when he accidentally stood on his TV remote control.

In 1964, Alan Mullery missed England's tour of South America after he put his back out while brushing his teeth. And Aston Villa's Alan Wright injured his knee stretching to reach the accelerator pedal in his new £50,000 Ferrari. 'The accelerator's position meant my right leg was bent slightly and my knee was giving me grief.' The diminutive defender was forced to sell the Ferrari. He bought a Rover 416 instead.

Arsenal legend Charlie George once famously amputated one of his toes while mowing the lawn. That was an accident. In 2003, on the other hand, Aston Villa striker Darius Vassell was taken to hospital after deliberately attempting to perform DIY surgery on one of his toes using a power drill. Vassell had a blood blister under the nail of one of his big toes and was attempting to drill through the nail to drain away the fluid. Not surprisingly, the haphazard and highly unsanitary procedure resulted in an infection. Vassell was taken to hospital, where half of his self-mutilated toenail was removed.

Brazilian Ramalho also ran into trouble when he attempted to self-medicate. The footballer was suffering from a dental infection and decided the best way to treat it was to swallow a suppository. He was laid up in bed for several days.

In 1999, Portsmouth striker John Durnin, nicknamed 'Lager', was playing golf with teammate Alan McLoughlin when he crashed his buggy into a bunker. Durnin claimed to have been distracted by the beautiful view. He dislocated his elbow and was out of action for six weeks.

Children are another danger best avoided by footballers. Leeds midfielder David Batty injured his Achilles tendon when his toddler ran over his foot on a tricycle. Danish international Alan Neilson missed several games after his daughter poked him in the eye. And Charlton's Mark Fish fell through a glass table while playing with his child. The broken glass slashed his shoulder blade, and the defender required 39 stitches.

Animals also represent a hazard. Barnsley's Darren Barnard was out of action for five months after slipping in a puddle of his new puppy's pee on his kitchen floor and damaging his knee ligaments in 1999.

In the 1970s, Norwegian international defender Svein Grondalen injured himself when he jogged into a moose. Grondalen was training for an upcoming international match when he collided with the animal. He missed the match, but the moose was unharmed. Indonesian player Mistar came off much worse when he bumped into an animal – he was killed. A herd of pigs overran the pitch where the player and his teammates were training for an upcoming cup tie. Mistar was trampled in the stampede and lost his life.

In recent years it has become clear that football has its own 'industrial diseases' with very serious consequences. Former West Bromwich Albion legend Jeff Astle scored 174 goals in 361 appearances for the club, and 'The King' also won five England caps. He died in January 2002 from brain injuries caused by heading footballs over his 20-year career. Consultant neuro-pathologist Dr Derek Robson told the coroner's inquest that Astle's brain had suffered injuries similar to those suffered by boxers and that the blood flow to his brain had been restricted. This led to dementia in his final years. All of this, the coroner decided, had been caused by heading a football.

In 2003, FA officials were presented with research carried out by the Italian Higher Institute of Health. The report looked at the medical history of 24,000 footballers and found a disproportionately high number of occurrences of motor neurone disease (MND). Again, this was linked to heading a football. Former Middlesbrough star Willie Maddren died of MND in 2000 aged just 49, and his widow said Willie had always been convinced that his illness had something to do with football.

The FA issued a cautious statement saying, 'We take any possible connection between medical problems and football seriously and would consult bodies who specialise in this area.'

The Italian research into the medical history of footballers also uncovered 70 suspicious deaths thought to be linked to drugs given to the players by their clubs. 'Out of 400 deaths since 1960, we are investigating 70 suspicious ones,' said Turin magistrate Raffaele Guarinello. The research showed an unusually high number of incidences of cancer, leukaemia and diseases of the nervous system among top Italian footballers. 'Many more players are dying of these diseases than members of the public,' said Guarinello. One such player was Gianluca Signorini, who played in Serie A for Roma, Genoa and Parma before becoming totally paralysed by amyotrophic lateral sclerosis, or Lou Gehrig's disease. The disease, which affects the nervous system and the spinal cord, is extremely rare, yet researchers found it had been contracted by 45 Italian footballers.

The wheelchair-bound Signorini appeared before fans at a May 2001 tribute match, where his daughter read out a message. 'I would like to get up and run with you,' it said, 'but I can't.' Signorini died in 2002, aged 42. Before his death, the footballer listed all of the drugs he had been given by his clubs. Other players from top clubs like Milan, Sampdoria and Inter came forward with similar evidence. The situation appears to have similarities to the outbreak of premature deaths suffered by East German sportsmen in the '70s and '80s, when the communist authorities secretly drugged their athletes without regard to side effects.

Footballing deaths on the field of play are rare, although football's early incarnations were notoriously violent. Thirteenth-century games, where entire villages competed over an inflated pig's bladder, were barely disguised battles. Personal and tribal disputes would be settled in a mass-punch up. Injuries and deaths were common, and calls were made to control the game. When football arrived in London in the early fourteenth century, Mayor Nicolas Farndon forbade the game, saying, 'There is a great uproar in the City through certain tumults arising from the striking of great footballs in the field of the public, from which many evils perchance may arise, which may God forbid, we do command and do forbid, on the King's behalf, upon pain of imprisonment, that such games shall not be practised henceforth within this city.' There were numerous arrests, but the game continued to grow in popularity.

By the seventeenth century, the game had become associated with raids on borders and neighbouring towns. A match in Kettering saw 500 players ransack a grain store, and the English authorities kept a close eye on Scottish footballers, fearing cross-border violence. A Frenchman who watched a football game in Derby commented, 'If this is what they call football, what do they call fighting?' The game was eventually tamed in the early nineteenth century, when the public school version of football introduced rules and gentlemanly conduct. But players continued to die.

In 1877, footballer James Beaumont was killed when he chased after a wayward ball and fell into a quarry. In 1897, Thomas Brice fell on his belt buckle during a match. The buckle punctured his stomach and the player died. A Spanish footballer was killed in 1924 when a ball brought down an electricity wire and he was electrocuted. William Walker died of internal injuries in 1907, and Sam Wynne died on the field in 1927 after contracting pneumonia. And in a September 1931 Old Firm clash, Celtic and Scotland goalkeeper John 'Jock' Thomson fractured his skull when diving at the feet of an opponent. Thomson died later that evening.

In the modern era, 24-year-old Nigerian international Samuel Okwaraji collapsed and died ten minutes from the end of a World Cup qualifier against Angola in Lagos in 1989. An autopsy showed he had died of a heart attack, and was suffering from an enlarged heart and high blood pressure. Adding to the tragedy, twelve spectators died at the same match in a crowd crush. In 1990, 25-year-old York City striker Dave Longhurst died during a League match with Lincoln City. He was suffering from a rare heart condition. And Oliver Petit, brother of French international and former Arsenal star Emmanuel, died during a match in 1987 aged just 20.

Four Romanian footballers died within 15 months of each other between 1999 and 2001. One of those who passed away was Stefan Vrabioru of Astra Ploiesti. He collapsed just minutes after being brought on as a substitute in his First Division debut against Rapid Bucharest and died on the way to hospital.

In 2003, Premiership star and Cameroonian midfielder Marc-Vivien Foe died during a Confederations Cup semi-final against

Colombia. The match was played in Lyon in stifling conditions and, 72 minutes into the game, Foe collapsed unchallenged in the centre circle. The former West Ham and Manchester City midfielder was immediately surrounded by medical staff, but their efforts were in vain. The 28-year-old was pronounced dead of a suspected heart attack 45 minutes later. A tearful final was played out between Cameroon and France as a tribute to Foe, and Manchester City retired their number 23 shirt in his honour.

In 1998, a lightning strike killed an entire football team in the Democratic Republic of Congo. The match, in the province of Eastern Kasai, saw the village of Bena Tshadi take on Basangana. The score was 1–1 when the lightning struck. All eleven Bena Tshadi players were killed, but none of the Basangana players were as much as scorched. The selective nature of the lightning prompted claims that witchcraft was involved. Kinshasa newspaper *L'Avenir* reported, 'The exact nature of the lightning has divided the population in this region, known for its use of fetishes in football.'

On the exact same day, South African television viewers watched open-mouthed as a live Castle Premiership match between Moroka Swallows and Jomo Cosmos was dramatically interrupted by lightning. Cosmos were leading 2–0 in Johannesburg's George Gogh Stadium when six players and the referee collapsed after being struck by lightning. None were killed, although several were badly injured. The fact that the lightning struck three players from each team plus the ref seemed to rule out witchcraft on this occasion. Swallows player Jaconia Cibi was in a critical condition for some time following the strike. 'Thank God and my ancestors for saving my life,' he said. 'I do not even want to entertain the idea that it could have been a *muti*-related act.'

In 2000, several Albanian footballers were electrocuted when lightning struck a metal crane close to their water-logged pitch. Flamurtari Vlore were leading Luftetari Gjirokaster 1–0 in the televised First Division game when the lightning struck. The lightning charge was conducted by the wet field, and players standing in heavily puddled areas of the pitch collapsed to their knees with their heads in their hands. Medical staff rushed onto the pitch to find players suffering from breathing difficulties and severe dizziness. Five were rushed to hospital. All survived, although Luftetari goalkeeper Erion Kristidhi lost his hearing and two of his teammates experienced speech problems.

In January 2004, a Chilean league match between rivals Bandera de Chile and La Gonzalina was suspended after rival supporters invaded the pitch and began to brawl. The referee was eventually able to restart the game after the pitch was cleared, but the controversy was just beginning. Just before the referee blew the full-time whistle, Bandera's top striker, El Rulo, popped up to score a dramatic last-minute winner. As he turned to celebrate, a Gonzalina player pulled a revolver from his shorts and fired at him three times. One of the shots hit El Rulo in the shoulder. The striker was taken to Rancagua hospital, but his gun-toting opponent disappeared. The local police said they knew who the shooter was and were confident of finding him. Presumably, they had checked the team-sheets.

Football and gunplay don't mix. Witness the appalling consequences of an own goal scored by the Colombian Andres Escobar in the World Cup finals of 1994. Twenty-seven-year-old Escobar, known to fans as 'El Caballero del Futbol', or 'the Gentleman of Football', was the linchpin of the defence in an exciting Colombian side tipped by Pelé to win the tournament.

Escobar scored his first international goal against England at Wembley in 1988, slotting a diving header past Peter Shilton. He scored his second international goal in June 1994, when Colombia played hosts the USA, in the Pasadena Rose Bowl in front of 93,000 spectators. Unfortunately, it was scored in his own net.

There had been worrying signs ahead of the game. Colombian coach Francisco Maturana received a death threat warning that his family and that of his midfielder Gabriel Gomez would be killed if the under-fire Gomez started the game against the USA. Did Maturana take the threat seriously? Unhesitatingly. Gomez was dropped and never played for his country ever again.

The fateful moment came 33 minutes into the crucial game. Escobar slid in to intercept a John Harkes cross. The ball ricocheted off his boot and ended up in the back of the Colombian net. The USA went on to win 2–1, eventually qualifying for the second round at Colombia's expense. The headline in one Colombian newspaper read 'Humiliated!' as the team returned home in disgrace. Escobar went back to Medellin, a city of just two million people, but with 7,000 murders every year.

On 2 July, he sat in a Honda Civic in a nightclub car park, after a night out with friend and fellow footballer Juan Jairo Galeano. A gang of men, including the notorious Gallon brothers, got out of two Toyota Landcruisers and began to chastise Escobar for his own goal. Escobar told the men that the own goal had been a simple mistake, but an argument ensued. Then the Gallons' bodyguard, 42-year-old Humberto Munez, approached the car and shot Escobar at point blank range six times with a .38, shouting 'Own goal! Own goal!' as he did so.

The killing sent shock waves throughout the world of football and beyond. Escobar was not the first Colombian footballer to have been shot dead. Felipe Perez and Omar Dario Canas of Nacional, Albeiro Pico Hernandez of Club Envigado, Arley Antonio Rodriguez of Independiente and Colombian referee Alvero Ortega were all murdered in the 1990s.

Tens of thousands of mourners attended Escobar's funeral, and many staged protests demanding justice in a country ravaged by drugs and gun crime. Escobar's friend Galeano, and brother Santiago, both quit football after his death. Escobar's killer, Munez, was arrested and sentenced to 43 years and 2 months in jail, despite concocting a bizarre cover-up involving deliberately sustaining a head injury, shaving off his moustache and claiming the Toyota used in the shooting had been stolen. Munez was placed in maximum security, partly for his own safety in a football-mad country enraged by the murder of one of its superstars. The Gallon brothers were not charged, with prosecutors deciding that they had not ordered Munez to pull the trigger.

Various rumours circulated surrounding the murder involving betting syndicates, drug cartels and hitmen, in a country where hired killers can be bought for as little as $10. But it seems likely Escobar's death stemmed from an argument. An argument over a simple football match. An argument over football's most tragic own goal.

Arsenal's Dennis Bergkamp has steadfastly refused to fly in an aeroplane throughout his distinguished career. He has subsequently been forced to endure long road journeys and has missed several European ties altogether. Had the Netherlands managed to qualify for the 2002 World Cup finals, Bergkamp would have found it very difficult to drive to Japan and Korea. His fear of flying, though, is not as misplaced as it may first appear, because plane crashes have killed more footballers than any number of other misfortunes combined.

On 6 February 1958, reigning English League champions Manchester United flew to Yugoslavia to take on Red Star Belgrade in the European Cup quarter-final. A 3–3 away draw saw the side progress to the semi-final 5–4 on aggregate. On the way home their plane, the twin-engine British European Airways airliner Lord Burghley, landed at Munich Riem airport to refuel. As the team sat on the runway, the wintry weather deteriorated and heavy snow began to fall. The pilot, Captain James Thain, made two attempts to take off, but aborted each one because of the snow. Then he made a third, fateful, attempt. Flight 609 failed to gain altitude, overshot the runway, clipped a house and crashed to the ground.

There were forty-four passengers aboard the plane. Twenty-three of them died. Manchester United players Geoff Bent, Roger Byrne, Eddie Colman, Mark Jones, David Pegg, Tommy Taylor and Liam Whelan were all killed in the crash. Duncan Edwards was pulled alive from the wreckage, but died two weeks later. Legendary United manager Sir Matt Busby was given the last rites on the runway, but made an unlikely recovery. Team trainer Tom Curry, coach Bert Whalley, secretary Walter Crickmer, supporter Willie Satinoff and travel agent BP Milos were not so fortunate. They all perished, alongside eight journalists and two BEA crew members. United players Jackie Blanchflower and Johnny Berry survived, but both suffered career-ending injuries. The official German inquiry into the crash reported that snow and slush on the runway was to blame, but others blamed ice on the wings.

Incredibly, only two matches were postponed after the disaster, and Manchester United were back in action just 13 days later. With Sir Matt Busby still in hospital, assistant manager Jimmy Murphy took the remains of his side, bolstered by youth players and emergency transfers, to play Sheffield Wednesday in the fifth round of the FA Cup. United won 3–0 and eventually reached the final, where they were beaten 2–0 by Bolton Wanderers and Nat Lofthouse. United struggled in the League, winning only one of their 14 remaining fixtures. They conceded the League to Wolverhampton Wanderers and finished ninth. It would be eight years before a rebuilt United reclaimed the League championship. In Europe, United were beaten in the semi-final of the European Cup by AC Milan. Red Star Belgrade petitioned UEFA to name United honorary Cup champions, but UEFA refused. They did, however, offer United automatic entry into the following season's competition, but the English FA refused the offer, and United failed to qualify.

A popular football urban legend says that a 1990s Premiership footballer survived the Munich air disaster – former Arsenal and Leeds goalkeeper John Lukic. The story reasons that Lukic was at the time being carried by his pregnant mother, who survived the crash. Unfortunately, this piece of footballing trivia isn't true. Lukic wasn't born until 1960, and his mother was not on board the Lord Burghley. Many myths, though, have their origins in facts, and it is true that there was another Mrs Lukic on the plane. This Mrs Lukic was the wife of the Yugoslavian ambassador to London. She was travelling with her baby daughter, and both mother and child survived the disaster.

Torino were the greatest Italian side of the 1940s, winning five consecutive Scudetti between 1943 and 1949 (with the league suspended in 1944 and 1945 due to the war). At that time 'Grande Torino' were among the most successful sides in Serie A history, and the Turin side provided many players for the Italian national side, including inspirational midfielder and captain Valentino Mazzola. On 4 May 1949, though, the Fiat-built plane carrying the squad back from a match in Portugal crashed into the Superga hills on the outskirts of Turin: 31 people were killed, including all 18 Torino squad members. The club never properly recovered from the disaster. After struggling in Serie A for ten years, Torino were relegated in 1959. Since then they have only won the Italian league championship once, in 1976.

All 20 travelling members of the Chilean side Green Cross were killed in 1961 when their Douglas DC-3 aircraft crashed into the Las Lastimas mountains near Lico in Chile. The plane was beginning its descent into the team's home city of Santiago when it fell from the sky. Four members of the airline crew also died. No official cause was ever found.

Similarly, no cause was ever found for the 1969 crash that killed 19 players and officials of the Bolivian side The Strongest. All 74 passengers and crew were killed when their DC-6B plane hit a 15,000 ft mountain near La Paz in the Andes.

In 1979, an error by Russian air traffic controllers caused a midair collision between two Tupelov 134A aircraft. One of the planes was carrying 14 players and 3 staff from Russian side Pakhtakor Tashkent, en route to a league match. The plane crashed over Dneprodzerzhinsk in the Ukraine. All 84 onboard the flight were killed.

Forty-three players, staff, wives and supporters of Peruvian side Alianza Lima were on board their Fokker F-27 when it ran into trouble on its approach to Lima airport in 1987. Dials failed, and the pilot performed a fly-by to check that the plane's landing gear was down. But the plane pitched up and crashed into the sea near the Peruvian capital. Just one passenger survived.

In 1989, Colourful 11, a Dutch side made up entirely of Surinamese players, were killed in a crash at Paramaribo while returning home from the Netherlands. Surinam Airways Flight 764 was attempting to land in fog. Two previous attempts to land had been aborted, but fuel was running out. On the third attempt, the plane hit a tree, and 176 of the 187 passengers and crew were killed.

And, in 1993, the Zambian national squad were on their way to play a World Cup qualifier in Senegal when the engine of their Zambian Air Force plane caught fire. The plane crashed into the sea off Libreville in Gabon. All 30 passengers and crew were killed, including the entire 18-man Zambian squad.

In the early 1980s, a light aircraft crashed onto a football field in South East London, during a Sunday League match. The players had spotted the plane was in difficulty and scattered towards the dressing room as it came down. It crashed onto the edge of the pitch and disintegrated. The Sunday Leaguers rushed to help, but the two people onboard had been killed in the impact. Police arrived and cordoned off the scene, with tape running along the touchline. The footballers, realising there was nothing further they could do, decided to restart their game. They played on for several minutes, until police found pieces of wreckage behind one goal and taped off the goalmouth.

If it is any consolation to worried footballers, football kills many more supporters than players. In 1902, 25 supporters were killed and 516 injured when Ibrox's West Stand collapsed during an international match between Scotland and England. 33 were killed and over 400 injured at Bolton's Burnden Park in 1946 when a wall collapsed before an FA Cup tie between Wanderers and Stoke City. In 1964, 318 fans were killed and 500 injured at the National Stadium in Lima, Peru. Rioting broke out after the referee disallowed a last-minute Peruvian equaliser in the match against Argentina. Then 74 fans were killed and 150 injured during an Argentinean league game between River Plate and Boca Juniors in 1968. Spectators were crushed against locked gates when they tried to flee after opposition fans threw burning torches onto them from an upper tier.

Back in Britain, 66 people were trampled to death and 145 injured near the end of an Old Firm match on New Year's Day 1971. Departing fans were attempting to get back into the stadium after a late Rangers equaliser. In 1974, 49 fans were killed in Cairo, Egypt, after a wall collapsed at the Zamalek Stadium. Six were killed in Port-au-Prince in 1976 during a World Cup qualifier between hosts Haiti and Cuba. A Haitian fan set off a firecracker, and the frightened crowd surged forward. A soldier was knocked to the ground and his gun went off, killing two young children. Two other people were trampled to death, one fell over a wall and the soldier committed suicide upon realising what he had done.

The world's worst ever sporting disaster happened at Moscow's Lenin Stadium in 1982. Fans were leaving the stadium towards the end of a UEFA Cup tie between Spartak Moscow and Haarlem, when a last-minute goal was scored. The crowd attempted to rush back into the stadium, and many were crushed to death. Official figures released at the time said 77 had perished. In fact, around 340 souls were killed.

In May 1985, a discarded cigarette butt set fire to accumulated rubbish under the main stand at Bradford City's Valley Parade ground. Fifty-six football fans lost their lives. Just three weeks later, thirty-nine fans perished before the European Cup final at the Heysel Stadium in Brussels. Fighting broke out between hooligans travelling with Liverpool and Juventus, and a wall collapsed on fleeing fans.

In 1988, 30 spectators were killed and 40 injured in Tripoli, Libya, during a friendly match against Malta. Panicked fans were crushed against a wall, which fell causing the collapse of a stand, after a man went berserk with a weapon. In the same year a freak electrical storm broke overhead during a match between Janakpur of Nepal and Muktijohda of Bangladesh at Nepal's National Stadium in Katmandu. Fans were caught in a stampede for the exits, and 70 fans were trampled to death.

Britain's worst ever sporting tragedy occurred on 15 April 1989. Liverpool were playing Nottingham Forest in the FA Cup semi-final at Sheffield Wednesday's Hillsborough Stadium. Wrong crowd-management decisions taken by the police caused a terrifying crush among arriving Liverpool supporters at the Leppings Lane entrance of the ground. Ninety-five fans were killed, both in the entrance tunnels and on the terracing. The death toll rose to ninety-six when another fan, Tony Bland, died in 1993 after being in a coma for four years.

In 1992, 15 fans were killed and over 1,300 were injured in Coresta, France, when a temporary grandstand collapsed during a cup semi-final between Marseille and Bastia. In 1996, 81 were killed and 147 injured when 60,000 fans packed into the 45,000-capacity Stadio Meteo Flores in Guatemala City one hour before a Guatemala versus Costa Rica World Cup qualifier. The crush was blamed on ticket forgers. In 2001, 137 fans were killed in Ghana at a match between Accra and Asante. Fans panicked and a stampede ensued when police began to fire tear gas into the stands in an attempt to quell crowd trouble.

One fixture that safety-conscious supporters would do well to avoid is the clash between South Africa's most popular teams, Kaizer Chiefs and Orlando Pirates. The rivalry between the two clubs is so intense that they are rarely allowed to play in their native Soweto, and few stadiums have the means to accommodate their huge bands of supporters. In 1991, 42 supporters died and 50 were injured during a friendly between the sides in the South African town of Orkney, after a refereeing decision triggered rioting. At the time it was South Africa's worst ever sporting disaster, but more was to follow. In 1998, 80,000 fans forced their way into Johannesburg's 64,000-seater Ellis Stadium to see the sides play, with tens of thousands more left outside battling cops in a full-scale riot.

Then, in 2001, disaster again struck at the twin-deck Ellis Stadium, primarily a rugby venue but earmarked as a key stadium in South Africa's World Cup bids. In front of a nationwide television audience, thousands of ticketless fans attempted to force their way into the stadium. Police tried to force them back with tear gas, but panic ensued, and fans were trampled and crushed against the six-foot barbed wire fence that surrounds the pitch. Officials opened gates in the fence and began to carry bodies onto the pitch. Ambulances were unable to get to the ground because of the chaos outside, so helicopters were called in to ferry some of the injured to hospital. The official death toll was 43, surpassing even the 1991 tragedy. Other estimates suggested the death toll could be as high as 57. Around 250 were injured.

And then we come to the biggest death toll ever associated with football. For four days in 1969 the world saw its first and only soccer war. Tensions were high between El Salvador and Honduras even before the two bordering countries faced each other over two qualifying matches for the 1970 World Cup. The first match, played at the Honduras capital of Tegucigalpa, was won by Honduras against a backdrop of violence and hatred aimed at the El Salvadorans.

The return match took place in San Salvador on 15 June 1969, and this time it was the Hondurans' turn to be beaten and insulted. El Salvador won the match 3–0, and the home fans celebrated by hurling rotten eggs and dead rats at the Honduran players. Then the El Salvadorans took to the streets of their capital and began looting and burning buildings owned by Hondurans, driving their rivals from their homes and chasing them to the border. Tens of thousands of Hondurans fled El Salvador for the safety of their own country, while many who remained were beaten or killed.

Honduras immediately broke off diplomatic relationships with El Salvador. El Salvador responded by sending troops and fighter jets to invade Honduras. The El Salvadoran army was larger and better equipped and made rapid progress across the border. But the Honduran air force offered stiff resistance and eventually destroyed the entire El Salvadoran air force. Stalemate was reached, the Organisation of American States intervened and a cease-fire was agreed. The Soccer War lasted just four days between 14 July and 18 July 1969, but more than 2,000 people were killed and tens of thousands were made homeless. So next time someone tells you that football is only a game . . .

AFTERWORD

Full-time, then, is blown on our foray into football's nether regions – probably by a drunken, colour-blind ref who suffers from alopecia. We've seen a game that has it all – punch-ups, sending-offs, own goals, penalties and genuine insanity. Along the way, we've encountered Nazis, transsexuals, elephants, robots and even the Son of God.

Footballers have been shot, imprisoned, hit by lightning, killed in plane crashes and sent for early baths (probably with Page 3 girls in close attendance). Managers have doped teams, taken bungs, attacked star players, offered outrageous post-match interviews and punched interviewers in the face. Chairmen have sacked managers via text message, been visited by aliens, bribed opponents, bought league titles and moved clubs to new towns. Fans have thrown celery, brandished guns, placed curses, rung football phone-ins and set up their own clubs. All typical behaviour in the weird, wide world of football.

But what does the future hold for the beautiful game? Almost certainly, more of the same. The stories on these pages run from the very beginnings of football right up to the present day, and there is absolutely no evidence that the game is getting any saner. In the future there will be new characters, fresh tabloid exposés and a whole new variety of footballers' haircuts. Football in the twenty-first century will continue to be fantastically mad, bad and stupid – until the year 2050, of course, when robot footballers will take over the world. We have been warned.

Until that apocalyptic day, football will continue to entertain and delight fans across the world. There will be great players, brilliant goals and wonderful games. But there will also be bad boys, idiotic incidents and crazy matches. Without villains there can be no heroes. Without moments of stupidity there can be no moments of genius. Without bizarre incidents there can be no thrilling unpredictability. These polarities are why football will never become boring. Whatever the future holds, football will remain the greatest game in the world.

FURTHER READING

The research for *Balls* covered hundreds of books, newspaper articles, websites and other sources. The following is a selection of sources that have been specifically quoted, or were particularly useful, and which should prove interesting as further reading.

ARTICLES

Baker, Danny, 'Revealing Truth Just a Nip and Tuck Decision', *The Times* (9 November 2002).

Gagliardi, Jason, 'Gaaoooool!', *Time Asia* (24 June 2002).

O'Hagan, Sean, 'Inside the Minds of Roy Keane' *Observer Sport Monthly* (1 September 2002).

Winter, Brian, 'Drugs, Sweat and Tears at Maradona Musical', Reuters (12 January 2004).

BOOKS

Adams, Tony, *Addicted* (Harper Collins, 1998).

Baggio, Roberto, *A Door in the Sky* (Una Porta nel Cielo) (Limina, 2001).

Beckham, David and Tom Watt, *My Side* (Harper Collins, 2003).

Bellos, Alex, *Futebol: The Brazilian Way of Life* (Bloomsbury, 2002).

Bowles, Stan, *The Original Stan the Man* (Paper Plane, 1996).

Green, Alan, *The Green Line* (Headline, 2000).

Gregg, Harry, *Harry's Game* (Mainstream, 2002).

Hulme, Chris, *Manslaughter United* (Yellow Jersey Press, 1999).

Jones, Vinnie, *Vinnie: The Autobiography* (Headline, 1998).

Keane, Roy and Eamon Dunphy, *Keane: The Autobiography* (Penguin, 2003).

Kelly, Ned, *Manchester United: The Untold Story* (Michael O'Mara, 2003).

Kuper, Simon, *Football Against the Enemy* (Orion, 2003).

McGuigan, Paul and Paolo Hewitt, *The Greatest Footballer You Never Saw* (Mainstream, 1998).

Marsh, Rodney, *Priceless* (Headline, 2002).

Matthews, Stanley, *The Way it Was* (Headline, 2000).

Roberts, David, *British Hit Singles* (Guinness, 2003).

Rollin, Jack, *Sky Sports Football Yearbook* (Headline, 2003).

Ronson, Jon, *Them: Adventures with Extremists* (Picador, 2001).

Rowlands, Alan, *Trautmann: The Biography* (Breedon, 1990).

Schumacher, Harald, *Blowing the Whistle* (W.H. Allen, 1987).

Wells, Steve, *One Hump or Two?: The Frank Worthington Story* (Polar Print, 1994).

Wilton, Iain, *CB Fry: An English Hero* (Metro, 1999).

WEBSITES

1000 People More Annoying Than Mick Hucknall, www.mickhucknall.com

AFC Wimbledon Official Website, www.afcwimbledon.co.uk

Balls Website (Paul Brown), www.ballsbook.co.uk

Danger Here: Ronglish, www.dangerhere.com/ronglish.htm

Danny Baker Internet Treehouse, www.internettreehouse.co.uk

Escape to Victory Website, www.spodrum.freeserve.co.uk/victory

Free Steve Ogrizovic Petition, www.petitiononline.com/fsteog/petition.html

Goalkeepers are Different, www.goalkeepersaredifferent.com

BALLS

International Football Hall of Fame: George Best,
www.ifhof.com/hof/best.asp

Internet Movie Database, http://uk.imdb.com

Ken Aston MBE Website, www.kenaston.org

Plane Crash Info.com, www.planecrashinfo.com/famous.htm

Reading Referees Association, www.readingrefs.org.uk

Rec. Sport Soccer Statistics Foundation (RSSSF), www.rsssf.com

RoboCup Official Website, www.robocup.org

INDEX